Knowing the Myst
of Life Within

But is it not strange,

that thou shouldst be of it, and not be able to know and own it, in this day of its manifestation; but call the light which is spiritual and eternal (and gives the true and certain knowledge of Christ) natural? What! of God, of Christ, (having received the Spirit, the living well) and yet not know the mystery of life within, nor its pure voice in this present day! but limit the unlimited One to a form of words formerly spoken by him!... Now, we are one with any of you (though ye know it not) so far as ye know and are of the truth, and feel true union with whatever is of God in you.

"Reply to Queries and Animadversions [Concerning the Rule of the New Covenant]" (1667/8), *Works*, IV.191

Knowing the Mystery of Life Within

Selected Writings of Isaac Penington in their Historical and Theological Context

Selected and introduced by
R. Melvin Keiser and Rosemary Moore,
manuscript transcriptions by Diana Morrison-Smith

Quaker Books 2005

First published July 2005 by Quaker Books
173 Euston Road, London NW1 2BJ

© Quaker Books 2005

© Introduction and commentaries Rosemary Moore and Melvin Keiser 2005

Illustrations on pp. xi, 2, 120 and 291, and front cover photograph © Library of the Religious Society of Friends, London. Drawing on back cover © David M. Butler.

The moral rights of the authors are asserted in accordance with the Copyright, Designs and Patents Act 1988. All rights reserved. No part of this book may be reproduced or utilised, in any form or by any means, electronic or mechanical, without permission in writing from the publisher. Reviewers may quote brief passages. Enquiries should be addressed to the Publications Manager, Quaker Books, Friends House, 173 Euston Road, London NW1 2BJ.

ISBN 0 85245 378 7

Design, typesetting and cover Andrew Lindesay at the Golden Cockerel Press, London

Copy editing Christopher Holdsworth, Deborah Padfield and Peter Daniels

Contents

General Introduction	vii
Notes and abbreviations	xii

Part I *The Life of Isaac Penington, from his Letters and Other Writings*

1. Origins of a Quaker Family, 1616–1658	3
2. Political Disruption and Quaker Dissension, 1659–1664	26
3. Aylesbury Gaol, 1664–1667	46
4. From Aylesbury Gaol to Reading Gaol, 1667–1672	72
5. The Last Years, 1672–1679	94

Part II *The Spirituality and Thought of Isaac Penington*

Introduction: Reading Penington Today	121
1. *The Way of Life and Death* (1658): Penington's First Quaker Writing	129
2. The Life	133
3. Process of the Spiritual Life	147
4. Life in the Church	158
5. Life in the Nation	169
6. Knowing, Sensing, Feeling, and Believing	178
7. Freedom, Virtue, and Wisdom	196
8. Prayer and Worship	205
9. Religion, Language, and the Self	213
10. Interpreting the Bible	228
11. Answering Theological Controversy	242
12. God	273

Appendices

Appendix A: Short titles used for extracts from *Works*, and notes on text	279
Appendix B: Quotations from Isaac and Mary Penington's writings in *Quaker faith and practice*	292

Bibliography	294
Index of Bible References	301
General Index	303

About the Authors

R. Melvin Keiser is Professor Emeritus of Religious Studies, Guilford College; author of several essays in Quaker theology published by the Quaker study centres at Pendle Hill in Pennsylvania and Woodbrooke in Birmingham; has written books on H. Richard Niebuhr and Stanley Romaine Hopper; and is a participant in the Quaker Theology Seminar (Woodbrooke). A member of Swannanoa Valley Friends Meeting, he lives in Black Mountain, North Carolina and is co-director of Common Light Meetingplace.

Rosemary Moore wrote a thesis on early Quaker writings for her Ph.D. at Birmingham University, after retiring from teaching religious education. She is a former President of the Friends Historical Society (Britain); author of *The Light in their Consciences: Early Quakers in Britain 1646–1666*; editor of *The History of the Life of Thomas Ellwood*. She is a member of Telford Quaker Meeting in Shropshire.

Amersham Meeting House as shown on the back cover is from *The Quaker Meeting Houses of Britain* by David M. Butler (London: Friends Historical Society, 1999). The left-hand side is a timber-framed house built in 1624, part of the scene at the time of Isaac's letter to Amersham Friends in 1667, although it was only enlarged and registered as a meeting house in 1689.

Acknowledgments

Many people have helped with this work. Robert Diamond, Emeritus Fellow of Christ's College, Cambridge, looked up information about Penington's time at the university, and Michael Frost, Assistant Librarian, Honourable Society of the Inner Temple, performed the same service regarding Penington's legal training. Alexandra Walsham, of Exeter University, made suggestions for the bibliography. The Services Sound and Vision Corporation allowed us access to their site at Chalfont Grove and provided a knowledgeable guide. The following people generously gave their time to provide information and show us other sites connected with the Penington family: Mr and Mrs Arthurton, George Bunney, Jacqueline Coombs, Sue Smithson, Mr and Mrs Swabey, and John Wilkins, while Derek Moore patiently drove the car.

As always, we owe a special debt to the staff of Friends House Library, London, without whom work such as this would be impossible, and we are particularly beholden to Josef Keith for his ability to decipher difficult handwriting. Finally, the authors want to express their gratitude to Christopher Holdsworth, who as editor extraordinaire exhibited grace and wisdom in his caring engagement with texts and authors, making many valuable suggestions on details and shaping this book into its final form.

General Introduction

"Our life is love, and peace, and tenderness; and bearing one with another, and forgiving one another, and not laying accusations against one another; but praying for one another, and helping one another up with a tender hand." (See p. 59.)

Most Quakers would recognise that quotation, and some could name the author. Vital with the life of the Spirit, Isaac Penington's writings have spoken to generations of Friends, from his contemporaries in mid-seventeenth century England up to the present day. He knew God in inwardness as Life that engenders life, Seed that grows within the self, Light that illumines, and Truth that leads daily into purity, justice, community, and fullness of being. His life was God-filled, seeking to be faithful to his measure of Life and Light, and to grow further in the way of the Spirit. He wrote with an evocative quality, joining religious and scriptural ideas with his own experience, and using metaphors, such as "spring", "seed", and "sweetness", that speak to our feelings and touch our hearts, immersing us in the mystery of the spiritual life and engendering trust in what is for ever beyond our grasp.

Because of the value of his writings, the Religious Society of Friends, or Quakers, has kept Isaac Penington in print – with a handful of other seventeenth-century leaders, Fox, Penn and Barclay – for over three hundred years. There have been several brief selections of his writings published during the second half of the twentieth century, but most present-day Friends encounter his words as extracts in *Quaker faith and practice*, the book of discipline of Britain Yearly Meeting, or in the books of discipline of other Yearly Meetings, or as brief quotations in Quaker publications. There has never been a scholarly selection made that portrays his life in his historical setting and presents a comprehensive view of his thought. Our volume attempts this, and was commissioned by the Literature (now Publications) Committee of Britain Yearly Meeting, originally as a co-operative effort between Mel Keiser, mainly handling theology, and Rosemary Moore, mainly handling history. However, it soon became clear that, if we were to avoid reproducing the preconceptions, not to mention the errors, of nineteenth-century studies, then a considerable amount of new work would have to be undertaken on the large corpus of practically untouched Penington manuscripts in the library at Friends House, London, and Diana Morrison-Smith took over this aspect of our study.

Penington's letters provide important insight into his life and times, and some of the most profound spiritual counsel within the body of Quaker writing. His essays explore many aspects of seventeenth-century Quaker spirituality and lay out Friends' theological perspective, clarifying, defending, arguing for the Quaker way of life, interpreting scripture and church doctrine, and defining the nature of prayer, religion, community, and God. Amidst spiritual and theological writing, he also writes personally of his long struggle to find a fullness of life; politically about the Puritan revolution and Restoration; prophetically about the nation's spiritual poverty, deceit, and oppression; and philosophically about the nature of the self in its doing and knowing.

In our selection of Penington's writings we have chosen passages that show his character and involvement in his times, and his spiritual depth and intellectual acuity, complexity, and indeed artistry: we hope to inform readers about one of Quakerism's major leaders in the past, and also to nurture spirits and minds in the present. We have chosen works to illustrate every period in Penington's life and the diversity of his thought. Although there is a bias towards devotional and pastoral writings, still of current interest, we have included examples that show Penington as family man, political commentator, prisoner suffering for his faith, supporter (for a time) of the Quaker schismatic John Perrot, and theologian engaged in fierce argument or incisive clarification of Quaker beliefs and practices. In selecting examples of his letters, we have given preference to those not previously published. We have included all passages quoted in Britain Yearly Meeting's *Quaker faith and practice* (listed in Appendix B), and provided more of their context.

Anyone who studies Isaac Penington soon realises that he was half of a couple, and cannot properly be understood except as a family man. We have therefore included a few of Mary Penington's letters. Isaac's and Mary's letters are sharply contrasted, Isaac's being mystical and theological while Mary's are practical and down to earth, providing a good illustration of the basis of their partnership. Mary's main work, not published during her lifetime, is *Some Experiences in the Life of Mary Penington*, which is readily available in a cheap paperback edition.

Part I of our book consists of Isaac Penington's life and its historical context as shown through his letters and some epistles to Friends, with commentary throughout. Part II presents Isaac Penington's spirituality and thought, mainly through the essays that were published during, or immediately after, his life. These are mostly excerpts, allowing us to represent more aspects of his life and thought than would be possible by reproducing just a few lengthy papers. A few of the more theological letters are placed in Part II, and examples of his letters to Friends' meetings appear in both halves of the book, according to their more personal or intellectual content.

Isaac Penington was, beyond question, a wordy writer. Even his contemporaries sometimes found him too much. George Whitehead, one of the weightiest of Friends at the time of Penington's death, was called upon to contribute a Testimony and clearly found it difficult, writing: "I hope I shall not need to write an apology [i.e. defence or advocacy] for this man's many writings...nor is it altogether proper for me to apologise in such a case, not having read all these his books" (*Works*, I. 430). But he believed Penington's books to be worthy, and that readers should not "censure" them if they found words they did not understand. Penington himself once commented, in response to a contemporary's criticisms: "The style is not my own (as standing in my own choice or will) but when the Lord requires me to write anything for his service, my soul in singleness of heart waiteth on him for the words" (John Penington manuscripts 1.31).[1] It is best to read Isaac Penington slowly, at the pace of the quill pen he used for writing.

---

1. This is an undated paper answering Allan Smallwood, who was the author of an anti-Quaker work called *Oaths no Gospel Ordinance* (York: Bulkely and Mawburne, 1667), replying to Penington, *The Great Question Concerning Swearing* (1661) and Francis Howgill, *Oaths no Gospel Ordinance* (1666).

With our selection of letters and essays we present a more comprehensive representation of Penington's writings than ever before. With our commentary we hope to make the manner and substance of Penington's thinking accessible to twenty-first-century Friends, and to others interested in early Quaker spirituality and thought.

The Writings of Isaac Penington

Isaac Penington was a prolific writer, publishing eleven titles during his pre-Quaker days, and fifty-seven afterwards. Most of these were short pamphlets, but a few were substantial books. In addition, he left a large quantity of unpublished papers at his death, and a number of these were printed in the first edition of his collected works, a two-volume folio: *The Works of the Long Mournful and Sorely-Distressed Isaac Penington* (London: Benjamin Clark, 1681). This was edited by his long-time friend Thomas Ellwood, no doubt with help and advice from Mary and eldest son John. It included most of Penington's writings published during his Quaker period. Family, local Friends and national figures contributed testimonies which provide some valuable biographical information. Subsequently, Penington's *Works* were republished in four volumes in 1741, 1761 and 1784.

After the publication of the *Works* a great mass of papers remained: letters written by Isaac and some by Mary, epistles to meetings and theological papers, as well as a large number of letters and papers written by other Friends, some of them important for the early history of Quakerism. John Penington copied them, over half a million words, into four manuscript volumes known as the John Penington Manuscripts which are now in the Library of the Religious Society of Friends at Friends House in London. A few Penington papers not copied by John Penington have survived in other manuscript collections.

In the late eighteenth and early nineteenth centuries Friends became interested in their origins, and sought out and printed selections from the unpublished correspondence of various early Friends, including Isaac Penington. Over a hundred of his letters were put together in one volume by John Barclay and issued in 1824, unfortunately with a number of unmarked omissions and minor alterations in the texts. This book is still available in many older meeting house libraries. The letters from Barclay's volume were included in the next edition of the *Works*, published in 1861–63. The most recent edition is based on the nineteenth-century text but also has some additional letters and a few printed papers not found in earlier editions. This is *The Works of Isaac Penington: A Minister of the Gospel in the Society of Friends, Including His Collected Letters*, in four volumes and supplement (Glenside, Pennsylvania: Quaker Heritage Press, 1995–1997). It is available freely on line at www.qhpress.org/texts/penington/index.html, and we cite it simply as *Works*. Penington's pre-Quaker works have never been collected, but the new edition of *Works* includes one example. Selections from the nineteenth-century edition were published during the later nineteenth and early twentieth centuries, and are listed in the bibliography.

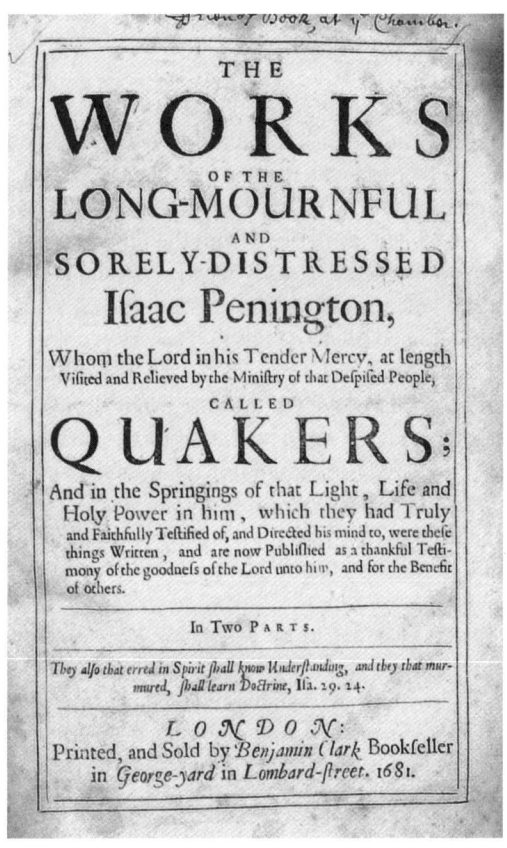

Notes and Abbreviations

Texts

For all works published in Penington's lifetime and in the seventeenth and eighteenth century collected editions, we have used the on-line edition issued by Quaker Heritage Press, which follows the text of the 1861–63 edition. Our omissions are marked by "..."

Letters have been transcribed from the John Penington or other manuscripts, or checked if already in print. Readers who know the previous printed editions of Penington's letters may notice some differences. We retained "hath", "doth", "goeth", etc., as Penington's prose reads better with these original forms, but otherwise we have modernised his spelling. We retained the original punctuation as far as possible, for Penington's punctuation though sparse was meaningful. We have increased the number of paragraphs, inserted inverted commas and apostrophes where appropriate, and occasionally added other punctuation.

Dates

At this time the year began on 25 March, so March was the first month and December the tenth month. We have changed the dates in headings to the modern style, but retained the original when quoting. Dates between 1 and 24 March present a problem: 24 March 1660 and 25 March 1661 would be consecutive days, but in Quaker style, the first date might be given as "24 1st month 1661". Sometimes, however, the same date would be given as "24 1st month 1660". In two cases definitely, and in other cases probably, Isaac Penington used the old year-date on letters written between 1 and 24 March, a practice that would be natural for an educated person. Note the form of date "4 of 1 month 6$\frac{8}{9}$" (p. 82) for 4 March 1689. This came into use in the later part of the seventeenth century.

Square brackets indicate our notes or explanations.

Biblical References

Penington and his readers knew the Bible well, so he did not often provide references; where he did, sometimes they were in the text and sometimes in round brackets. Our additional references are square bracketed. All abbreviated references, Penington's or ours, are given in the form of the New English Bible, unless otherwise specified as RSV (Revised Standard Version). An index of biblical references is provided at the back of this book.

Initials

In the letters, individuals are often referred to by initials only. "G.F." becomes George Fox. In other cases where identification is moderately certain we have used square brackets, as in "W[illiam] R[ussell]".

Obscure Words

Explanations of obscure words are given in square brackets, with the exception of a few words which occur on a number of occasions. These are:

Bowels The bowels were supposed to be the part of the body where feelings of pity and compassion came from, and by extension the word itself came to mean "compassion" or "mercy". The best known example is Cromwell's, "I beseech you, in the bowels of Christ, think it possible that you may be mistaken".

Flesh Used in the same sense as in Paul's epistles, that is, not necessarily the physical body, but rather ordinary human nature, prone to sin, lacking divine influence.

Tender Sensitive to spiritual influence.

Travel In the seventeenth century there was no distinction between the words "travail" and "travel". Penington used "travel" to mean labour, but usually in the sense of a spiritual journey.

Notes and Abbreviations

> In nineteenth-century editions the word was most often rendered "travail". Since "travail" is now becoming obsolete, we have reverted to "travel".

Virtue   Generally to be understood as "strength".

Abbreviations

JP   The John Penington Manuscripts, which are copies of Isaac Penington's letters and papers made by his son John and now in Friends House Library, London, manuscript volumes MS Vol 341–44.

NEB   The New English Bible. Cambridge: Cambridge University Press, 1961.

RSV   The Revised Standard Version of the Bible.

Qfp   *Quaker faith and practice: the book of Christian discipline of the Yearly Meeting of the Religious Society of Friends (Quakers) in Britain.* 1994.

Works   Penington's collected works. Volume and page references are to the Quaker Heritage Press edition (see p. xi).

Short titles used for references to Penington's works within our text are listed in Appendix A (pp. 279–91), with notes on publication history.

Part I

*The Life of Isaac Penington,
   from his letters and other writings*

Rosemary Moore

Isaac Penington senior, father of Isaac the Quaker. Copy (1800) of the frontispiece wood engraving to *A True Declaration and Just Commendation...* by W.S. (1643), praising his improvements to the fortifications of London.

CHAPTER I

Origins of a Quaker Family, 1616–1658

Isaac Penington was born about 1616, son of Alderman Sir Isaac Penington and his first wife Abigail, daughter of John Allen of London. The Peningtons were a wealthy London merchant family, whose riches had been largely built up by Isaac senior's father, Robert Penington, a prosperous London fishmonger who diversified into landed property in Norfolk and Suffolk. Isaac senior continued the fish business and acquired further estates near the Chalfonts in Buckinghamshire.

The young Isaac Penington grew up in a time of political and religious controversy. Unable to agree with his parliament, Charles I dissolved it in 1629 and for the next eleven years ruled alone, financing his government by taxes which were considered highly objectionable if not unlawful by the people who had to pay them. He was also suspected of favouring Catholicism, a sure route to unpopularity at a time when there was living memory of the Spanish Armada and of a pope who had encouraged Elizabeth I's Catholic subjects to assassinate her, and when Catholicism was associated in the popular mind with John Foxe's *Acts and Monuments,* otherwise known as the "Book of Martyrs", with its lurid woodcuts of burnings at the stake.

Moreover, the King and his archbishop, Laud, preferred church worship to be ceremonial, and there was now a considerable body of people who strongly disapproved of such practices, advocating simpler forms of worship, and church government with no bishops at all. Such people, who included the Penington family, usually called themselves "godly", for by this time the word "Puritan" had developed overtones of disapproval. They were not all of one kind, and included Presbyterians who favoured a state church governed like the present-day Church of Scotland, Independents who later metamorphosed into Congregationalists and who favoured separate churches each governed by its own church covenant, and several kinds of Baptists. Other people, known as Seekers, considered that the true church had been lost at the end of the Apostolic age, and waited in hope for its reappearance. Some of the "godly", in varying degrees, disapproved of sports and the theatre and practised simplicity in everyday life. Theological differences added to the complications, for most of the "godly" held to a form of Calvinism, believing in human depravity and the salvation only of those predestined as elect, while Laud and his supporters (and likewise some of the "godly", especially Baptists and later the Quakers) favoured the theology known as Arminian, that God would save anyone who sincerely turned to him.

At last the King, having no more financial resources, was forced in 1640 to call a parliament, and by that time nobody was willing to compromise. The merchants and country gentry, who were increasingly the power in the land and a much wider group than the "godly", had had more than enough of bad government and over-taxation, and after two years of acrimony the country drifted into civil war. Isaac Penington senior, a wealthy City alderman, twice Lord Mayor of London and a member of the 1640 parliament, was prominent among the supporters of the revolt.

Isaac senior had six children of whom Isaac junior, the Quaker, was the eldest. The second son, William, became a City merchant, and also a Quaker, though tending towards the unofficial "fringe".[1] He may have been the same person as a William Pennington who in 1655 published descriptions of a number of visions which he experienced between 1649 and 1654, very anti-monarchical and supportive of the Fifth Monarchists, a group that looked for a political Kingdom of God and was prepared to use violence to achieve its ends.[2] The

---

1. See letters to William, pp. 23 and 66.
2. *Mr Evans and Mr Penningtons Prophesie concerning seven Yeers of Plenty and seven Yeers of Famine and Pestilence... Together with the coming of the Fifth Monarchy* (1655). "Mr Evans" would probably be Arise Evans, a leading Fifth Monarchist, though all the visions were William Pennington's. They got their name from the kingdom of God which was to follow the four evil kingdoms as prophesied in Daniel 2:44. The standard work is B. S. Capp, *The Fifth Monarchy Men* (London: Faber and Faber, 1972).

youngest of the three brothers, Arthur, turned Roman Catholic in 1676, and the parallel development with Isaac is worth noting, for both Catholics and Quakers were subject to official disapproval in the seventeenth century.[3]

One Penington sister makes an appearance in Samuel Pepys's diaries, although her first name is not mentioned there, Pepys always referring to her as Madam or Mrs Penington ("Mrs" was a courtesy title). Pepys first met Mrs Penington on 8 October 1665 at a dinner party, where the guests were his regular men friends "and a very fine lady one Mrs Penington", and he recorded that he had "most witty discourse with this lady, a very fine witty lady, and indifferent handsome". Two weeks later, at the same house, he wrote that he "was mighty merry with only Madam Penington, who is a fine, witty lady. Here we spent the evening late with great mirth". They saw a good deal of each other for several months that autumn, Pepys being rather surprised at her freedom of behaviour, although he never quite managed to get her into bed. Madam Penington was evidently in control of the situation, and when she had had enough of Pepys, she locked him out of the house. After that we hear no more of Madam Penington (Pepys, Oct.–Dec. 1665). In her own way, she was like her brothers Isaac and Arthur, in that she was a strong character who followed her own bent without regard for anyone else's opinion.[4]

These were Isaac Penington's siblings. Isaac himself had the education of the eldest son of a good family. According to Isaac's stepson-in-law, William Penn, his "education was suitable to his quality among men, having all the advantage the schools and universities of his own country could give him, joined with the conversation [acquaintance with] of some of the knowingest and considerablest men of his time" (*Works* I.3). At school he would have spent his time on classical languages, becoming fluent in Latin to speak, read and write, also learning Greek and possibly some Hebrew. However, unlike some educated Quakers of the time, he never, in his career as an author, wrote in Latin or made use of his knowledge of classical and early Christian authors.[5] Further education for young men of

---

3 Letters to Arthur and his friend, p. 97.
4 Letter to Judith Penington, thought to be the "Madame Penington" of Pepys's Diary, p. 106.
5 Samuel Fisher, Robert Barclay and Thomas Ellwood wrote in Latin, and William Penn and Robert Barclay, in particular, show knowledge of early Church Fathers.

his social class usually involved some time at Oxford or Cambridge and also legal studies. Records of the Inner Temple show that Isaac was admitted in 1634, and called to the Bar in 1639, while Cambridge University records show him spending time at St Catherine's College, which he entered in 1637. After completing his education he lived in his father's house in Coleman Street in the City of London, though there is no indication that he was involved with the family business (Penington, *Light or Darknesse* 1650, 16). He was evidently provided with adequate means, so that he could pursue his own interests, which were mainly theological. He was a deeply religious young man, not at ease in the world in which he found himself, with a tendency to depression from which he suffered for the whole of his life. His friends and family were well aware of this, describing him on the title page of his collected works as "long-mournful and sorely distressed", though it is beyond the scope of this book to discuss the question whether he suffered from actual depressive illness. No doubt his politically active, go-getting father found him a considerable disappointment.

The family church was St Stephen's in Coleman Street, where Isaac Penington senior gained some notoriety in 1645 by engineering the dismissal of the vicar, an eminent minister named John Goodwin. Goodwin tended to both Arminianism and Independency, both of which Penington senior disliked. At some point Isaac junior left this church, possibly under the influence of Goodwin, and joined an Independent congregation. In 1648 he published his first book, *A Touchstone and Tryall of Faith,* a brief exposition of passages of John's Gospel with some notes on "Spiritual Practices of Christians", which is the only one of his pre-Quaker writings included in his collected *Works*. It is a straightforward pastoral pamphlet, with no hint of his coming spiritual upheavals, warning of the dangers of political and religious controversy, and advising people to wait quietly upon God (*Works* IV.515–38). He had already moved away from conventional doctrine, for he interpreted the phrase "born of water and the spirit" (John 3:5) as a purely spiritual birth, not involving water baptism.[6]

---

[6] There is a good account of Penington's development during this period in Douglas Gwyn, *Seekers Found* (Wallingford: Pendle Hill Publications, 2000), pp. 265–288, which cites the letter to a friend reproduced on p. 9. See also R. Melvin Keiser, "From Dark Christian to Fulness of Life: Isaac Penington's Journey from Puritanism to Quakerism". Greensboro, NC: *Guilford Review 23* (Spring 1986) 42–63.

1. Origins of a Quaker Family, 1616–1658

That year politics came to the fore. The second civil war was over, and the King was put on trial. Oliver Cromwell and his associates believed that the elimination of the King, "the Man of Blood", was an essential preliminary to the coming of the Kingdom of God that they were expecting. Penington senior was a member of the Commission that tried the King for treason and condemned him to death, although he would not, or at least did not, sign the death warrant. Charles I was publicly beheaded on 30 January 1649, to the horror of many people who believed quite literally in the divinity that hedged a king. One can imagine the atmosphere in the Penington household, at the centre of these events. Isaac junior's reaction was to withdraw. His book published that year was called *The Great and Sole Troubler of the Times, Represented in a Mapp of Misery, or A Glimpse of the Heart of Man which is the fountain from which all Misery flows, and the source unto which it runs back. Drawn with a dark pencill, by a dark hand, in the midst of Darkness*. "Abundance of wickedness", he wrote, "hath broken forth in these few years. ... It appears in the King's party, in the Parliament's party, in the Army's party; among the Episcopal sort, Presbyterian, Independent, etc. All these see it plainly enough in one another ... but who suspects it at home?" A few months later he wrote that the civil commotion had resulted in religion receiving "a blow within, a wound at heart". He wondered whether "the establishment of ... any form of government, or church discipline, can heal this breach within." Certainly the Kingdom of God was not imminent. "If ever there was a time for tears without, and a grief of spirit within, this seems the season ... when after such an expectation of Light and Glory, of settlement and establishment in the things of God, such thick darkness, such universal shame, such dreadful shatterings, have so apparently overtaken us, and are so likely daily more and more to overtake us..." (*A Voyce out of Thick Darkness* 1650, 3, 12, 17). Before long Penington was in a state of religious crisis, which he described some years later:

Expositions with Observations Sometimes on Several Scriptures (1656) 592–593

> ... when I was almost at the top, filling my heart and soul to the very brim with knowledge, faith, love, obedience, humility, and the fatness and riches of the ... dispensations of God's grace; even then was I shaken and thrown down

> into the depth of so great misery, darkness, and anguish, as my soul yet trembles at the remembrance of.
>
> The thing which I could not fear, overtook me: He, who I looked upon as my indissoluble friend [i.e. God], became my greatest enemy, bringing that upon me, which I thought it utterly impossible for him to suffer to befall me, much more for him to lay it upon me with his own hand. These breakings were very sudden, they came upon me in one hour very violent, they rushed in by main force against all the oppositions of my heart and soul: very unexpected, for indeed I then looked for somewhat of another nature, and not for that: very piercing, for they entered deep, seizing upon the very life of my spirit. ... They were also universal, for there was nothing spared, no knowledge that was not overclouded, no holy inclination that was not borne down, and made visibly sin and darkness to me (for in this fire and great darkness there was a kind of light.)
>
> And these breakings were not only in the lump, but particularly (for though I received the great blow at once, in one day, in one hour, in one moment: yet it was perfected [completed] gradually afterward). The inmost, and most practical light and knowledge, which God hath bestowed on me, was broken piece by piece... so that I as really, and sensibly, felt myself lost and undone, as even man did in his outward estate; against which, all reasonings and considerations were of no value.

Did anything really matter? Perhaps good and evil, nature and spirit, God and human, were all the same. Around 1649 and 1650 the people commonly called Ranters, who were not an organised group and were very varied, were speculating along these lines. Penington, briefly, turned his thoughts the same way. The following letter was written when his crisis was unresolved:

A Voyce out of Thick Darkness (1650) 18–20

> *This pamphlet was purchased on 1 April 1650 by George Thomason, a London bookseller whose collection of pamphlets is now in the British Library.*

The Sense of a poor shattered Soul, Concerning his Spiritual Loss and Misery thereby, Expressed in A LETTER to an intimate Friend

My dear Heart, mine own Soul; what shall I call thee? I can call thee any thing in word, in form; but nothing in light, in power. I have not been unwilling to write to thee, otherwise than I am made unwilling towards all motions: But this I must confess, I am unwilling so far to grieve thee, as my writing necessarily will occasion. How canst thou bear to hear how I have been tossed up and down, stripped of all; not of the outside, but of the inside; not of my corruptions, (which I hoped had been burning up, and wasting away), but of the vigour and life of my spirit? Not one branch of knowlege, not one sweet motion of my spirit, but hath been confounded, condemned, taken from me, and made odious to me. Very shy have I been of new notions, till extremity made me desirous to entertain any thing that might in any respect mitigate my torment, and then fain would I believe anything, imagine anything, be anything, for ease sake. And yet to this day am I still held off from everything. I can neither receive anything that is new, nor return to anything that is old: but everything is darkness, death, emptiness, vanity, a lie. Thus they still appear to me, and yet my spirit presently judgeth me for so thinking and judging, while I know them not, nor what they may be. I am rent from all things, but have nothing to turn to. My hopes, comforts, enjoyments, are all dashed, but nothing new brought in their stead. I am like a wild bull in a net, entangled with misery and torment, which I know not what it is, nor whence it comes, nor whither it tends, nor see no likelihood of any issue. I am perfectly weary of my self and all things, but continually more and more beset with what I hate; and have quite lost the remembrance of what I desire, or could love. Nor is there any use of any means for me, for there is no principle left in me for any man, or means, to work upon...

I am weary of all things, of religion, reason, sense, and all the objects that these have to converse about: but yet there is somewhat instead of these that I would fain find within, and somewhat instead of those objects I would fain meet with without, which if once my spirit might be satisfied in, I should find some rest; till when I cannot but remain truly miserable, and be fit for nothing, but to torment, and to be tormented.

18 February 1649 [1650]

Penington's distress continued for some months. In a sermon included in his next book, *Light or Darknesse* (purchased by Thomason on 22 May), he wrote, "I have been so tossed and tumbled, melted and new moulded, that I am changed into that which I thought it impossible for me ever to be. I am grown at peace, if not in love, with Folly". He had been accused of favouring "pure sporting with sin", an idea put forward by some Ranters, but he did not mean practising sins, he said, but rather that, since everything came from God, so evidently did sin. In its present state "the Creature sees it as unlovely". He then began to develop the idea of different levels of reality: "But come deeper, beyond thy state, beneath the law; look with a true eye, and you shall find all this unloveliness pass away, and an excellency appear, that the Creature could never so much as imagine or dream of". But in spite of these speculations Penington never went to the extremes of some Ranters, who abandoned conventional morality entirely. Two months later, as shown by Thomason's dating, he was arguing with those "Mad Folks" or Ranters, who thought they were not under any law, and could not sin. He published another letter, probably to the same friend, beginning "Dear Heart, I have looked upon thee as the Captain of that Generation whom my soul loveth". It was true, at one level, that God was all, that all things were good, and all things alike. It was true of God, and it would be true of "those who are one with him and perfectly live in him", but it was not true of "creatures in their creaturely state". "And the present form of these earthly moulded tabernacles seemeth to me...quite void of any capacity of entertaining and enjoying absolute perfection" (*Several Fresh Inward Openings* 1650, 28–30).

By the autumn of 1650 Penington was in a calmer state of mind. In his next work, purchased by Thomason in November, he returned to an academic discussion of religion in opposition to the "Mad Folk". God was not the same as human, and good was not the same as evil. Penington was again hoping for the coming of the Kingdom of God: "The appointed time of his absence is wearing out amain, and the time of his return approaching." Christ "sows his seed in the heart, the seed of life, his own seed, the seed wherein the very Godhead is contained, and which cannot but grow up into God" (*An Eccho from the Great Deep* 1650, 40–41).

Naturally enough, in an age when politics and religion were so closely related, he now turned to politics; his next two works, *The Fundamental Right, Safety and Liberty of the People* (1651) and *A Considerable Question about Government* (1653) concerned the practice and limitations of parliamentary government. After Cromwell expelled the remnants of Charles I's parliament in April 1653, there were great hopes that the Kingdom of the Lord would now arrive, but Penington was dubious, seeing no sign that Christ's spirit was yet poured out. Meanwhile, he continued to develop the theme of different layers of reality.

The Life of a Christian (1653)

From the Epistle to the Reader

The most excellent kind of things is hid, and those kinds which appear, in their greatest worth and excellency are but veils to that life wherein lieth our happiness. Miserable were the estate of man, could he enter into that estate of life which he desireth and seeketh to enjoy; but more miserable is his condition, in that he is not only fallen short of that glory which is perfectly satisfactory [complete] in God [Rom 3:23], but of that glory which belongs to him to adore and solace himself in, in his estate and condition. All Truth is a shadow [symbol, prefiguration] except the last, except the utmost: yet every Truth is true in its kind. It is substance [a real entity] in its own place, though it be but a shadow in another place, (for it is but a reflection from an intenser substance) and the shadow is a true shadow, as the substance is a true substance. But this is the exceeding great misery of man, he meets not with Truth either in substance or shadow; but (that which the world is full of) vanity, a lie, a fiction of his own heart and the Devil's, in imitation of the Truth of God: A doctrine of his own framing out of the Scripture, graces of his own forming in his Soul, and a worship and ordinances [usual Protestant term for Baptism and the Lord's Supper] of his own creation for his public or private devotion. And yet such hath always been the thick darkness of man,

*Qfp §
27.22*

that he could never see the lie (though never so palpable) in his right hand. When the light shineth, we shall all see where we are; but in the dark who is it that doth not mistake! We are all justifying ourselves and condemning one another, but who is it that shall be found able to stand before the righteous judgment of God? Who is it in whom the true light and life of God is sown, and in whom doth it truly spring up and shoot forth?

Surely if there was ever need of provoking one another to love and good works, the season is now proper: Religion is grown so outward, and hath spread forth into such various forms, pleasing itself so much in that dress which it most affects, that the inward substantial part, viz. the life and power of it, is almost lost in the varieties of shapes and shadow: The excrescences of religion are become so exuberant, that the vigour of it is much drawn from the heart. I profess I can hardly blame men for growing out of love with religion, both it and the professors of it being grown so unlike what it is and they once were, and still pretend to be. The worth of a religion consisteth not in a name or a profession, but in such a life, power, righteousness and holiness as the spirit of man, with all the art and strength of man, cannot attain. Where this is and appears in truth, it will gain esteem in the spirits, hearts and consciences of men; whereas a name and profession of religion, falling short of that common righteousness and goodwill which is formed in man, cannot but most deservedly become a reproach. Love, true love, the love of Christ (sown and springing up) is the life of true religion; which as it is like the love in Christ, so it will appear and act like it. This love being of a deep intense and most pure nature, goeth forth with mighty strength and entireness towards the fountain of life from which it came, and towards all the branchings forth of this life into such as are changed and renewed by it: nay it extends itself to all men, even the greatest enemies, blessing them that curse, and wishing well to them that use the subjects of it in the most despiteful manner; nay to all creatures, expressing itself in sweetness, meekness; tenderness, pity, mercifulness, and in what way else soever it can vent itself doing good to any sort of things, persons or creatures. This love in its way of acting (according to the pattern) to the household of faith [Gal 6:10], is in part here described and exposed for the view of such as may stand in need of such an help, and shall find hearts to make use of it.

In 1654 Isaac's life changed when he married Lady Springett, born Mary Proude, a young widow with a small daughter. Mary was born in 1625 of a wealthy family, but was orphaned and brought up by relations in Kent. Even as a child she had felt ill at ease with conventional religion, to the point that she was told by her guardians that she was jeopardising her chance of making a suitable marriage. However, another young man of the household, Sir William Springett, was of the same way of thinking, and they were married very young, in 1643. According to Mary's account they were extremely happy; she had a small son and another baby on the way when her husband, now a colonel in the Parliamentary army, died of fever while on active service (*Experiences*, 72–108). A daughter, named Gulielma after her father, was born soon afterwards. (This name is the feminine of the Latin form of William, the G is hard, and she was known as Guli for short.) Mary would not have Guli baptised, for she and her husband had decided there was no justification for this practice. Her little son, as so often in the seventeenth century, died as a young child. Mary's mother-in-law, to whom she was devoted, lived with her till she also died in 1647. Mary was left isolated and depressed, "wearied in seeking and not finding". Isaac Penington seemed to her to be another person in similar case. She later wrote of him: "All things that appeared to be religion and were not so, were very manifest to him; so that, till then, he was sick and weary of all appearances. My heart became united to him, and I desired to be made serviceable to him in his disconsolate condition; for he was as one alone and miserable in this world" (*Experiences* 38). Mary and Isaac, who were living in London at the time of their marriage, soon had a son, John, born in London in 1655. A second son, Isaac, followed, and a daughter, Mary, was born in 1657. They soon moved out of London, at first to Datchet and then probably to Caversham, near Reading (Ellwood 11).

Isaac had not rediscovered his early assured faith, but he was in a calmer frame of mind, awaiting the leadings of God. In 1656 he wrote: "I am now a dark thing, still in the dark, being neither what I formerly was, nor yet formed into a vessel by the Potter. Not yet perfectly broken, (though to my own sense perfectly broken long ago) and very little made up [Jer 18:1–6, cf. Isa 45:9]." He was content to "wait quietly for the descent of life and power from above" (*Expositions* (1656), 595, 603). It was around this time that the Peningtons first encountered Quakers, who had spread over most of England and Wales during 1654 and 1655.[7] The Quaker movement had started in the East Midlands during the 1640s, growing rapidly during 1651 and 1652 when the charismatic young preacher George Fox travelled widely in the North and gained many adherents. The Quakers taught that there was no need for formal worship and a paid ministry, for "Christ had come to teach his people himself", and in their meetings they quaked with the power of the Lord. They believed in the equality of all human beings before God, and therefore addressed everyone with the familiar "thou" and refused to offer customary honour, such as bowing or, for men, removing one's hat to social superiors.

Like most people of their social standing, Isaac and Mary were not favourably impressed at first. Isaac wrote of them: "They were for the most part mean, as to the outward; young country lads, of no deep understanding or ready expression. ...How ridiculous was their coming forth and appearance to the eye of man! About what poor, trivial circumstances, habits, gestures and things did they seem to lay great weight!...How far did they seem from being acquainted with the mysteries and depths of religion" (*Some Deep...Israel, Works* II.376). But Mary was interested in what she heard, and thought she would like to go to a Quaker meeting.

---

7 There is a suggestion that the Penington's home was already known as a Quaker centre in 1655, in a note in the second edition of William C. Braithwaite *The Beginnings of Quakerism*, (Cambridge University Press, 1955, page 582). This depends on the year dating of a letter from Richard Hubberthorne (Swarthmore MSS 1.106) to Margaret Fell and other Friends, addressed to Gerrard Robert's house in London, and written on the 5th October, which from Hubberthorne's references to other days of the week appears to have been a Friday or possibly a Saturday, and in which he stated that their route to London would take them 12 miles from Isaac Penington's house. Geoffrey Nuttall, "Early Quaker Letters" 1952, gave the year date as 1655; however, 5th October was also a Friday in 1660, and Saturday in 1661. 1660 seems the most likely date. Margaret Fell was in London during 1660, but not in 1655.

Then, one day, when they were out walking in the grounds of a friend's house, Mary and Isaac were accosted by a passer-by, who turned out to be a rather newly convinced Quaker. Mary recorded what happened: "He cried out to us against our pride, etc., at which I scoffed.... He drew nigh to the pales [fence], and spoke of the light and grace which had appeared to all men. My husband and he engaged in discourse. The man of the house coming up, invited the stranger in: he was but young, and my husband too hard for him in fleshly discourse." So the young man promised to bring further support, and the next day two well-known Quakers came to call, Thomas Curtis, a draper from Reading, and William Simpson who is best remembered for his habit of "walking naked as a sign".[8] By this time, Quakers had lost much of their early charismatic fire, and were making efforts to present themselves in a more sympathetic manner. Mary, who may have been more impressed than Isaac by the young man of the day before, wrote: "Their solid and weighty carriage struck a dread over me. I now knew that they came in the power and authority of the Lord" (*Experiences* 40–44).

Isaac and Mary probably attended a Quaker meeting in Reading in February 1657 (Alexanders Parker's "Testimony", *Works* 1 [App. A].445), but nothing is known about their further relations with Quakers during that year. Isaac, who had intellectual difficulties in accepting Quakerism, later gave an account of this time:

"A true and faithful relation, in brief, concerning myself, in reference to my spiritual travels, and the Lord's dealings with me," 15 May 1667 (*Works* 1.7–11)[9]

Isaac's friend Thomas Ellwood found this paper, which was written when Isaac was imprisoned in Aylesbury Gaol, when he was sorting Isaac's papers after his death, and he included it in his "Testimony" to Isaac.

At the very first they [the Quakers] reached to the life of God in me ... but still in my reasonings with them, and disputes alone (in my mind) concerning them, I was very far off from

---

8 For this and similar practices of early Quakers see Kenneth L Carroll, "Early Quakers and 'Going Naked as a Sign'", *Quaker History* 67.2 (Autumn 1978).
9 See Introduction p. xii for an explanation of this use of the word 'travel'.

owning them, as so knowing the Lord, or so appearing in his life and power as my condition needed, and as my soul waited for. Yea, the more I conversed with them, the more I seemed in my understanding and reason to get over them, and to trample them under my feet, as a poor, weak, silly, contemptible generation, who had some smatterings of truth in them, and some honest desires towards God; but very far off from the clear and full understanding of his way and will. And this was the effect almost of every discourse with them; they still reached my heart, and I felt them in the secrets of my soul; which caused the love in me always to continue, yea, sometimes to increase towards them: but daily my understanding got more and more over them, and therein I daily more and more despised them.

In January 1658, a large meeting of Quakers from the surrounding area was held near Ampthill in Bedfordshire at the house of John Crook, who was one of the few Quaker converts from the class of landed gentry. Quakers sent reports of such meetings to Swarthmoor Hall, the home of Margaret Fell and the original Quaker base in Cumbria, and noted that on this occasion some people "great in the outward" were there, among them Isaac Penington, who "grows sensible into the knowledge of the truth". Mary and probably Guli were also present (Caton MSS 3.111). Quakers, whatever their theoretical views on the equality of all, were not immune to excitement when the rich and powerful attended their meetings and, even better, actually joined with them.

During the following months Isaac and Mary evidently made up their minds to follow the Quaker way. On 5 May 1658 Edward Burrough, a very able young man who was at this time probably the most influential Quaker after George Fox, wrote them a letter beginning: "Isaac Penington and thy dearly beloved wife: My dear Friends, whom I do love and salute in the Lord, because of your love to the precious truth, which now the Lord hath made manifest". Burrough was very pleased that "to you is the way of life and truth discovered", but pointed out that the Peningtons would need to make some changes in their way of life: "Let it not seem hard to you to lay down your crowns of honour and glory in the world" (JP IV.179).

On 31 May Isaac was present at another big meeting at John

Crook's, where George Fox and many other leading Friends were present. According to Alexander Parker, a Friend who wrote one of the "Testimonies" to Isaac after his death, it was on this occasion that Isaac definitely decided for Quakerism. More likely, judging by the evidence of the letter from Burrough, this meeting clinched a decision that had effectively been taken some weeks before. Isaac's "Spiritual Travels" may compress the experience of several meetings:

Qfp §
19.14
After a long time I was invited to hear one of them (as I had been often, they in tender love pitying me, and feeling my want of that which they possessed); and there was an answer in my heart, and I went with fear and trembling, with desires to the Most High, who was over all, and knew all, that I might not receive any thing for truth which was not of him, nor withstand any thing which was of him; but might bow before the appearance of the Lord my God, and none other. And indeed, when I came, I felt the presence and power of the Most High among them, and words of truth from the Spirit of truth reaching to my heart and conscience, opening my state as in the presence of the Lord. Yea, I did not only feel words and demonstrations from without, but I felt the dead quickened, the seed raised; insomuch that my heart (in the certainty of light, and clearness of true sense) said, This is he, there is no other: this is he whom I have waited for and sought after from my childhood; who was always near me, and had often begotten life in my heart; but I knew him not distinctly, nor how to receive him, or dwell with him. And then in this sense (in the melting and breakings of my spirit) was I given up to the Lord, to become his, both in waiting for the further revealing of his seed in me, and to serve him in the life and power of his seed.

There was now a process of adjustment to go through. Mary recorded that it took much heart-searching over a period of months before she herself was ready to be counted as a Quaker, not for their doctrine, but because she was "exercised against taking up the cross to the language, fashions, customs, titles, honour and esteem in the world". Her relations, she recalled, "made this cross very heavy" (*Experiences*, 44; *Qfp* §19.13). Isaac's "Spiritual Travels" continued:

> Now what I met with after this, in my travels, in my waitings, in my spiritual exercises, is not to be uttered: only in general I may say this, I met with the very strength of hell. The cruel oppressor roared upon me, and made me feel the bitterness of his captivity, while he had any power: yea, the Lord was far from my help, and from the voice of my roaring. I also met with deep subtleties and devices to entangle me in that wisdom, which seemeth able to make wise in the things of God, but indeed is foolishness, and a snare to the soul, bringing it back into captivity, where the enemy's gins [traps] prevail. And what I met with outwardly from my own dear father, from my kindred, from my servants, from the people and powers of the world, for no other cause but fearing my God, worshipping him as he hath required of me, and bowing to his seed, which is his Son, who is to be worshipped by men and angels for evermore, the Lord my God knoweth, before whom my heart and ways are; who preserved me in love to them, in the midst of all I suffered from them, and doth still so preserve me; blessed be his pure and holy name.

Social relationships also changed, as described in the following account of what happened when two friends paid the Peningtons a visit. Walter Ellwood had known Mary in London during her widowhood, and his son Thomas, a few years older than Guli, had sometimes played with her (Ellwood 4). Young Thomas, who later became a Quaker and a life-long friend of the whole Penington family, told this story of what happened when his father decided to visit the Peningtons, who had recently moved to a considerable property called The Grange, at Chalfont St Peter in Buckinghamshire. It had presumably been made over to Isaac junior by his father, and still exists, though much altered. It has been occupied by the Holy Cross convent school since 1929.

> **From *The History of the Life of Thomas Ellwood, Written by Himself*, 11–12 (2004 edn)**
>
> But very much surprised we were when, being come thither, we first heard, then found, they had become Quakers; a people we had no knowledge of, and a name we had till then scarce heard of.

So great a change, from a free, debonair, and courtly sort of behaviour, which we formerly had found them in, to so strict a gravity as they now received us with did not a little amuse [puzzle] us, and disappoint our expectation of such a pleasant visit as we used to have, and had now promised ourselves. Nor could my father have any opportunity, by a private conference with them, to understand the ground or occasion of this change, there being some other strangers with them (related to Isaac Penington), who came that morning from London to visit them also.

For my part I sought and at length found means to cast myself into the company of the daughter, whom I found gathering some flowers in the garden, attended by her maid, who was also a Quaker. But when I addressed myself to her after my accustomed manner, with intention to engage her in some discourse which might introduce conversation on the foot of our former acquaintance; though she treated me with a courteous mien, yet, as young as she was, the gravity of her look and behaviour struck such an awe upon me, that I found myself not so much master of myself as to pursue any further converse with her. Wherefore, asking pardon for my boldness in having intruded myself into her private walks, I withdrew, not without some disorder (as I thought at least) of mind.

We stayed dinner, which was very handsome, and lacked nothing to recommend it to me but the want of mirth and pleasant discourse, which we could neither have with them, nor by reason of them with one another amongst ourselves; the weightiness that was upon their spirits and countenances keeping down the lightness that would have been up in us. We stayed, notwithstanding, till the rest of the company took leave of them, and then we also, doing the same, returned, not greatly satisfied with our journey, nor knowing what in particular to find fault with.

Inevitably, there was a breach between Isaac and his father, and several letters written during the next few months indicate that relations between them were in a poor state. Much of the trouble was due to Quakers' refusal to observe customary forms of politeness.

Part I The Life of Isaac Penington

Sons at that time were expected to remove their hats in the presence of their fathers, and to address them with the polite "you" rather than the familiar singular, "thou". The following letter, probably because of its strong language, has never previously been printed. Isaac is evidently replying to an even stronger letter from his father.

To his father [1658–9] (John Penington manuscripts, cited as JP, 1.122.2)

> *The letters to Penington senior are placed together in JP 1.120–122.2. One is dated 14 February 1659, and probably the rest date from around this period. The two that were printed in John Barclay's* Letters of Isaac Penington *(1828) were designated as "to a near relation", presumably because of the unfilial tone (Works 1.421 and IV [supp].18).*

> Dear Father,

> How can I hold my peace, and behold thy ruin, thy eternal ruin! This spirit (whereof thy letters savour) I am sure is not to inherit the kingdom of God: and there is but a moment left for thee to be severed from that spirit, or to perish with it. How strangely and slightly doth my Father take liberty to speak, concerning the worship which I perform to my God, in the depth of the seriousness of my soul, calling it a "knack" [artificial contrivance], not to scare crows but to drive away my nearest and dearest friends? Ah my Father, that which I have waited for all my days, hath not been a knack, but the true guidance of the spirit of the Lord; and upon no other account could I be drawn to do what I do, but in obedience to the Lord: and I am sure that that which is pleasing to the fleshly part is not of him. Ah Father what is it that makes it thus harsh to thee? Is it meekness of spirit? Is it humility? Or is it loftiness, and a fleshly desire which the better to hide itself from God's witness in thy heart, takes hold of a Scripture, "Honour thy father and thy mother" [Ex 20:12], but doth not humbly wait to know what that honour is, but concludes it to be a fleshly honour, which pleaseth not the Lord, but is forbidden: for he that will be Christ's disciple, must deny whatever the flesh calls for both in himself or others? There is an honour which is of flesh,

and there is an honour which is of God only. The one of these the true Christian seeks, the other he takes up the cross to. What, be a Christian, and seek the honour of the part which is to be crucified? How can these stand? To be a believer and seek the honour of this world can no more stand together, than the love of God and the love of the world can. Did not Christ keep the law? Did not he honour his father and mother? Yet he showed not that to them which you would call honour, for he regarded no man's person. And when the Jews might watch him in this thing (telling him his mother etc. stood without to speak with him) to see what reverence he would show to them, he saith, "Who is my mother, etc" [Mt 12:46–50, Lk 8:20–21]. The honour due to parents is of the Lord, and of a right kind and nature, not such as the flesh calls honour, which is gratifying to the fleshly part, but loathsome to the living heir who is not of this world, nor can give or receive its honour.

Ah, dear Father, the Lord knows I cannot do this without the utter hazard of my soul, and without nourishing of that in my father, which I beg of the Lord to destroy in him. Would my father have me throw away my soul to put off an hat to him? Or would he have me to contribute to feed that in him, which is too fat already? This might a little gratify the fleshly part at present, but what comfort would it be hereafter? Ah Father, we have pleased one another (setting up one another, and honouring the fleshly part one of another too long already) and robbed God. Now God is come to require his own. O do not strive for that honour which is due to him alone, but wait for receiving of that humility from the Lord, which knows not how to strive about outward honour. If my father were not exceedingly overborne in his mind in this particular, he would rather rejoice that his son (in tenderness of conscience to God) should deny such a thing, than be so much troubled for the loss of it. O that that which loves the honour and esteem of this world were subdued in thee, and this would soon be no such harsh thing.

And then what an unsavoury passage is that, "If thou wert at a further distance, thou couldest pass it by as a whimsy and brainsick toy". Suppose it should be of God (for I am sure my father doth not know the contrary) whence then do these words come, which speak so reproachfully of it? I came not to it by the workings of the brain; but against the workings of the brain; and my heart was torn in pieces, and my strength broken before I could submit. And this I may venture to say, that if such a thing were laid upon my father, he would find it much harder to yield to it, in true obedience to the Lord than he is now aware of.

And whereas I am charged as having "ever been full of fancies", my conscience clears me, in the sight of God, that from my childhood (in singleness of heart) I have pressed after the truth and substance of religion, and to avoid fancies. But I know the charge will in due time light (from the righteous God) on many, who now unrighteously lay it upon others: for the very faith, love, hope, peace, joy etc. which hath not the true virtue in it, is but a fancy, and will appear so when men awake.

And then I am charged with "cross carriage" [perverse behaviour]. Wherein hath my carriage been cross? Mine own conscience doth not accuse me: yet if I were informed wherein, I think I should beg strength of God to remove the occasion. But if my father hereby means, that which I perform in singleness of heart, and in obedience to the Lord my God, I must then plainly profess, my God and my soul are dearer to me than my father, although he be exceedingly dear.

And now, dear Father, let the bowels of a son at length pierce [those things] which have rolled over [covered] thy soul ever since I had any sense of God, and be persuaded to improve that little time thou hast, not towards the changing of a notion, or outward practices, but mourn bitterly to the Lord to slay this spirit in thee (which otherwise will undo thee) which all thy religion hitherto hath not done.

Ah, dear Father, the old root is standing in thee (which brings forth sour grapes [Isa 5:1–7]) whereof Christ is not the head, but the serpent [devil] is the head; and so notwithstanding all thy long profession, many performances, and applying of promises, and thou are not yet come to feel the virtue of the first promise wrought out in thy heart, viz. To have the head of the serpent bruised by the seed of the woman there [Gen 3:15]: but what is good in thee, is in bondage, and the evil one rules over it, and thou art yet a captive in a strange land, and not come out of Egypt from under Pharaoh [Ex 3:7–9 et al.]. O that thou mightest know (before thou goest hence, and be no more seen) that which washes and makes the heart clean from such a spirit: for the way of eternal life is a way of holiness (a pure way, a living way) and the unclean spirit cannot walk in it, but must be cut off here in this world, and that is the circumcision, which he that goes out of this world without, must not enter into the holy land. Dear Father open thy heart (if it be his pleasure) that thou mayest live and not die.

Despite these problems with his father, Isaac remained on good terms with various other members of his family, and letters survive to his two brothers and to one sister, besides a cousin and an uncle. The following could have been addressed to either brother, but was more likely written to William. Isaac wanted to share his newly found certainty:

To his brother, 14 February 1659 (JP 1.127)

My desire is that thy soul might come to live, by a true feeling of the power of him, who alone can quicken it. And if thy soul live, the bond of sin and death may be broken, and the hasty, peevish, selfish, imperious, profane nature cut down by the sword of the Lord: yea all thy religion and wisdom in the first birth must perish and come to naught, for this will judge the wisdom of God foolishness, and the ways thereof weak, and will never suffer thee to become such a fool and child, as alone can enter into the kingdom and know the things of God [Mk 10:15, cf. 1 Cor 1:20–25]. God hath made us fools to the world, yea to the wise worldly part in ourselves, where the wisdom of the first birth scoffed at Isaac, the seed of promise: yet this shall inherit the everlasting kingdom, when the other (with all his religion and devotion) shall be thrust by [Gen 21:2–12]. Therefore fear before the Lord God, and be not conceited, but wait to know his counsel, and to feel the guidance of his spirit, which will make thee also a fool to the world, and to all thine own wisdom, if ever it make thee wise to salvation. The wise, the reasoner, the disputer in thy self, shall never know God: but if thou canst feel an eternal seed sown in thy soul; and a birth of it born to God, to that babe will God reveal his infinite wisdom, and save him by the arm of his everlasting strength: and in joining to it, mayest thou be saved, and no otherwise. It is the eye of this child, which can see the light of the scriptures, but the eye of man's wisdom cannot, but understands them in a light beneath that wherein they were written, and so falls short of the spirit and life of them. Ah dear Brother, do not throw away thy precious soul, but beware of that wisdom which will destroy it, and wait for the redeeming wisdom, for the wisdom which is from above, which grows not in man's understanding, but in the understanding which is given from above. God makes a new-creature, and in this new-creature he forms a new understanding and into this understanding he pours the treasures of the wisdom and knowledge of himself. Therefore seek out wisdom's gate, and wait there for the gift, that thou mayst live: but take heed of treasuring up a stock of knowledge in that spirit which is to perish.

I remain
Thy truly affectionate Brother
14 of 12 Month 1658 [1659]

Isaac had at last experienced what he described to his brother, and it was worth any difficulties. "Spiritual Travels" concludes:

Qfp § 19.14   But some may desire to know what I have at last met with? I answer, I have met with the Seed. Understand that word, and thou wilt be satisfied, and inquire no further. I have met with my God; I have met with my Saviour; and he hath not been present with me without his salvation; but I have felt the healings drop upon my soul from under his wings. I have met with the true knowledge, the knowledge of life, the living knowledge, the knowledge which is life; and this hath had the true virtue in it, which my soul hath rejoiced in, in the presence of the Lord. I have met with the Seed's Father, and in the Seed I have felt him my Father. There I have read his nature, his love, his compassions, his tenderness, which have melted, overcome, and changed my heart before him. I have met with the Seed's faith, which hath done and doth that which the faith of man can never do. I have met with the true birth, with the birth which is heir of the kingdom, and inherits the kingdom. I have met with the true spirit of prayer and supplication, wherein the Lord is prevailed with, and which draws from him whatever the condition needs; the soul always looking up to him in the will, and in the time and way, which are acceptable with him. What shall I say? I have met with the true peace, the true righteousness, the true holiness, the true rest of the soul, the everlasting habitation, which the redeemed dwell in: and I know all these to be true, in him that is true, and am capable of no doubt, dispute, or reasoning in my mind about them; it abiding there, where it hath received the full assurance and satisfaction. And also I know very well and distinctly in spirit where the doubts and disputes are, and where the certainty and full assurance are, and in the tender mercy of the Lord am preserved out of the one, and in the other.

CHAPTER 2

Political Disruption and Quaker Dissension, 1659–1664

Fox probably took the opportunity of their meeting on 31 May 1658 to speak with Isaac about his future service to the Quaker movement. The Peningtons' house soon became a staging post for the distribution of Quaker books and correspondence, and among the Penington papers are copies of 81 epistles of George Fox, as well as other important documents of early Friends.[1] Isaac began his long career as a Quaker apologist, his first Quaker book being *The Way of Life and Death*.[2] The following letter is undated, but the reference to "Oliver" places it before Cromwell's death in September 1658. Many people at the time were critical of Cromwell's government and declared that the Lord, who ruled all governments, would not tolerate its failure to fulfil its promise.[3]

> *To the Council* [1658] (JP II.242.2)
>
> Hearken to me, ye rulers of this nation, in what I have to say on the Lord's behalf, that the Lord may hearken unto you in the day of great distress, which he is bringing upon all the earth.

---

1. See Portfolio MSS 36.46, in LSF, a letter from Alexander Parker, sent from Chester prison 13th October 1660, the original or early copy of JP 4.104. There is a note at the end: "Let this be sent into Sussex to be read amongst Friends there at their meetings. Let a copie be sent to Isaac Penington to be read amongst friends in Buckinghamshire, as the Lord makes way, and moves any thereunto."
2. See Part II pp. 129–134.
3. See also Part II, *Some Considerations proposed to the City of London*, p. 172.

Ye are as a vessel in the hand of the potter. This power, this authority which ye have in the nation is not for yourselves, but for the Lord. If the Master find you fit for his use and service, it may please him to continue you, and make use of you: but if otherwise, he can easily break you upon the wheel, and form another vessel fitter for his service.

The King and Bishops were not for the Lord's use and service, but greatly against it [i.e. not suitable]: and though it might then seem to man impossible, yet the Lord found a way to break them. The Parliament after them proved not such as the Lord might justly expect: the Lord laid them aside too, first the House of Lords then the Commons. And how the hand of the Lord hath been upon the army, and how they have lost their day, is hard to speak. (O Oliver, Oliver, what a crown hast thou lost!)

Now, of a truth, ye are fallen into the snare of, and deeply entangled in, that wisdom and interest which hath undone all these. Ye have forgotten the pit from whence ye were digged [Isa 51:1], and the snare wherein the feet of those that went before you were taken; and so have wheeled about, and centred in that which God began to draw you out of. O remember your first works, remember your first leader; quit your station in the fleshly wisdom, quit your hold of the fleshly Interest, lest the Lord smite and overturn. If the Lord hath raised up a seed to serve him, he will break their bonds: if your government be bonds to the just, it must be broken.

I have a word to say to you. I have a clue of the Lord's wisdom opened in me, to lead you out of the snare: but I am exceedingly afraid, lest the fleshly spirit in me should bring it forth, and lest it should be set before the fleshly part in you, by either whereof it may lose its virtue [Penington knows he has a leading from God, but is uncertain whether he can express it without distorting it according to his own understanding]. But this I am sure of, that if the right thing in me speak, and the right thing in you hear and obey, it will strike at the root of that (and save you from that) which otherwise will ruin you. Yet do I not find, that I am to impose anything upon you, by way of authority, but only speak to your consciences in the sight of God, and they shall answer me. But if the [human] wisdom get up in you, and bear down the testimony in your consciences, because it suits not with the wisdom, and with your interest in the flesh, it may go hard with you.

Therefore seek the Lord, and beg earnestly, that what is of him may not be rejected by you; and that ye may no longer be of yourselves; or for yourselves; but of him and for him.

I am a true friend to your souls, to your government (so far as it is of God) and to this nation and the whole creation.

I.P.

Mary also used her contacts to further the Quaker cause, and wrote to a kinswoman of hers who was married to Cromwell's son Henry, the governor of Ireland, asking her to use her influence to help Quakers.[4] Note her comment on the social status of a Cromwell wife. Ishmael was the exiled son of Abraham by his concubine (Gen 21: 9–21), and his descendents are frequently depicted in the Old Testament as being opposed to the true Israelites.

From Mary to Henry Cromwell's wife [1658] (JP IV.181.2)

Dear Friend,

The fire of the Lord is kindled in my bones, and is burning up in me the love of acceptation with men, by being found in their customs and frothy language: I that have abounded in that which pleases men and my own flesh, must now witness a putting off worldly greatness and a vain show of pride and pomp. Therefore I write not compliments but a declaration of love to thee, whom I hope not to find in the Ishmael nature of scorning, but in the tendernesss of

---

4. The exact relationship is not known. Henry Cromwell had considered Quakers a serious danger to the discipline of his army, and imprisoned many. The situation of Quakers had eased by 1658–9, but in the confused political situation Mary presumably thought that her appeal would be appropriate. For Quakers in Ireland see W.C.Braithwaite, *The Beginnings of Quakerism* (2nd edn Cambridge University Press, 1955) 215–223; T.C.Barnard, *Cromwellian Ireland* (Oxford University Press, 1975) 109–112.

the Lord's seed which he hath made the promise to. Dear friend, there is an opportunity put into thy hand of showing kindness to the Lord's particular people; know wherefore thou art raised above thy people and father's house, not to abuse his mercy, but to intercede and stand between them and ought [anything] that goes forth from thy husband upon the innocent, the fear of the Lord will keep thee clean in thy place and make thee of great service to the servants of that God who hath set thee amongst princes.

This from thy kinswoman in the flesh,

Mary Penington

Richard Cromwell, Oliver's eldest son, succeeded his father as Lord Protector in September 1658, but he proved unable to retain the confidence of the army. He resigned the Protectorate in April 1659, and the country rapidly descended into anarchy. Established authors like Penington had much to say about the situation, and his writings reflect the changing fortunes of the years 1659–1660.[5] Despite the disturbed political situation, Quaker ministers continued to travel the country, and if they passed within reach of The Grange they would be entertained by the Peningtons, as happened on an occasion described by Thomas Ellwood (Ellwood 13–15):

> My father, having gotten some further account of the people called Quakers, and being desirous to be informed concerning their principles, made another visit to Isaac Penington and his wife, at their house called the Grange, in Peter's Chalfont, and took both my sisters and me with him.
>
> It was in the tenth month [December], in the year 1659, that we went thither, where we found a very kind reception... while we were there a meeting was appointed at a place about a mile from thence, to which we were invited to go, and willingly went...
>
> To this meeting came Edward Burrough, besides other preachers, as Thomas Curtis and James Nayler, but none spoke there at that time but Edward Burrough, next to whom, as it were under him, it was my lot to sit on a stool

---

5. See Part II, pp. 171–177.

by the side of a long table on which he sat, and I drank
in his words with desire; for they not only answered my
understanding, but warmed my heart with a certain heat,
which I had not till then felt from the ministry of any man.

When the meeting was ended our friends took us home
with them again; and after supper, the evenings being long,
the servants of the family (who were Quakers) were called
in, and we all sat down in silence. But long we had not so sat
before Edward Burrough began to speak among us. ...

The subject of the discourse was, "The universal
free grace of God to all mankind", to which [my father]
opposed the Calvinistic tenet of particular and personal
predestination. ... Edward Burrough said not much to him
upon it, though what he said was close and cogent; but
James Nayler interposing, handled the subject with so much
perspicuity and clear demonstration, that his reasoning
seemed to be irresistible; and so I suppose my father found
it, which made him willing to drop the discourse. ... As my
father was not able to maintain the argument on his side, so
neither did they seem willing to drive it to an extremity on
their side; but treating him in a soft and gentle manner, did
after a while let fall the discourse, and then we withdrew to
our respective chambers.

Soon afterwards, Thomas Ellwood declared himself a Quaker.

Meanwhile, the political situation was reaching a crisis. Parliament had lost control, and General Monck, who had been Cromwell's commander in Scotland, marched his army south and was invited by Parliament to secure London, which he entered on 3 February 1660. To begin with, Penington was hopeful of the outcome, and in a pamphlet dated 12 February he wrote, "This is the thing which the Lord hath determined to do ... namely, to pull down the mighty from their seats [Lk 2:52]. ... This work has the Lord begun already; for his great and notable day has appeared" (*Question...England, Works* 1.293). But the situation was still confused and unstable, and people's minds turned towards a restored monarchy as the best means of achieving an effective government, provided that the existing system of religious toleration could be maintained. After hurried discussions between London and Charles II's court in Holland, Charles issued the

2. Political Disruption and Quaker Dissension, 1659–1664

Declaration of Breda on 4 April, promising freedom of worship provided that Parliament consented. Charles was then proclaimed King, and returned to England on 29 May.

Everything had happened so quickly that many people were taken by surprise. Quakers, who were considered dangerous extremists by many people, had a hard time. Meetings all over the country were attacked and broken up. Penington's pamphlets from the later part of 1660 and from 1661 show attempts to grapple with the situation, appeals to the new government, and explanations of the Quaker faith which were designed to show that Quakers posed no threat to the new order. Like many other people at the time, Isaac and Mary both wrote directly to the new King. Isaac's letter is very long, so we reproduce Mary's. Compare it with the attitude to kings expressed in Isaac's earlier letter to Cromwell's government. The key to understanding Quaker thinking at this time is the phrase "since thou art by the Lord brought into this nation". The Lord had effected the change of government, and his will must be respected. This letter was presumably written during the early summer of 1660, when proposals for a new religious settlement were under discussion. The reference to a "weak silly woman" was typical of the time, not to be taken too literally.[6]

> ### From Mary, to the King [1660] (JP II.249)
>
> O King, since thou art by the Lord brought into this nation, and not by might, courage, wisdom, policies nor outward strength, let the Lord God be thy interest and thy counsellor. O King, fear no party, nor make not a league with any sort of men, for to preserve thee in thy dominion over these nations; but fear the Lord, trust confidently in him, and be safe; do equal justice to all sorts, and his blessing will be thy strength and defence. O King, have a care of making an arm of flesh thy trust, it hath not served thee, nor been the cause of thy possessing these dominions, nor it shall not prevail against thee, if thou, O King, be but found upright before the Lord: and singly mind the good of all, the succouring of all, and redressing the grievances of all; O King, in this and for this, none can nor shall harm thee, nor disappoint

---

6. Compare the tone of Mary's letter to the women's meeting at Armscote, pp. 109–113.

thy happy governing of this people. O King, there will be a majesty and authority in thy government, if thou love mercy and do justice and as a father of this nation, takest care of all mankind in it, be they Papists, Protestants, Presbyterians, Independents, Anabaptists [Baptists], Seekers, Quakers.

O King, thy power is given of God to preserve the persons of all and not to make a league with any sort against the other. O King, there is a generation who love to exercise lordship over the heritage of God, whom the Lord hath cursed; their God is their belly; they can pray for thee or against thee as thou, O King, art in prosperity or adversity; the soul of the Lord loathes them, and he will spew them out of his mouth; they can be any thing for filthy lucre [Titus 1:7]: O if thou shouldst join with them, the Lord would soon withdraw his favour from thee, and depart from thee and thy council, and then thou wouldest be as weak as water. But O King, my desire and prayer to God for thee is, that thou mightest meet with in thy government the blessing, wisdom, salvation of the Lord: nothing, O King, will make thee faint, and distract thy councils, but a departing from the counsel of the Lord in thy own heart, and a leaning to thy own understanding, and the vain consultations and policies of men, who see not the wheel within the wheel, by which all things are governed, but like Nebuchadnezzar [Dan 4] boast of their might and wisdom, as if that brought great things to pass, when alas their wisdom is blown upon, and their counsels turned backwards in a moment. Despise not O King this love, it is a love from the Lord to thee, though conveyed to thee through a weak silly [simple] woman.
O King, I am

Thy faithful subject, as thou rulest for the Lord. Mary Penington.

Isaac had personal reasons for concern at the change of regime, because of his father's record as a prominent supporter of the previous government. Not having signed Charles I's death certificate, Isaac senior was not executed, but he was imprisoned for life and his property confiscated. He died in the Tower of London in December 1661. This family connection was a major reason for the financial problems that dogged Isaac junior thereafter, and also for some of the lengthy periods that he spent in prison. A letter from Burrough dated 6 August 1660 indicates that the Peningtons had serious troubles during that summer: "All thy outward afflictions, which come upon thee from the wrath of men, the Lord will make easy unto thee, and carry thee through it all. ... And be not impatient or hopeless; for how knowest thou whether the Lord may not work thy deliverance from the hand of thy enemy?" (JP IV.25). The details are not known, but it seems that there was some flaw in Isaac junior's title to his estate. According to Mary, their relations took legal action against them. Quakers would not take oaths, as they considered the practice contrary to Scripture and indicative of a double standard of truth (Mt 5:33–37).[7] Consequently, not being able to swear to the facts of the matter, the Peningtons lost all Isaac's estate and a part of Mary's (*Experiences* 53).[8] Tenants refused to pay their rent, and neighbours looked down on them. Isaac's lack of practical skills probably exacerbated the situation. He was, as Thomas Ellwood later wrote of him, "to the world and its affairs very much a stranger" (*Works* I.3).

Then, in January 1661, there was a revolt in London organised by the Fifth Monarchists, and Quakers were suspected of being implicated.[9] Quaker and Baptist meetings were immediately banned, and 4,000 Quakers were arrested, including Isaac Penington, who was one of 63 Quakers imprisoned from his district. Edward Burrough, who was travelling the country in support of the many Quaker prisoners, visited The Grange, and afterwards wrote to Isaac: "My very dear love in the Lord. I hope in thy patience and faithfulness in this thy day of trial". He himself was now on his way to London, "to suffer if the Lord

---

7. For the Quaker testimony against oath-taking see Rosemary Moore, *The Light in Their Consciences: Early Quakers in Britain 1646–1666* (University Park: Pennsylvania State University Press, 2000) 118.
8. Perhaps, given the confiscation of Isaac senior's property, some members of the family thought it might be possible to find a flaw in Isaac junior's title, since he would not swear to it, and thereby recoup their lost inheritance from Isaac senior. But which members of the family? Isaac remained on good terms with several of them, though not with his father. Perhaps his brother-in-law? On another occasion Mary said that Isaac had lost his estate "upon his Father's account" (*John Penington's Complaint against William Rogers*, Benjamin Clark 1681, 10–13). Either way, it appears that Isaac's title to the estate was not secure.
9. For Fifth Monarchists see p. 4, note 2.

will" (Gibson MSS 1.49, JP IV.1 20, Feb 1661). Thomas Ellwood was also arrested, and was held in prison in Oxford (Ellwood 55–64). Isaac wrote to him from his own prison, and Ellwood kept the letter:

To Thomas Ellwood, 14 Feb 1661

Known only from Ellwood's History, *62–3, no manuscript copy. Works* II.457.

> Dear Thomas,
> Great hath been the Lord's goodness to thee, in calling thee out of that path of vanity, and death, wherein thou wast running toward destruction; to give thee a living name, and an inheritance of life, among his people: which certainly will be the end of thy faith in him, and obedience to him. And let it not be a light thing in thine eyes that he now accounteth thee worthy to suffer among his choice lambs, that he might make thy crown weightier, and thine inheritance the fuller. O that that eye and heart may be kept open in thee, which knoweth the value of these things! and that thou mayst be kept close to the feeling of the life, that thou mayst be fresh in thy spirit in the midst of thy sufferings, and mayst reap the benefit of them: finding that pared off thereby, which hindereth the bubblings of the everlasting springs, and maketh unfit for the breaking forth and enjoyment of the pure power! This is the brief salutation of my dear love to thee, which desireth thy strength and settlement in the power; and the utter weakening of thee, as to thyself. My love is to thee, with dear Thomas Goodyear [a Quaker from Cumbria] and the rest of the imprisoned Friends.
>
> I remain thine in the truth, to which the Lord my God preserve me single and faithful.
> I. P.
> From Aylesbury Gaol, 14th of 12th month, 1660 [1661]

Two of Isaac's personal letters to Mary from prison have been preserved. Note that Isaac's parentage was evidently a major cause of his detention. The oath tendered in court was the Oath of Allegiance and Supremacy, recognition of the King as secular ruler and head of the state church.

To Mary, 17 March 1661 (JP III.494)

AH is Guli's maid, Anne Hersent. JW is John Whitehead, a well-known Friend who was imprisoned with Isaac.

My dear,
Yesterday I with some few others, was sent for before the court. There was none called in but I, but J. W. thrust in with me. The judge asked me if I would take the Oath [of Allegiance and Supremacy]. I delivered him a paper which was an appeal to the Court, whether it was fitting for us, as the case stood with us, to take the Oath. He thought it had been the paper delivered him before by Friends in other places, and so asked me again about the Oath. I told him the paper was an appeal to him and the Court, and so desired it might be read, that the Court might hear it, which he endeavoured to put off, but I pressing it hard as exceeding equal [important] and necessary in a case which so nearly concerned us, he promised it should by and by (as I understood him) but called on some other business, and so we were ordered to withdraw for the present, but were called in no more.

I am told we are appointed to appear tomorrow at the sixth hour in the morning: what they will further propose to us, I do not know, it is believed they will release some and detain others. William [his brother] stays to know, whom I suppose thou mayest expect tomorrow night. J. W. remembers his love to thee and the family. There is one, who can hardly be called one of us, who formerly did warp, at present stands beyond expectation, and may hold out if he be not too confident, but wait on the Lord in his fear. My dear heart, my dear and tender love is to thee. I know thou dost believe that is most equal that the Lord should dispose of me, and will not desire me, unless he please in the freedom of his life and in clearness of conscience to return me to thee. I am thine very much and desire to be thine much more, even according to the purity and largeness of my love in the inner man. When the Lord pleaseth our innocency shall be cleared, and that which is now our reproach, be our beauty and honour in the sight of all the world. My dear love to Guli, to A. H., and all Friends in the family, and my dear little ones.

Aylesbury Gaol, 17 1st month, 1660 I.P.

The next letter needs some explanation. Isaac was asked to provide sureties (guarantors) for his good behaviour. It was the principle of Quakers not to do so, as they would not admit they had been guilty of any offence. If he had been at fault, he said that he would have been willing to enter into a bond, but he had no estate left.

To Mary, 1661, a few days later (JP III.494.2)

J. Brierly is not known.

My dear,

When I was called before the Judge on the second day, he again asked me if I would take the Oath. I answered I had put in my appeal to the Court whether it was fitting for me, in that state I stood, to take the Oath. He did not much press it on me, but took a paper of J.W. containing the substance of the Oath, which the Justices looked on, and (as we were told) confessed that it was the substance of the Oath, and that there wanted nothing but the formality. At last he told me I must put in sureties for the peace, which I said I durst [dared] not do, I think as often as he pressed me thereto. The next morning I was brought before him again (with J.W. and J. Brierly) Then he told me he would not require the Oath of me nor yet sureties for the peace, but he had heard I was the son of such a person, etc., and so he could do no less than require sureties of me for the performance of what was promised in the paper J.W. had delivered, to wit, that I would neither plot or conceal any plot, which I knew or did certainly hear of. This as far as I remember was the substance. I was sore distressed, and had not a word to say a long season, but my soul breathed to the Lord to preserve my innocency, and to make me willing to stand as a fool before them [I Cor 3:18–19], if he did not give me wherewith to answer them. Indeed I felt that I could not do the thing, but how to avoid the reasonableness and fair dealing which appeared to be on their side, I knew not. At length I told the Judge, that to perform the thing, that was to keep out of plotting, etc., this I could easily do, but to come into bond I could not.

Then he and the officers of the Court much disdained and derided me, and asked if I did not take bond of my tenants etc., which the Lord enabled me to bear with meekness and stillness of spirit. Then I told him I could give it under my hand what he required, which was more to me than a bond; but it was little with him. I told him likewise I was so far from plotting, notwithstanding I had lost my whole estate, that I did never so much as grumble in my mind, or wish the change of government, that I might enjoy my estate again. He seemed to be satisfied concerning my innocency, and said (as JW testifies) that he believed I would keep my promise, but he could do no less than require this of me, considering what my father was. So he committed me referring me to the Justices to be released, either upon my own recognizance or upon sureties.

Since which time three of the Justices sent for me to the White Hart, with whom I was a pretty season [length of time], who seemed very willing to release me, urging me much either to enter into bond myself or put in sureties; but otherwise they were tied by the Judge's order, which they could not recede from. I told them I was innocent in the sight of the Lord, and did in my heart believe the Lord would justify me in this thing at the great day, and so durst not do that thing which did appear to me to draw a cloud or doubt over my innocency. So I asked what I or the sureties were to be bound in. He said, I [should promise] £200 or the sureties £100 apiece. I told him if I had any estate left me of my own, I told him I could freely subscribe myself willing to bear the penalty of £400, if I were found in any such thing, nay, I did not care what hazard I ran, so free I was from any danger of the thing, but be bound in this case I could not. Since this last refusal, I have found great peace and satisfaction from the Lord as concerning this thing, and great rest in my spirit: and let all that love me bless his name for me, for I see clearly I had been a miserable man had the Lord suffered me for the gaining of my liberty, to have betrayed mine innocency, and have transgressed the law of my life. Indeed I was pressed very sore in the natural [the 33 pages following were excised from the manuscript at an early date, apparently by John Penington himself since there is no reference to them in the original index].

The other Quaker prisoners were soon set free, but Isaac, because he was his father's son, was held for seventeen weeks until all political prisoners were released by royal proclamation. The following details, and some others concerning his various imprisonments, come from an unpublished manuscript, a notebook consisting of an account of Isaac's early imprisonments, corrected and added to in another hand using the first person singular. It ends with an account of Isaac's arrest in Reading in 1670 (Gibson MSS II.45). The style and wording suggest that the author was probably Mary, and that Isaac made the corrections. Ellwood apparently had this document before him when writing the account of Isaac's imprisonments that forms part of his "Testimony" to Isaac (*Works* I.11–13), but Ellwood's version is much smoother in style. The judge had ordered that Isaac should have good accommodation and some liberty, but the local justices had other ideas, and Isaac was held during cold winter weather "in a very inconvenient room, a low room next the street door, without a chimney, over the cellar, with great holes in the boards under the bed and very noisome by reason of its joining to the common gaol. This very bad room procured him a very sore distemper", so that for several weeks after, he was not able to turn himself in bed.[10] Judging from a letter from a friend, Morgan Watkins, written in February, he also suffered a return of depression: "Put a strict watch on thy own thoughts and doubts, which arise in thee, and judge them out, for these be the enemies of thy own house, that many times veil thy comforts and and cloud the sunshine of thy father's strength in love to thy soul, and take no thought for thy state outward, nor doubt of thy state inward" (JP IV.9.3).

Despite these troubles, 1661 was another productive year for Isaac, and he managed to publish several books, while the threat to

---

10. The date of his release is not certain, but it was after 12 May, as a letter of that date, JP 2.313, was written from the prison. A release shortly after that would fit in well with the estimate of seventeen weeks, given in Gibson MSS. II.45 and used in Ellwood's "Testimony". The anti-Quaker proclamation was issued on 10 January, and the wholesale arrests began the next day.

their home did not materialise. Thomas Ellwood's relationship with his father had soured following his conversion to Quakerism, and in 1662 he joined the Penington household as tutor to the children, also acting as Mary's estate manager. Son of a Justice of the Peace, a country gentleman who kept a farm in his own hands, Ellwood had the necessary experience and authority, and the Peningtons appear to have had no more trouble with their business affairs.

Meanwhile, during the summer of 1661, the Peningtons became acquainted with one John Perrot, a talented Quaker travelling preacher, just released from prison in Italy.[11] He was greatly admired by many Friends, but this admiration was not shared by George Fox and other Quaker leaders, who considered Perrot a disruptive influence, for Perrot had made public his objections to the convention that men should remove their hats when prayer was offered during public worship.[12] Perrot thought that this practice had no more justification than any of the other formalities that Friends had given up, and he expressed his views vehemently without consulting the leadership. Fox and his colleagues thought that to encourage diversity of practice, especially at a time of persecution, was a sure road to disunity in the movement and hence to weakness. Perrot was required to explain himself, and had a gruelling session with Fox and other leaders. After further travels in Britain and Ireland he was finally imprisoned in London with many other Quakers, and the authorities gave him the choice of facing charges or emigrating. He departed for Barbados in the autumn of 1662, but his followers continued to promote his views.

George Fox issued an epistle to Friends emphasising that the real problem was one of a divided movement: "You ... have given occasion to the world to say, that the people of God called Quakers are divided, some with their hats on, and some with them off" (Fox, *Friends, the Matter concerning not putting off the Hat at Prayer* 1663, Postscript 3, and Epistles No. 199).

---

11. For Perrot the standard account is Kenneth L. Carroll, *John Perrot, Early Quaker Schismatic* (London: Friends Historical Society, 1970). See also Nigel Smith, "Exporting Enthusiasm: John Perrot and the Quaker Epic" in Thomas Healy and Jonathan Sawday, eds, *Literature and the English Civil War* (Cambridge 1990) 248–264.
12. See Thomas Edwards, *Gangraena* (1646) I 65 and III 96 for soldiers keeping their hats on during church prayers that they disapproved of. See William Mucklow, *Tyranny and Hypocrisy Detected* (1673) 10 for variations in practice; apparently, in East Anglia it was usual in all churches to keep one's hat on during prayer.

Among the people attracted by Perrot were William Penington and his friend John Pennyman; they introduced him to Isaac.[13] Perrot was invited to spend some time at the Peningtons' house after leaving London, and Isaac was deeply impressed. There was an unpleasant incident when some abusive letters to Perrot from the Quaker leadership were delivered to The Grange, and Isaac may have seen them. Isaac said nothing at the time, but the matter was upon his mind.[14] Some years later, in connection with another dispute, he wrote to his friend Thomas Curtis:[15]

Part of letter to Thomas Curtis, 25 February 1678 (JP IV.144)

> I did not esteem J. Perrot, but I looked upon him as an injured person in some respects, and said in my heart, truth can injure none, and I must stand by the injured against that which injures them, without respect of persons. Nor was I for keeping on the hat in prayer: but I was against the imposing of putting off the hat, believing that no man was to have a law laid upon him by others what to do in the particular, nor to lay a law upon himself but to wait what the Lord would have him do. I had likewise a fear begotten in me, that there was an eldership and authority of man coming over us, and that we were not left so nakedly to be guided by the principle of truth, which we were first directed and turned to.

After spending some time considering his position, Isaac circulated several manuscripts among Friends, of which the following is an example, giving his opinion that Perrot's ideas deserved fair consideration.[16]

"Some things have been very observable and wonderful to me concerning John Perrot" [1663] (Crosse MSS page 6, and T. Edmund Harvey's collection 13 page 5)

---

13. Letters concerning these relationships. For Pennyman, see Moore, *Light in Their Consciences* 223.
14. It is possible that Penington consulted with John Pennyman. See JP 1.154, 29 May 1675, where Penington accuses Pennyman of having once led him astray.
15. See pp. 104–105 for more of this letter.
16. These included a set of pro-Perrot queries, Harvey 13/5, later reproduced by William Mucklow in *Tyranny and Hypocrisy Detected* (1672), 63–65, see p. 94.

The two versions are practically identical; Harvey is followed here.
Some things have been very observable and wonderful unto me concerning John Perrot, as

1stly. The great sufferings which he underwent in Rome for truth's sake which I had a deep sense of when I was in prison and did cry unto the Lord to carry him through.

2dly. The precious sparklings of life, which broke forth from him while he was in prison, in several papers sent over by him, which deeply refreshed the life and raised the love in many towards him.

3dly. His delivery from there, which is a thing very rare concerning any so testifying against them, and standing to his principles.

4thly. His deep reaching, raising and refreshing the life of many after his coming hither; insomuch as the meetings, where he was ordered to be, were much fresher than lately had been known before his coming. This is a true upright testimony, which the hearts of many who felt the same thing, can set their seal unto.

5thly. His different practice and holding forth about the hat, which (now I am drawn to confess that) the fleshly and reasoning part in me did exceeding stiffly rise up against, insomuch as I cried earnestly to the Lord concerning it, that he would cool my spirit, and bring me to wait on him for judgment, and not let that up in me which I was sure was not appointed by him to be the Judge. And my spirit was quieted and drawn to let him alone, and leave the thing to the Lord, whose servant he was, and to whom he was to give an account of what he required or did not require of him.

6thly. The great owning of him by divers friends, herein, and the dissatisfaction and disowning of others: both which I desired in my heart to be kept clear from, and not to set up a rule in my mind either for or against the thing, but to wait singly how the Lord would draw me in the action (who is either to justify or condemn me about it) to whom my heart was desirous to stand subjected, according as I felt his light leading me therein, just at the action.

7thly. The freshness and power which was reported to break forth through him in Barbados, contrary to the expectation and predictions of some.

8thly. His present retiring, upon a particular command of the Lord's, as he signified in a letter.

All these things are weighty unto me, and my heart is fixed to wait on the Lord concerning him, and not to admire or lift him up on the one hand, not to throw him down on the other hand. But this I must confess, that I have often had a testimony in my heart concerning the uprightness of his heart to the Lord, and I am sure my life hath owned the life in him, and seen sparklings of true glory break forth through him. And I can by no means think hardly concerning him till I find the life in me disown him. But if any thing be really amiss in him, I have cried, and still do cry, to the Lord to sever it from him, that he may be a sanctified vessel to him; and that the glory of life, which hath broken forth through him in the sight of many, may yet more abundantly break forth in him or others (as the Lord shall please) to the refreshment of the weary and to the praise of the mercy and powerful name of the Lord. And so far as the Lord hath formed my heart aright in this thing, I desire the hearts of others may be so formed, by the power of the same life, that the glory of God and his peace may rest upon Israel, and no prejudice, nor fighting with carnal reasonings, nor striving to draw any faster than the Lord leads, nor by any other light save the springing up of his own light in their hearts, may be found in Israel.

    Isaac Penington

This is my desire, that this paper may be communicated to the tender and upright-hearted, and kept out of the hands of contentious spirits, for it was written, not for contention's sake, or to strengthen one party against another; but in true drawings to refresh the upright hearted, who with me

have received a testimony from the Lord concerning this thing, which if the watch be not kept to that which gave the testimony, the testimony of man may weaken.
IP

Isaac also put out a printed pamphlet with the title *Many Deep Considerations have been upon my Heart Concerning the State of Israel*, Israel being the true church, that is, the Quakers.[17] (The title is changed in the collected *Works* to *Some Deep Considerations*.) He reminded his readers about the high hopes "about the beginning of the late troubles of the nation" which had been disappointed when people became involved in "disputes and contention about forms of worship and church government". Then came "the precious breaking-forth of the Lord...in some hidden vessels.... and who can utter what the glory of this light was...!" They had prospered, the Lord had "enriched them with gifts and abilities, and in every way fitted them for the service and employment he had had for them". But now they were in danger, more danger than when they had been poor and weak. They were in danger of arrogating to themselves the powers that belonged to God, and God would not tolerate it. Then came three queries: the first, how a man, whom the Lord had exalted, could be prevented from falling; the second, if such a thing happened, how could the little ones (ordinary Quakers) be kept safe; and the third, how could such a fallen leader be recovered. He ended with an appeal to Friends to abide in the Life, and keep to the Power and the Principle.[18]

Discussion of this kind was normal practice in the Independent churches and Seeker groups from which Penington had come, but it was not welcomed among Quakers who valued unity, and the "man whom the Lord had exalted" could only be George Fox. Edward Burrough had died in prison, and Fox was occupied in the north, so it was Francis Howgill, one of Fox's most experienced colleagues, who attempted to deal with the matter. He wrote Isaac a lengthy letter in which he took a long time to come to the point, clearly finding it difficult to address Isaac Penington on a matter of discipline. No other Quaker of Penington's status had gone so far in support of Perrot.

---

17. Extract, pp. 165–66.
18. The date [1664] for *Many Deep Considerations* in Wing's *Short Title Catalogue* should be 1663, as this pamphlet is mentioned in Howgill's letter of 20th June 1663, JP 4.3.

Part I The Life of Isaac Penington

Most of Howgill's preliminaries and circumlocutions have been omitted from the following version of his letter.

Francis Howgill to Isaac Penington, 20 June 1663
(JP IV.3, Portfolio III.83)

>Dear Isaac
>In unfeignedness of heart and spirit I greet thee in the immutable life of Christ Jesus. I greatly desire thy increase and settlement in that, wherein perfect peace is witnessed... and seeing that thou hast been a man of sorrows and sometime acquainted with grief [Isa. 53:3], and hath been poured from vessel to vessel, till the Lord appeared in such a way out of his love for thee. ... In the bowels of true love I write unto thee, that which hath been in my heart divers [several] days.
>
>I am no man of strife, neither ever loved contention among them that did believe. ... If there be a beating one another the destroyer gets place, and at last devours and consumes the good, and I desire not to be found in this work. I have been sparing in writing lest deceit should get advantage on any hand and must tell thee plainly, we have no such custom nor practice this many years among us, as to write one against another, or anything that might lead to division. ... Dear Isaac, these few things was in my heart to write unto thee, that thou do not hurt thyself about these things... divers papers I have seen, which indeed have a tendency in them to weaken the faith of some, and beget doubts and fears in others, and a bad construction some will make of them, howbeit thou may intend them as for good. Thou sayest, "Let it be no wonder in Israel, if the Lord should suffer the greatest to fall". We have spoken of a state which could not fall... again thou sayest, "Let none be prejudiced against a further appearance of the Lord". ... such things... weakens us in the sight of our adversaries. ... Dear Isaac, I do not deal with thee as an enemy... as I hope thou wilt not look upon me for speaking plainly unto thee. I would have thee stop writings and papers of this nature, and send them not abroad, but be quiet and still and banish evil thoughts and surmises, and let them

have no place in thy heart, against any whom God hath made serviceable in this work. ...

Divers things more I could say about that business of the hat, but I desire that it may die with that spirit that brought it forth: and fill not thy mind with things of this nature, for it will beget trouble and thoughts of hurt. These things were upon me in brotherly love to lay before thee, not desiring nor expecting any answer, as in way of contending, but as being sensible that divers writings and papers from divers hands hath done hurt, and have had a bad effect. No more, but my dear love to thy wife, remaining,

Thy true friend, Francis Howgill
London, 20 of 4 month 1663

Other Friends offered similar advice.[19] There is no contemporary record of how Isaac reacted, but references in later letters show that he was aghast at the furore he had caused, and very distressed at his apparent breach with Friends. He wrote an explanatory letter to Fox, which has not survived.[20] By the autumn of 1664 good relations seem to have been restored, but Isaac was still unhappy in his mind.[21]

---

19. Notably, William Smith, JP 4.7, and Richard Farnworth, JP 4.40, a general letter to Friends on this subject. See also JP 4.4.2 from Alexander Parker, 4.2 from Josiah Coale, 4.4 from Richard Hunt.
20. The relevant letters include JP 4.143.2, 25 Feb 1678, and 145 [1678], both to Thomas Curtis, in connection with the Wilkinson-Storey dispute, where Penington was telling the tale of his early experiences. JP 4.12 from Watkins and 4.5 from Alexander Parker suggest that relations were returning to normal by late 1664.
21. It came to light after this manuscript was completed that Guli, accompanied by her maid Anne Hersent and probably with Morgan Watkins in the same party, visited George Fox and Margaret Fell in Lancaster Gaol during the summer of 1664, afterwards staying at Swarthmoor and meeting other Friends in the area, before being interrogated by the civil authorities in Kendal (Cumbria County Records Office, Kendal, Sir Daniel Fleming Public Offices JP General Papers 1661–1692, Box 3, information kindly supplied by John Gowling). Whatever the exact circumstances, it seems likely that this visit would be linked to the rapprochement between Isaac Penington and George Fox that appears to have taken place about this time.

CHAPTER 3

Aylesbury Gaol, 1664–1667

From late 1664 until the end of 1667 Isaac was, for much of the time, imprisoned in Aylesbury gaol.[1] To explain this, it is necessary to go back to the situation when a new parliament, known as the Cavalier Parliament, assembled in May 1661. For reasons of political stability, this Parliament was determined to establish the worship of the Church of England and permit no other. Quakers were considered likely to be a particular danger to the state, and Parliament began a move against them during the summer of 1661, introducing a bill "for preventing the mischiefs and dangers that may arise by certain persons called Quakers and others, refusing to take lawful oaths".

The bill became law in May 1662, and is known as the Quaker Act. It was made unlawful to refuse to take a legally tendered oath, or "by printing, writing or otherwise go about to maintain and defend that the taking of an oath...is altogether unlawful". It forbade Quakers above the age of sixteen years to assemble together "under pretence of joining in religious worship, not authorised by the laws of this realm." The penalties were fines and imprisonment, with the possibility of transportation, normally to plantations in Barbados, for a third offence.

Quakers now faced serious persecution. Meetings were broken up, and people attending them were beaten and imprisoned. In the crowded prisons there were soon deaths, the greatest loss to the

---

1. There are slight incompatibilities between Ellwood's *History* and his "Testimony" to Penington in *Works* on the one hand, and the manuscript datings on the other, but the general story is clear.

Quakers being Edward Burrough, who died in January 1663. In 1664, Parliament passed the First Conventicle Act, whch extended the provisions of the Quaker Act to all Dissenting bodies. The persecution was not, however, uniform all over the country, as much depended on the attitude of the local authorities, and the Peningtons were for a while left in peace.

Sometime towards the end of 1664 a meeting at The Grange was interrupted by the authorities, and a number of those present were arrested, among them Isaac himself, his brother William and George Whitehead, a long-standing Quaker from the north who was at this time the leading Quaker at liberty. Most of the prisoners were quickly released, but Isaac was held for about seventeen or eighteen weeks till the assizes, when a jury refused to convict him.[2] Then, in July 1665, he was arrested again while attending a Quaker funeral in Amersham, and imprisoned for about a month (Ellwood 135–6). Not long after his release he was again arrested, this time when he was at home "in his wife's chamber who had lately lain in" (having given birth to their third son, William). A "rude soldier" arrived, without a warrant, to arrest him. One of the servants "being not a Friend" protested that "it was an unfitting hour" and promised that his master would come in the morning. Isaac was ordered to be imprisoned during the pleasure of the Earl of Bridgwater, the Lord Lieutenant of Buckinghamshire. It appears that the Earl said that Isaac "should never be released until he had made him bow to him in giving him his titles" (Gibson MSS 2.45).

The letter that follows is one of very few in Isaac's own hand that survive. At this stage Isaac did not want Mary to plead for his release, though later, like other imprisoned Quakers, he composed appeals to the authorities and permitted other people to be active on his behalf.

To Mary Penington, 1 September 1665 (Cash Collection, Temp. MS 747/3A)

This letter is dated on the reverse in another hand.

1st of 7th month 1665.

My dear true love,
I have hardly freedom to take notice of what hath passed so much as in my own thoughts: but I am satisfied in my very

---

2. JP 1.88.2, 4 March 1665, is dated from Aylesbury gaol.

heart that the Lord, who is good, hath ordered things thus, and will bring about what he pleaseth thereby. Why should the fleshly, wise, reasoning part murmur, or find fault. O be silent before the Lord, O all flesh within me, and disturb not my soul in waiting on my God for what he is working in me and for me, and which he maketh these uncouth occurrences conduce unto. Thou wilt perceive by these few lines that I am quieted, satisfied and pleased. One thing have I desired of the Lord, even that I may be his, perfectly disposed of by him, know nothing but him, enjoy nothing but in his breathing life and leadings: thus must I forget and part with thee, my most dear and worthy love, or I cannot be happy in my own soul or enjoy thee, as I desire. I find my heart deeply desire and pant, breathing after the pure power and life of the Lord to reign in me; yet dare I not choose, but beg to be taught to wait; and to be made willing to drink the residue of the cup of suffering, both inward and outward, until the Lord see good to take it from my lips.

O, my dear! say little concerning me; plead not my cause, but be still in thy own spirit, wait what the Lord will do for me, that all the prayers which in the tenderness of my soul I have often put up for thee, may have their full effect upon thee, that thou mayest abundantly be the delight of my soul in the Lord, and mayest take notice of, see and be delighted with his exceeding precious and tender work on my heart, which after my long, great and deep captivity, indeed I hope for, from the Lord. My dear, be my true yoke-fellow, helpful to draw my heart toward the Lord, and from every thing but what is sanctified by the presence and leadings of his pure life. O my dear, I feel, and thou knowest that I am, very dearly thine,
  I.P.

Isaac again suffered from bad conditions in prison, and although there was plague in the gaol, Lord Bridgwater refused to allow Isaac to be given better quarters. To add to their troubles, the family were now forced to leave The Grange.[3] At this time Guli was a young woman in

---

3. JP 4.8.2, 16 Nov. 1666, from Elizabeth Walmsley, mentions their recent removal, which apparently had taken place since her previous letter dated July.

her early twenties, and the children were John aged ten, Isaac and Mary rather younger, and the baby William. Both Mary and Ellwood blamed the Penington relatives for the expulsion (*Experiences*, 53; Ellwood 141). Probably it had taken several years for the whole legal process to go through, and bad will on the part of the local civil authority may have brought things to a head. Mary went with the children to Aylesbury to be near her husband and, when the gaoler was away, the gaoler's wife allowed Isaac to move out of the close prison to a house for the servants and children of prisoners. Guli went for a few months to visit relations in Bristol. Mary then took lodgings in a farmhouse called Bottrels in Chalfont St Giles, which was occupied by a Quaker family named Grimsdale (Elwell, *Bottrells Close*, 1973). It was too cramped when the whole family was present, and Ellwood, who also spent some time in prison during 1666, found roomier accommodation for them in a large farmhouse called Berrie House (now The Old Farmhouse in the Bury Farm estate) on the outskirts of Amersham, where they moved in the autumn of 1666 (Ellwood 145).

Isaac wrote a number of letters to Friends and meetings during his long imprisonment. His troubles had the effect of heightening his sensitivity, and some of his finest work dates from this period. Here is some advice on the tactful handling of Sarah, the wife of one Nicholas Bond, who was not as committed to Quakerism as her husband. Isaac also wrote directly to Sarah herself (JP III.377, *Works* IV [Supp].11).

To Nicholas Bond, 1 November 1665 (JP III.378)

Dear Nicholas

As thou lovest thy wife and desirest the salvation of her soul, so be watchful in thy carriage towards her, and let thy words be few and weighty, spoken in the Lord's time and wisdom, and not in thine own, that she may be overcome by and subject to the pure wisdom of God, and may not receive anything of God's truth in the wisdom of the flesh, but in the evidence and demonstration of his spirit. And let her alone about the things of this world, do not intermeddle more than thou art necessitated from the Lord, that life in thee may have dominion, and in its dominion and true authority may awaken life in her, and be helpful to it.

O my dear Friend, be exceeding watchful, that thou do not obstruct that which thou exceedingly desirest, but mind thine own heart, night and day, that that which is superfluous may be cut off, and that which is wanting may be supplied, that in true wisdom and understanding thou mayst be helpful to others: and not according to the wisdom or will of the flesh wherein the things of God are not wrought, nor in that land do they prosper: but the beginning must be right, the additions and growth right, and that which is of a contrary nature in all its disguisings must be watched against, that it may be kept out, that the whole building of life, faith and obedience in the heart may be purely and perfectly of God, from first to last. O that thou mayest grow, O that thou mayest witness the separation from flesh, and be silent in spirit and words concerning all things, further than God leads and approves, that thou mayest reach the witness in thy wife, which being reached, will witness to truth and gain upon her heart, to the joy of thine: but if thy desires and endeavours be managed otherwise, even out of the leadings and limits of life, thou wilt get little ground of her; but rather drive her further off, for they are not words or seeming advantages which will catch her, but the demonstration, life, and power of truth, in which the Lord guide thee, that thou mayst therein reach her heart, and obtain every pure and righteous desire of thy heart concerning her.

From Aylesbury Gaol I.P.
1st of 9th Mon. 1665

The next letter is to Bridget Atley: Isaac wrote to her several times. Ellwood, making a collection of local Friends' sufferings, described her as a widow living in Horton, a village halfway between Aylesbury and Dunstable, who in 1670 was fined £8 for attending a Quaker meeting, and had goods distrained consisting of two goosefeather beds – "all she had" – two feather bolsters, one coverlet, one bedstead with curtains, vallance and curtain rods, one trundle-bedstead (this fitted under another bedstead when not in use), one folding table, one cupboard, two pots, a platter, and a candlestick (Harvey MSS 15). There was much dissension in the meeting at Horton, and Bridget Atley was disturbed and unhappy, very torn in her mind as to what she should do.

3. Aylesbury Gaol, 1664–1667

To Bridget Atley, 1665 (JP III.371, *Works* II.463)

Dear Friend,

I know thy soul desires to live, and my soul desireth that thou mightst live: O why art thou so backward to hearken to the voice which is nigh thee, wherein is life? Why dost thou reason? Why dost thou consult? Why dost thou expect? Why dost thou hope? Why dost thou believe against thine own soul? The snares of the subtle one will entangle for ever, unless thou wait for, hearken to and obey the voice of the living God, who leads the single-hearted and obedient out of them. Is there any way of life but one? Is not the Lord leading his children in that way? Must not all that come after, follow in the foot-steps of those that go before? Is there any Saviour, but the seed of life and the Father of it? Is it not the same in thee, as in others? Hath it not the same voice?

O that thou hadst the same ear and the same heart, that thou mightest hear, receive and live! They wait aright, dost thou wait so? They hope aright, dost thou hope so? If not, what will thy waiting and expecting come to? In that which hath sometimes inclined thy heart, there is truth, there were the beginnings of salvation; but in that which draws thee out to expect some great matters, and dries up thy present sense, and hinders thy present subjection, therein is deceit and the destruction of thy soul. Therefore, if thou desire and love the salvation thereof, O hasten, hasten out of it, wait for the reproofs of wisdom; and what it manifests to be of the earthly and worldly nature in thee (the words, ways, thoughts, customs thereof), hasten out of. O, turn thy back upon the world with speed, and turn thy face towards the heavenly wisdom and light eternal, which will be springing up in thee, if thou turn thy back upon the world, and wait for it.

Qfp §
19.43

And do not look for such great matters to begin with, but be content to be a child, and let the Father proportion out daily to thee what light, what power, what exercises, what straits, what fears, what troubles he sees fit for thee: and do thou bow before him continually in humility of heart, who hath the dispose of thee, whether to life or death for ever. Ah, that wisdom which would be choosing must be confounded, and the low, humble thing raised, which submits and cries to the Father in every condition. And in waiting to feel this and in joining to this, thou mayst meet with life; but death, destruction and separation from God is the portion of the other for ever. O that thou mayst be separated from it, and joined to the seed and birth of God, that in it thy soul may spring up to know, serve, and worship the Lord, and to wait daily to be formed by him, until thou become perfectly like him. But thou must join in with the beginnings of life, and be exercised with the day of small things [Zech 4:10], before thou meet with the great things, wherein is the clearness and satisfaction of the soul. The rest is at noonday: but the travels begin at the breakings of day, wherein are but glimmerings or little light, wherein the discovery of good and evil are not so manifest and certain: yet there must the traveller begin and travel; and in his faithful travels (in much fear and trembling, lest he should err) the light will more and more break in upon him.

Qfp § 19.43

This have I writ in tenderness to thee, that thou mightest not miss of the path of the living which is appointed of the Father to lead, and alone can lead the soul to life: O that thou mightest be enlightened and quickened by the Lord to walk therein, and mightest be thankful for and content with what he gives thee, and walk therein from the evil to the good, from the earthly to the heavenly nature daily, and mightest not despise the cross or shame of the seed: for I know there is a wisdom in thee which will despise and turn from it, until the Lord batter and crucify it: and I can hardly put up a more proper request for thee, than that the Lord would draw out his sword against it, and deeply perplex and confound it in thee.

1665 I.P.

Elizabeth Walmsley was a close friend of the Peningtons who became a Quaker after attending meetings at their house. It was Elizabeth who was given charge of Isaac's letters to Chalfont Meeting: "I think it will fall again to thy lot to read this enclosed. Look not out [i.e. do not look for other than divine guidance], for if the Lord make thy heart willing, and be with thee in it, it will be an acceptable service from thee to him, though it be outwardly hard" (JP 1.89.2). Several of Isaac's letters to Elizabeth Walmsley are included in his collected *Works*, but this one has not previously been published:

To Elizabeth Walmsley, 23 May 1666 (JP 1.89.1)

Dear Friend,
whom I dearly love in the truth, and for the seed's sake, which the God of mercy hath revealed in thee, and truly gathered thy heart in a measure into, insomuch as thou hast witnessed true breathings after him, and true union and peace with him. Yea in his tender mercy he hath stood by thee in the needful hour. And his loving kindness and tender care doth not abate, but increase towards thee, whose delight it is to spread his skirt over thee, preserve thee and nourish thee up in his pure living presence [Ezek 16:8]. Blessed be the God of thy mercy and salvation, saith my soul, and let the daily sacrifices of his praise rise up in thee from his pure brightness, that his name may be glorious in thee, and his precious fountain of life open to thee, for the refreshing and satisfying of thy soul, according to thy desire in his will, and according to all thy needs.

The Lord is tender of me and merciful to me, though indeed I have felt much weakness both inwardly and outwardly, yet my strength doth not forsake me, but the free mercies of the Lord are renewed to morning by morning. I could almost sing to his glorious name, seeing (in the pure, powerful overcoming life) the death of all that troubles Israel. O the gates of Hell, you shall not prevail against the least Lamb of my Father's preserving. Glory be to his mercy, to his love, to his power, to his wisdom, to his goodness for evermore. My dear Friend, my heart cleaves unto thee, and the Lord God of tender bowels ever preserve thy soul and mine (with the souls of all that love and fear him) in that which knitteth and uniteth in him.
Thy Friend in truth and tenderness of affection I.P.
From Aylesbury 23 of 3 Month 1666

After some nine months in prison, probably in July 1666, Isaac was released as a result of the intercession of the Earl of Ancram, who took a kindly interest in Quakers.[4] The Earl of Bridgwater, however, had not finished with the Peningtons, and Isaac was re-arrested after only three weeks at liberty. "They took him in bed and behaved themselves very uncivilly in the house [and] carried him to prison where he lay one part of the time in an earthen floored room without a chimney and the other part in a very cold upper high roofed room without a ceiling...he was like to have died in the gaol, nobody lying in his room or near him, he lay weak several months of this distemper" (Gibson MSS 2.45). Altogether he was held for around eighteen months, but, despite the conditions, the Peningtons managed to conceive their last child, Edward, who was born on 3 September 1667.[5] Presumably there were again interludes when Isaac was allowed to move into a house nearby.

During his time in prison Isaac became acutely depressed and unhappy regarding his earlier support for Perrot and separation from the main body of Friends. He was a man of his time, and it was natural for him to feel that his imprisonment, with the loss of his estate and his home, were the Lord's punishment. His letter to Thomas Curtis (JP IV.144, 25 February 1678), describing this time, was quoted in the previous chapter, and continues:

> ...a wrong sense and judgment stole upon me, which it was long before the Lord gave me to see, and I afterwards bore his dreadful hand for a long season, and felt a bar between me and his living people.... And I was brought even to the pit of despair, and lay there gasping and bitterly mourning and crying to the Lord night and day: but at last it pleased the Lord to show me mercy and by degrees to restore me, though I often feared the Lord would never fully bring me back to that state again, wherein to he had led me before this my grievous temptation and fall.

His friend Morgan Watkins, a Welsh Quaker minister, was a regular correspondent (JP IV.9–19, 1661–1668) and did his best to

---

4. Charles Kerr, second Earl of Ancram. He was in correspondence with Margaret Fell in 1685 (Elsa F. Glines, ed., *Undaunted Zeal: the Letters of Margaret Fell* (Richmond, Indiana: Friends United Press, 2003) 444), and in 1689, together with some of his family he attended a meeting at which George Fox spoke (*Itinerary Journal* 201, 348).
5. Birth and death dates of the Penington children, where known, are in the "Dictionary of Quaker Biography", in Friends House and Haverford libraries.

comfort him. Watkins, himself in prison at the time, wrote to Isaac in May 1666 that he was "satisfied that through the sea of afflictions and great tempest of temptations, the Lord will arrive thee in the land of his everlasting rest and peace." Isaac should listen to his friends and thereby save himself much sorrow, as he could not see things clearly himself. A week later, having had another letter from Isaac, he wrote that Isaac should not be worried at the loss of his property. "The more I behold thy true poverty; may God make thee poor enough and bring thee a morsel of bread." God would help him: "Thou went out in thy own will [i.e. deliberately disobeyed], but thou may come back in his. Thy innocent life was betrayed into the hands of wicked spirits...but blessed be the Lord who strives to transform thee." The next month he wrote again: "O my Dear Brother, receive a little strength from me, at this time, as a token of his love through me to thee...feel that which did not leave thee in thy distress." Meanwhile, he advised that Isaac should write to the Earl of Bridgwater and "lay his wickedness upon him, in tenderness and moderation".

This advice was taken; Isaac wrote three times to the Earl during the next few months (JP 1.4.2, 1.5, 1.8). Note the use of "you", plural. Isaac would not have used this word out of politeness, and he evidently intended this letter to be read by other persecutors besides the Earl: see the third paragraph especially.

To the Earl of Bridgwater, 24 August 1666 (JP 1.4.2)

From Aylesbury jail, 24th of 6 month 1666.
These are for him that is called the Earl of Bridgwater to read in meekness and coolness of spirit, and so reading he will not repent thereof: for it was writ to him in the love that desires his outward prosperity and eternal happiness.

Why do you persecute and afflict a man, who desireth to live in the love and peace of God toward you? Will nothing satisfy you, unless I deny the Lord, whom I have sought and been acquainted with from my childhood, and whose favour and presence I cannot but value above all things? God appeareth not in outward shapes or voices, but in his truth revealed in the hearts and consciences of them that fear him and wait upon him: and he that denieth subjection to any manifestation of the pure light revealed there denieth God, and shall be denied of him. This I dare not run the hazard for (or through) fear of man.

You are men, great men (many of you) but I know God to be greater, and that his power and authority over me is greater than yours; and therefore I am not to be blamed in yielding subjection to him in the first place. You have not power of making laws in your own will, not in your own wisdom; but ought to do it in fear and subjection to God, and according to the true sense and light of that of him, which is in your consciences; which, when so made, that which is of God in every conscience will answer and witness to, as just and good. (Here is the true foundation of righteousness, peace and love among men.) But if they be made in the will and wisdom of the corrupt part they are against that which is of God, and cannot be submitted unto by it, but rather witnessed against, in such ways as the Lord requireth.

O what are you doing? O that you could yet consider. Can poor worm man contend against his maker and prosper? Alas, what are we? But if the Lord our God hath appeared to us and in us, and you in that respect are offended at us, and make war with us; do you not contend against God? What will be the end of these things? Ah, what will you bring this poor nation and yourselves unto? For of a truth God is righteous, and what you have sown in the day of your power, that you must reap in the day of his righteous judgment; and all the sufferings, oppressions and cries of the innocent will then come upon you in full weight and measure, though, the Lord knoweth, it hath been and still is the desire of our souls, that (if it be possible) you might escape that cup of wrath and sore vengeance from God, which, as with cart ropes, you are pulling upon yourselves [Isa 5:18]. I write this in love, tenderness and true goodwill, as the Lord knoweth (who justifieth me therein) however you may interpret it, who after all my other sufferings from you, could freely lay down my life for your sakes (as a sacrifice for you) if it were the will of God, who have been and still remain,

A patient sufferer for well doing (blessing the Lord, who redeemeth and preserveth the souls of his, out of that evil doing, which brings his indignation and wrath, with great perplexities and miseries upon nations and persons. O read Isa ch. 24 and Rom ch. 2.v.9. and fear before him: for it is good for man to be abased, and found in the true fear before his maker)

From Aylesbury IP
23rd of 4 month 1666

At this time there was a dispute among Chalfont Friends, probably connected with Perrot's ideas, and Isaac begged them to hold to their first leaders, the "pillars" of the church (Gal 2:9) and not be led away by new ideas. In his reaction against Perrot, Isaac had become a strong supporter of George Fox as leader.[6] The main letter is available in the collected *Works*, so we have not reprinted all of it, but we have included a previously unpublished part of the postscript. Compare with 1 Corinthians 12:31, where Paul exhorts the members of the church at Corinth to respect each other, for even the lowliest is an essential part of the one body; note also Penington's rewriting, in the second paragraph of the postscript, of Christ's saying "He that receiveth whomsoever I send receiveth me" (John 13:20). Penington's emphasis, by contrast, is on the status of the leaders.

To Friends in the Chalfonts, 25 January 1667 (JP I.10, *Works* II.479)

To the Friends in truth in and about the two Chalfonts

As a father watcheth over his children, so do I wait, and desire to feel the Lord watching over my soul continually: and in his Love, care, wise and tender counsel, is my safety, life, and peace; and I never yet repented either waiting for him or hearkening to him. But if I have hearkened at any time to any thing else, and mistook his voice, and entertained the enemy's deceitful appearance, instead of his pure truth (which it is very easy to do) that grievous mistake hath proved matter of loss and sorrow to my soul. Now, O my Friends, that ye might know and hear the voice of the preserver, so shall ye be preserved, and kept from the voice of the stranger which draweth aside from the

---
6. See Part II, p. 159.

pure principle of life and the true, feeling sense. There is that near you, which watcheth to betray, O the God of my life, joy, peace, and hope watch over your souls, and deliver you from the advantages which at any time it hath against any of you. The seed which God hath sown in you is pure and precious. O that it may be found living in you, and ye abiding in it!

[...]

I. P.

Aylesbury Prison, 25th of Eleventh Month, 1666

POSTSCRIPT

And, my Friends, once more it is in my heart to beseech you, exceedingly to cry unto the Lord, and to watch in his fear, that a wrong thing judge not in you, nor a wrong sense get up: for that will approve and justify that which is wrong, and condemn the innocent: and if it be thus with you, into what spirit are you then entered, or what is your path and end like to be! The great danger and subtle betraying of the soul, after it is turned towards the Lord, is not so much by that which is manifestly evil, and apparently of the enemy, as by that which appears as good and as of the Lord; yet he that swallows down that bait at any time, even of that which appears to be good and of the Lord, is really strake [struck] with the hook and caught by the enemy, as he that enters into that which is manifestly evil. Therefore watch against all false appearances and devices of the wicked one, both within and without, that you may discern that which is pure, and be gathered thereto and abide therein, and not drawn therefrom by any device or subtle appearance of the enemy whatsoever, whether within your own hearts or without from others...

And Friends, you that are weak, bless God for the strong: you that have need of a pillar to lean on, bless God that hath provided pillars in his house, and in fear and the guidance of his Spirit make use of these pillars [Gal 2:9], who are faithful, and have ability from God in his power and glorious presence with them to help to sustain his building, even as they had ability from the Lord to gather unto him. He that despiseth him that is sent, despiseth Him that sent him: and he that undervalues any gift, office or work, that God hath bestowed upon any person, despiseth the wisdom and disposal of the giver. Are all Fathers? have all overcome the enemy? are all grown up in the Life? are all stars in the firmament of God's power? hath God made all equal? are there not different states, different degrees, different growths, different places, etc.? Then if God hath made a difference, and given degrees of life and gifts different according to his pleasure, what wisdom and spirit is that, which doth not acknowledge this, but would make all equal?

Qfp § 10.27

O my Friends, fear before the Lord, honour the Lord in his appearances, and in the differences which he hath made among the children of men and among his people. He gave Prophets of old, and the rest of the people were not equal with them. He gave Evangelists, Apostles, Pastors, Teachers, etc. [Eph 4:11], and the other members of the churches were not equal with them. He hath given Fathers and Elders now, and the babes and young men are not equal with them. Thus it is in truth from the Lord, and that which is of God in you (its eye being open by him, and its speaking in you from him) will so acknowledge it. Therefore watch every one to feel and know his own place and service in the body, and to be sensible of the gifts, places, and services of others, that the Lord may be honoured in all, and every one owned and honoured in the Lord, and no otherwise. I. P.

Qfp § 10.27

26th of the Eleventh Month, 1666

A letter to the nearby meeting in Amersham avoids Isaac's usual fault of over-wordiness:

To Friends in Amersham, 4 May 1667 (JP II.311, *Works* II.486)

Friends,

Qfp § 10.01

Our life is love and peace and tenderness and bearing one with another, and forgiving one another, and not laying accusations one against another: but praying one for another, and helping one another up with a tender hand, if there has been any slip or fall, and waiting till the Lord

Part I The Life of Isaac Penington

give sense and repentance, if sense and repentance in any be wanting. O wait to feel this spirit, and to be guided to walk in this spirit, that ye may enjoy the Lord in sweetness, and walk sweetly, meekly, tenderly, peaceably and lovingly one with another. And then ye will be a praise to the Lord, and anything that is, or hath been, or may be amiss, ye will come over in the true dominion, even in the Lamb's dominion, and that which is contrary shall be trampled upon as life rises and rules in you. So watch your hearts and ways, and watch one over another in that which is gentle and tender, and knows it can neither preserve itself, nor help another out of the snare, but the Lord must be waited upon, to do this in and for us all. So mind truth, the service, enjoyment and possession of it in your hearts, and so to walk as ye may bring no disgrace upon it, but ye may be a good savour in the places where ye live, the meek, innocent, tender, righteous life reigning in you, governing of you, and shining through you in the eyes of all with whom ye converse.

Your Friend in the truth, and a desirer of your welfare and prosperity therein.

I. P.

Aylesbury, 4th of Third Month, 1667

About this time the elder Penington children were sent to a new school in Waltham Cross, run by a Quaker named Christopher Taylor. The following letter to them is given in full despite its length, because of its interest as an example of contemporary advice to children.[7] One may be surprised to find Isaac Penington threatening his children with hellfire if they misbehave. He was a loving and hands-on father, but he was nevertheless a seventeenth-century parent with the ideas of that time.[8]

---

7. Fox's *Journal* 520 states that this school was founded in 1668 at his own instigation. (The note in this edition that it was for boys is not in the original manuscript.) Mary's *Experiences* gives the impression that the children were sent to school soon after the loss of The Grange. The letter "to his Children" suggests they were at school, or going to school in the near future, in the spring of 1667, but the letter to Mary in the following chapter, written in the spring of 1668, suggests that they were at home then.
8. See also Part II ch. 11 on "Last Things", p. 248.

To his children, 10 May 1667 (JP IV.106, *Works* II.487, *Letters of Early Friends* ed. A.R.Barclay 1841, page 397)

For my dear children J[ohn], I[saac], and M[ary] P[enington].

MY DEAR CHILDREN,
Two things I especially desire in reference to your learning: one is that ye may learn to know and hearken to the voice of God's witness in you. There is somewhat in you which will teach you how to do well and how to avoid the evil, if your minds be turned to it. And the same thing will witness to you when ye do well and against you when ye do evil. Now to learn to know this, to hear this, to fear this, to obey this, that is the chief piece of learning, that I desire to find you in. And your Master or any of the family that turns you to the witness minds you of the witness, reproves you for not hearkening to or obeying the witness, O love them, and bless God for them in that respect: and remember this, that he that hearkens to reproof is wise, but he that hates or slights it is brutish [Prov 12:1; 13:18; 15:5]. That is the dark spirit, which would please itself in its dark ways, and therefore loves not the light which makes them manifest and reproves them: and that spirit is the brutish spirit beneath the nature of man: for man was made in the likeness and Image of God [Gen 1:26]: but this spirit which hates the reproof of the Light, and would continue its vain foolish ways and delights which the Light testifies against, that spirit debaseth man, bringing him beneath the state, wisdom and nature of a man, into a beastly and brutish state, whose state it is to live and act without the understanding of a man. Now as you bear the shape of man's nature, so you should grow up into man's image and wisdom. God hath not made you beasts, O do not join to that which makes you beasts: for out of the wisdom of man, out of the nature of man, in the unreasonableness, in the headiness and wilfulness, you are but beasts. Therefore mind the witness which discovers these things to you, and leads you out of them, as ye hearken to it, and come to know, fear, and love the Lord God, by its instruction and testimony. The way of youth is vain, dirty and foolish, and defiles the mind: O my children, wait for the

cleansing, watch to that which cleanseth the foolish way of children, which is that which discovers and witnesses against your foolishness and vain tempers, and temptation of your minds, and leads out of them. Therefore, my children, do not follow the vain things, which will daily be rising in the minds, but watch out for somewhat to rise after them, to discover your vanity to you, to rebuke it and draw from it; and follow that which rebukes vanity and draws from vanity, and not that which leads into it. Learn to bear the yoke in your tender years. There is a vain mind in you, there is somewhat would be feeding and pleasing that vain mind: and there is somewhat near you appointed by God to yoke it down: O give not scope to the vanity (it will be an occasion of woe and misery to you hereafter), but the yoke which keeps under the vain mind, O take that yoke upon you, and then ye shall become not only my children, but the disciples of Christ and children of the Most High. This is the first thing which I mainly and chiefly desire you should apply yourselves to learn.

The next thing is (which will also flow from this) that ye learn how to behave yourselves as good children, both in the family and to persons abroad, in a meek, modest, humble, gentle, loving, tender, respective [respectful] way (avoiding all rude, rough, bold, unbeseeming carriages towards all) honouring your Mother and Master (as God teacheth and requires) dearly cleaving to one another in the natural relation, which is of God, wherein ye our love [sic, possibly 'are loved'] even a great proportion of natural affection and kindness one to another, not as dogs, snarling and biting and quarrelling, not as Cain, who fell upon his brother [Gen 4:8], but as such who are near in nature and ought to be very kind and tender one of another. So to the servants carry yourselves very lovingly, sweetly, meekly, gently that none may have any cause of complaint against you, but all may see your lowliness and be drawn to love you. And to strangers carry yourselves warily, respectfully, in a sober, submissive, humble manner of demeanour, not disputing and talking, (which becomes not your age and place) but watching what ye may observe of good in them, and what ye learn of those that are good, and how ye may avoid any such evil, as ye observe in any that are evil. Thus your time will be spent in profit, and ye will feel the blessing of God, and of your parents, and be kept out of those evils which your age and natural tempers are subject to, and which other children (who are not careful nor watchful) are commonly entangled in. Mind these things my children, as ye will give an account to God, who through me thus instructs you, who am your imprisoned father, and have been much grieved when I hear of any ill concerning you, it being more matter of trouble and sorrow to me, than my imprisonment or any thing else I suffer, or can suffer from men.

Your father, who desires your good, and that it may go well with you both here and hereafter.

I. P.

10th of Third month, 1667

And remember this one thing, which as a father I admonish you of, and charge you in the authority of God to take notice of and observe, which is this, that ye do not fly out upon one another or complain of one another because of the evils ye observe in one another, but first take notice of that evil in yourselves, if by the true Light ye find your own hearts cleansed from it, bless God who hath done it, and keep to his Light and the testimony of his witness in you whereby he did it, and watch that ye be not overtaken in it for the future: but if ye be guilty of the same evil, or have lately done the same thing or are liable suddenly to do it, O for shame forbear accusing or blaming another, and in the fear of God wait on him and pray unto him, that ye may be delivered from it, and kept out of it. And then in tender pity, love and meekness, admonish thy brother or sister of his or her evil, and watch to be helpful to preserve or restore them out of, and pray to God to direct thee how to be helpful to them. But that is the bad spirit and nature (which God will sharply punish) that is ready to accuse others: and though it be never so bad and guilty yet will be excusing itself and laying the fault upon others or remembering some other fault of another when it should be sensible of and ashamed of its own.

Dear children, if ye bend your minds to learn these things, the Lord will help you therein, and become your teacher, guide and preserver, and pour down his blessings on you, and ye will be a comfort to me and your mother, and an honour to his truth; and he also may give me wise fatherly instructions to teach you further: but if ye be careless, foolish, vain, following your own minds and what riseth up there from the wicked one, ye will grieve my heart and provoke God against you to bring evil upon you both in this world and for ever. Therefore children, mind that which is near you; the light of God which discovers the evil and the good is near you. His witness which observes all ye do is near you. Yea, he himself is in that light and with that witness, therefore know ye are in his presence at all times, who is an holy and just God, hating that which is vain and evil, and loving that which is good and right before him; and hath appointed a day and set time, wherein he will either reward you with peace, joy, and eternal happiness, if ye have been good and done that which is good or with misery, destruction, and unsufferable pain both of soul and body, if ye have been evil and done that which is evil. And God takes notice how many instructions ye have heard from friends in truth, and from your parents, and how many meetings ye have been at wherein ye have been taught and warned of these things, so that if ye turn your back upon his Light, and will not hear its reproofs, but be vain, and idle, and foolish, and rash, and quarreling and fighting, and doing that which is naught, and then covering it with lies, and so be as bad if not worse than children who were never thus taught and instructed, God will be exceeding angry with you, and may in his just judgment and sore displeasure separate you from his Light, give you up to the black dark spirit from whom all this wickedness is, to sow in sin here and to so suffer the flames of [a line seems to be missing here] eternal life hereafter, which is his reward and the reward of all that are persuaded by him to be of his nature, and that hearken to him and let him work through them.

O my children, mind the truth of God in you, and that will let you see and understand the truth of what I now write, and in what fatherly love and tender care of you I write these things; that ye might be warned of the great danger of neglecting the time of your visitation by God's light and witness in you, and of going on in the evil ways of the dark crooked spirit, who will be tempting you to evil, and hindering you from God as long as ye hearken to him. Therefore be not fools to be led by him to destruction in the evil way and evil works, which lead thereto, but be wise to hearken to the light, and follow it out of that which is evil, into every thing that is good, to the salvation of your souls.

I desire that friends in the family watch over them in these respects, and when they find just occasion, putting them in mind of any of these things, in the fear and wisdom of God, with tenderness and gentleness, that they may reach the witness, but to take heed of upbraiding them, or aggravating any thing, lest they be thereby hardened, and the bad raised and strengthened in them. And my dear G[uli] and Friends, watch over your hearts and ways, that ye may be as examples to them, that they may not only read these things from my writing, but in your carriage towards them and one towards another, that they meet with nothing to strengthen or raise up the bad thing, but to reach the witness, and bring and keep down the evil in them: So the Lord bless your watchfulness, care and endeavours herein, that I may hear good of them, and be comforted in the mercy and kindness of the Lord towards them.

The following letter from Isaac to Fox, which by modern standards appears to grovel, needs to be read in the light of Isaac's state of mind. It may be that Fox, who was now reorganising the Quaker movement following his release from Scarborough Castle in September 1666, wanted assurance that the Peningtons had truly given up their association with the followers of Perrot. He was evidently satisfied, for he wrote two encouraging letters to the Peningtons during the following weeks (JP IV.23.4 and IV.2.3).

To George Fox, 15 July 1667 (JP III.389, *Works* II.493)

Dear G. F.
I feel the tender mercy of the Lord, and some proportion of that brokenness, fear and humility, which I have long

waited for and breathed after. I feel unity with and strength from the body, O blessed be the Lord who hath fitted and restored me, and brought up my life from the grave. I feel an high esteem and dear love to thee, (whom the Lord hath chosen, anointed and honoured) and of thy brethren and fellow labourers in the work of the Lord. And dear G. F., I beg thy love, I intreat thy prayer in faith and assurance that the Lord hears thee, that I may be yet more broken, that I may be yet more filled with the fear of the Lord, that I may be yet poorer and humbler before the Lord, and may walk in perfect humility and tenderness of spirit before him all my days. Dear G. F., thou mayst feel my desires and wants more fully than my own heart. Be helpful to me in tender love, that I may feel settlement and stability in the truth, and perfect separation from and dominion in the Lord over all that is contrary thereto.

I. P.

Aylesbury Gaol 15 of 5 Month 1667

I intreat thy prayers for my family, that the name of the Lord may be exalted and his truth flourish therein. Dear G. F., indeed my soul longs for the pure, full, undisturbed reign of the life in me.

Isaac's imprisonment was evidently not harsh when he wrote the following letter to his brother, as he was "going out to walk". It concerns what appears to have been an ongoing discussion of William's relationship with Perrot. Note, in the postscript, a curious reversed use of one quotation, for "cut out of the land of the living" comes from Isaiah 53:8 or Jeremiah 11:19, both references to the persecuted servant of God, not to God's enemy.

To his brother, 7 October 1667 (JP 1.58.3 and 1.59, part in Works 11.502)

The point of division between the letters is not clear in the manuscript.

Dear Brother,

This morning, as I was going out to walk, somewhat sprang up in my heart freshly and livingly; and as it sprang up there sprang a motion to write to thee: whereupon I consulted not, but immediately turned back so to do. Now, if the Lord make it useful to thee, thou wilt have cause to bless his name, and so shall I also, who heartily desire the life and welfare of thy soul in the living God, and thy avoiding all such snares as the enemy lays to betray, and to keep it in death and bondage. The thing that rose up in me was this.

God gave some apostles, some prophets, etc., for the work of the ministry, for the building up of the body, for the perfecting of the saints [I Cor 12:28, Eph 4:12]. This was God's gift, in mercy and love, to them in those days, of which gift they were to walk worthy, and to be thankful for it.

And in these days, the Lord hath given gifts to some for this work, which the body hath need of; and the body is to wait on the Lord in the use of his gift, in fear and humility. ... It is easy, still, to despise God's messengers and servants; but, he that will truly and rightly esteem them, must lie low, must dwell in the pure fear, and in the sense of life, that he may be taught of God so to do. It is an easy matter to have objections enough against them but, to see through all prejudices and objections, to the pure and precious life in them, and to the gift and spirit and power of the Lord, wherein and whereby they minister, this requires a true eye, and an heart opened by the Lord. ...

And dear Brother, mind this advice which just springs in my heart, pick out some of the faithful ones of the Lord's servants, and open thy heart to them, as in the leadings of the Lord and waiting upon him thou findest freedom therein. Indeed, Brother, I have had for a long time a deep sense of danger towards thee; the Lord prevent it; that thy soul may live to him, and not die from him. There is a wisdom, a will near thee, which will destroy thee, unless the Lord destroy it in thee.

O that thou mightest come to wait aright for the motion of his Spirit, and mightest be kept in that by him, which knows the drawing; then wilt thou hunger and thirst after the righteousness of his kingdom [Mt 5:6], and long after times of meeting and assembling with his people, and find thy sense of them living, and thy life refreshed therein. For God is with his people of a truth; and they meet not without him; but his presence is in the midst of them, causing his life to flow into every vessel that stands open to him. And death is not come over his people (whatever the enemy suggests, where he gets an ear open) but life grows more and more in freshness and into dominion in them. O Brother, the Lord fully gather thee into and preserve thee in that wherein thou mayst feel this, that thou mayest witness the freshness of life and the power thereof (in them) in thy own particular, that thy heart, also, may be as a watered garden, and as a living temple, wherein the pure living God dwells.

I am satisfied in my heart, that not only my love, but my life speaks to thee. O that thou couldst hear, and feel, and fear, and bow down before the Lord, that he might raise thee up in his life and power among his people in his due season, purifying thee and preserving thee pure and living to him for ever.

[...]

Aylesbury Gaol, 7th of 8th Month, 1667.

POSTSCRIPT

Dear Brother, There is one thing more springing up in my heart towards thee, which is this, J. Perrot had a more than ordinary sense of thee, and a deep unity with thee. Whence did that arise? but that he felt his own [spirit] in thee. And if it spring up in thee, as it did in him (and be not discovered by the light and hammered down by the power of the Lord, through his tender mercy to thee) indeed, it will destroy thee, as it did him. For this I say to thee, Brother, Come to the true feeling in the life, and thou shalt feel his name cut out of the land of the living, and from the memory and unity of the righteous seed. And O, Brother, come from the tents which that spirit pitcheth, lest the earth open her mouth and swallow thee up also [Ps 106:17]. Dear Brother, bear with me: for I have been long filled with the workings of love, and with dread concerning thee. For I was near being swallowed up alive in the pit without remedy: and the Lord shewed me great mercy, breaking the net and the snare, wherein my soul was taken and deeply entangled [Ps 124:7 et al.]. And now I am nothing (poor, weak, able

to help none) but the Lord show mercy to others also, and
particularly to thee is the desire of my heart.

Three days later Isaac wrote to members of his own local meeting, describing to them how he had worked through his inclination towards Perrot:

To N[icholas] N[oye] and others, 11 October 1667 (JP 1.60)

Nicholas Noye was a Friend who is mentioned on several occasions in the minutes of the local Monthly Meeting, and is the only likely possessor of the initials N.N. (Saxon Snell).

Dear Friends,
It is somewhat strongly on my heart this morning to
acquaint you, how that after that hour of darkness and
sore temptation, which it pleased the Lord to suffer to befall
me, wherein I have since seen in the light of the Lord, my
great danger of utter perishing from the Life and power of
the Lord. (I say after that) how that the Lord manifested
to me his great tenderness and mercy in preserving me
from the snare of the hat, where with I was very sorely
and strongly assaulted many ways, with all manner of
temptations, to draw me into and entangle me therein:
but I knew not then that they were temptations but was
questioning, and doubting, and fearing in spirit, and crying
to the Lord and waiting for his light and motion therein, as
I doubt not but others also have been.

But after the sore storm was over, the Lord visited me,
and brake the snare wherein I was entangled [Ps 124:7], then
he gave me clearly and sensibly in the stirrings of his life to
discern the motion of his spirit therein, and that the thing
was of him: and shewed me the ground from whence the
other temptations did arise; and that the other was not of
him; but of the enemy to darken the minds of Friends, and
bring in a practice which was against his witness even in
them that practised it, though while they were held in that
which blinds and darkens the mind, they could not discern it.

Now my Friends, I have not been forward to testify this
to you, nor any else: but indeed at present it doth lie upon

me, and with it this counsel springs up in me to you, so wait to feel the pure seed, and in it breathings to the Lord that his witness may speak in you, and that the ear may be opened to hear its voice, and your heart to distinguish the motion of his spirit, that you may feel true unity with him, and with the people of the Lord in all that is of him: and that that part at which this entered, and the way of its entrance, may be discovered in the spirit of life and in the feeling sense thereof unto you, that the enemy's entrance there may be stopped up.

Little did I think what the enemy brought into me at that one passage, wherein he brake in upon me about the hat: and perhaps the enemy may have brought more into you of this passage of the hat than you are aware. The Lord discover things to you as they are, and not suffer you to lodge, rest and enjoy peace, in the snares and devices of the enemy, which are against his Spirit and life, and the evidence of his witness in the hearts of his people.

This is the naked simplicity and true love of the heart of your friend in the fear, love and truth of God, who desires your perfect union and fellowship in the life and spirit of the body, and with all that is of God therein: and your deliverance and preservation from all that is not thereof, that you may never be suffered to err (much less to abide in any error, either of heart or judgment) from the truth, to the grief of God's spirit, the wounding of his life in you, the setting backward the work of your redemption, and the endangering of your souls: for every snare of the enemy hath all these in it (and much more) though he strives to hide both the snare and all its dangerous effects from the sight of the bird.

Aylesbury Gaol 11 of 8 month 1667 IP

Isaac was finally set free, sometime in the late autumn of 1667, after a relation of Mary's made an application for Habeas Corpus.[9] He had been charged with no crime. Morgan Watkins (see chapter 2) wrote to him that he had prayed to the Lord who had replied "I will

---

9. Ellwood's "Testimony" says Penington was released in 1668, but late 1667 fits better with the evidence from manuscript datings.

come in a full stream of love", and would not deny consolation to Isaac. It was fortunate that "thou hast been most of thy days a man of sorrows... that was his mercy to thee, for hadst thou been high thy danger had been greater, but being low and simple-hearted, the easier beguiled and the sooner come to see it and find mercy" (JP IV.17, 7 December 1667).

CHAPTER 4

From Aylesbury Gaol to Reading Gaol, 1667–1672

A change of government ministers in 1667 brought to power a group of men who were less enthusiastic about enforcing laws against Dissent, so that for the next few years Dissenting groups of all kinds gained some respite from persecution. George Fox took advantage of this interval to reinforce and where necessary establish the Quaker administrative system of monthly (district) and quarterly (county) meetings. The Penington family lived quietly at Berrie House.

Ann Fleetwood was the recipient of several letters and was mentioned in others. She was evidently an old friend, presumably belonging to the family of Sir George Fleetwood, regicide, whose estate at the Vache, near Chalfont St Giles, was confiscated after the Restoration.[1] It is not known whom Isaac proposed to take with him on the visit to her friend, but John Crook would have been a possibility.

To Ann Fleetwood's Friend, 11 December 1667 (JP 1.65.2)

Friend,
It hath pleased the Lord, after my long misery, sore distress of heart and longings after him, to manifest to me the way of his truth, even to the satisfaction, great joy and rejoicing

---

1. George Fleetwood's wife Hester became a Quaker, and in her old age lodged at Jordans Farm (see preamble to letter "To One Possessed of Prejudice" p. 74), which had at one time been part of the Fleetwood's estate. (Robert Huxter, *Jordans Meeting*, Jordans Preparative Meeting, 1989).

of my heart in his sight. And indeed I (with others) cannot conceal, but are required of the Lord to testify of this rich treasure, that others also might be stirred up rightly to seek after, sell all for, and enjoy it. But the enemy to the Lord, and to the soul's right serving and true enjoyment of him, stands stiffly and subtle in the way of truth's testimony, distilling into and filling the mind with prejudices, that there might be no room for it to enter. It is possible it may be thus with thee, and that through mistakes thou mayest think hardly of and speak to the dishonour of that which thou oughtest to honour, and which perhaps if thou rightly knowest thou wouldest.

Therefore it is in my heart to propound in true love to give thee a visit, with a friend of mine (who is meek, tender, singlehearted, and has sought after the Lord from his childhood) to see if the Lord please to give us any opportunity of service to him and one to another, in the love, meekness, sobriety, tenderness and fear which is of him. Friend, the intent of my heart is not to come to dispute with thee, but rather to keep out of disputes, in the tender sense of God's presence. And if he give me anything to speak, that would I speak; and if he give me not to speak, I would abide in silence, with my spirit retired towards him. In the meantime look up to the Lord, that thine heart may be opened by him to let in anything that is of him, and only shut against that which is against him.

If thou acquaint A[nne] F[leetwood] with this, remember my dear love to her, whom I in true love desire may be present with us, and that her heart also may be opened and shut by the Lord, to what is pure and of him, and against that which is impure and deceitful.

11 of 10 month 1667

I. P.

At this time, Isaac was confronted with a problem in his local meeting at Chalfont, probably a matter of incompatible personalities. A certain Friend would not attend meetings at "W.R.'s" house, and Isaac wrote to remonstrate. His advice echoes that given in many Friends' papers of advice on the resolution of disputes between

Friends, and derives from Matthew 18:15–20. W.R. was presumably William Russell, who lived at Jordans farm where Friends met before Jordans meeting house was built.

To one possessed with prejudice against a friend, 13 December 1667 (JP 1.66.2, *Works* II.505)

Dear Friend,

I have heard that thou hast somewhat against W[illiam] R[ussell] whereupon thou forbearest coming to meetings to his house, which thou oughtest seriously to weigh and consider, that thy path and walking herein may be right and straight before the Lord.

Is the thing, or are the things which thou hast against him, fully so as thou apprehendest? Hast thou seen evil in him or to break forth from him, and hast thou considered him therein and dealt with him as if it had been thy own case? Hast thou pitied him, mourned over him, cried to the Lord for him, and in the tender bowels of love and meekness of spirit laid the thing before him? And if he hath refused to hear thee, hast thou tenderly mentioned it to others, and desired them to go with thee to him, that what is evil and offensive in him might be more weightily and advantageously laid upon him, for his humbling and for his recovery unto that, which is a witness and strength against the evil? If thou hast proceeded thus, thou hast proceeded tenderly and orderly according to the law of brotherly love, and God's witness in thy conscience will justify thee therein. But if thou hast let in any hardness of spirit or hard reasonings against him, or hard resolution as relating to him, the witness of God will not justify thee in that.

And if at any time hereafter thou hast any thing against others, oh learn from that of God in thee, to show bowels of compassion towards them, as the Lord has had pity on thee. And keep to his witness in thy heart, wait to feel the seed, and to keep thy dwelling therein, that thou mayest abide in the peace and rest thereof, and not depart out of thy habitation, out of the sense of truth: for that will let in temptation upon thee, give the enemy strength against thee, and fill thy soul with anguish and perplexity. So the

4. From Aylesbury Gaol to Reading Gaol, 1667–1672

Lord God of infinite tenderness renew his mercy upon thee, and keep thee in that wherein his love, life, rest, joy, peace, and unspeakable comfort of his Holy Spirit (which is able to keep the mind out of all the snares and temptations of that which is unholy) is felt and witnessed, by those who are taught and enabled by him to abide and dwell in that into which he gathered them, and in which he hath pleased to appear unto them. This is in the love and tender goodness of the Lord to thee, from thy friend in the truth, and for the truth's sake,

13th of 10th Month, 1667 I. P.

In the spring of 1668 Mary went to London with Guli. She was not well, perhaps as a result of the birth of Edward, or "Ned", the previous autumn when she was 42, and she apparently intended to consult doctors. Isaac's short letter consists mainly of family news and messages to friends. Baby Ned has been boarded out, but Isaac is looking after the toddler Bill, then two and a half.

To Mary, 19 March 1668 (Gibson MSS II.45.1)

Addressed on reverse "To William Penington Merchant at the corner house in Sen Mary [next word illegible, presumably St Mary Axe is meant] near Bevis Marks, London, for M.P." This part of the City had escaped the Great Fire, and was mainly occupied by merchants and their warehouses. Most of the people referred to by initials have not been identified, but Dr P. and his wife were probably Doctor and Judith Parker, owners of Bottrells in Chalfont St Giles where the Penington family had lodged in 1666. "Phanatiques", or fanatics, was a general term of abuse for groups like Quakers and Fifth Monarchists.

19th of First-Month, 1667

My dear love, whom my heart is still with, and whose happiness and full content is my great desire and delight.

Leaving thee in so doubtful a condition, and there being such an earnestness in my mind to hear how it was with thee, it was pretty hard to me to miss of a letter from thee on the 3rd day [Tuesday]. T[homas] E[llwood] had one from W[illiam] P[enn] on the 4th day, wherein there was very

75

good and welcome news concerning thy health. On 3rd day night here called E.F., W[illiam] R[ussell] and G.S. not having been called at the Assizes. They said the judge spake much against the Papists at the Assizes and also gave a short charge relating to the Phanatiques. I heard by a Windsor friend that they were very forward and preparing to be very sharp at Windsor.

Yesterday I saw thy boy Ned at T. Lanes, looking very well and fresh, if not too well, I mean, too fat. W. Cowper hath [illegible] his desire and it is to be next first day, if the Lord should so order that T.B. were free to come, perhaps it might do well. Bill and thy children are well. Bill expects thy coming home at night, I bid him write to thee to come home, but he said no, he would go to London to thee. I said, if thou camest not quickly, father would get all the love from thee: (for he was exceeding loving to me this morning in bed). He said, no, no must not get all the love from mother.

My natural love to thee makes me express these things, yet not without some fear, lest I should be instrumental to draw thy mind too much into that part and nature which I myself wait to be daily further and further drawn out of. My dear love is to thee and my dear Guli, and to my dear brother W[illiam]. Mind it also to S.H. and J.B. and W. and S.B. and Doctor P. and his wife, and the Pagets, if thou see them, which perhaps it might be convenient so to do if thou hadst opportunity; for it seems some have endeavoured to instil into them, as if we were neglectful of them, and had not love for them answerable to theirs to us. O my dear, the Lord lead us more and more into his precious life and holy power, and into the sense of and subjection to his pure truth, that therein we may live to him, and feel the daily change more and more into his holy image.

Thine in all dearness and truth and love,
I. P.

P.S.—Thomas Ellwood desires me to mind his love to thee and Guli.

Indeed my dear, my soul hath been poured out in prayer for thy health and ease (if the Lord might see good)

and for his doing thee good by the pain wherewith he
pleaseth to afflict thee, and for thy growth and prosperity
in his truth, which just now it runs in my heart to express
to thee which I hope the Lord will not despise, but hear
the voice of his own in me for thee. I desire of the Lord
tenderness and wisdom in me towards my children, which
I have also have a breathing for: for the Lord knows, I never
have desired a child in me for [sheet torn] self, but for him,
that they might be of his generation and for his service.

That letter mentioned William Penn, who had recently joined with Friends, and he and Guli were quickly attracted to one another. Ellwood had probably been somewhat in love with Guli, but he now realised that he was not going to succeed in winning her. In 1669 he married a local Quaker and left the Penington household, although he continued to act as land agent for Mary Penington and Guli (*Experiences* 56–7, Ellwood 158).

Soon Isaac, still acutely unhappy about his backsliding, was again in correspondence with George Fox. The only surviving letter from Fox to which Isaac might be referring is a short note of personal encouragement written in February 1668 (J.P.4.2.4), but there may have been others.

To George Fox, 4 April 1668 (JP 2.217.2)

Most Dear G.F. whom the Lord hath exceedingly honoured,
and whom I truly love and honour in the Lord.

Some passages thou hast writ unto me of late, have
been often on my heart, and indeed I do earnestly desire
them of the Lord, to wit, that I may be faithful to him and
his truth fully and in every respect, and that he that never
sinned may wholly and perfectly reign in me according to
his right, and that I might wear the pure linen without any
mixture of the woollen [Lev 19:19], and so stand and abide
spotless before him among his redeemed ones. Now dear
G.F., this desire hath not been only often in my own heart,
but it hath also been often with me to request thy prayers
for me to the Lord in these respects, believing that the Lord
heareth thee, and that the cry of thy life to him for me
may be helpful to me herein. And dear G.F., though I have

been very unworthy of the Lord's love (and of the tender care of his faithful ministers and servants over me) having been foolish, blind and dark and conceited, exalting the apprehensions of my own wisdom and understanding above the pure light and sense of truth in them, and have done that whereof I am ashamed, and might justly in the righteous displeasure of the Lord have been cut off from him and his people forever: yet if the Lord please th[o]roughly to cut down the root in me from which all of that kind sprang, I shall be so no more, but shall walk the more in fear, and true subjection and abasedness of spirit, and in the tenderness and true humility of love, before him and in the midst of his people, all my days. So dear G.F., I believe thou canst feel my spirit, either through words or without words, and I pray thee in the tenderness of love (wherewith the Lord hath given thee to abound) be helpful to me, that I may at length feel my soul fully the Lord's, perfectly redeemed by him and perfectly living to him, in that which is pure of him, even in his own heavenly seed, all that is contrary brought under and kept under by his holy power for ever more.

4 of 2.m 1668 My dear love in fear and humility salutes thee. I.P.

Isaac continued to correspond with local Friends and acquaintances. The next letter was written to Elizabeth Walmsley's husband, who was not a Quaker. Note especially the postscript, which summarises the Quaker belief that Christ had returned in spirit, and was truly present.

To Thomas Walmsley, 18 February 1669 (JP 1.21.2)

Thomas Walmsley,
"God is love and he that dwelleth in love dwelleth in God" [1 Jn 4:16].

By this we know that we are of God even by the love which he hath given us. For he hath translated us out of the enmity, wherein deceit and death lodges, into the love where the life and power of truth is felt. Now this love we have not obtained of ourselves, but by his gift who hath shed it abroad in our hearts [Rom 5:5]. Nor could we ever learn it but as we were taught of him first to love him who begat, and then to love one another in the birth which is of him. Nor is our love limited here (though here it flow most strongly). But the same which teacheth us to love our God, and one another in his life and spirit, teacheth us also to love all that breathe after him in any measure, and desire for them, that they also might come to feed on that which truly satisfies the soul. Yea, we do not only read a precept, which commands us to love enemies; but love is also given us unto enemies, insomuch as we feel the love of Christ working in us towards enemies so far, as that we are freely willing to expose ourselves to many sufferings for their sakes, and could even lay down our lives for the rescue and salvation of their souls.

Now being in this love, which flows from the father and the son, we are here in union and fellowship with the father and the son: and none can speak against us or blaspheme our dwelling place but they speak against them also. And the great reason why several sorts of men (yea the Professors [professing Christians] of this age generally) do so, is because they truly and rightly know not, either the father or the son. O Friend, that thou mightest truly and rightly know them! I have often, in simplicity and sincerity of heart, had this desire in me for thee; O that it might at length take place upon thee, and not the power of the dark spirit deceive and captivate thee to thy destruction! O wait on the Lord, to receive the understanding (from him) which is true and pure, that in it thou mayest know him that is true, and the things that are true, from those which are false; that thou mayest not go out of this world in the deceit and darkness of the night and so perish for ever; but mayest come into the light of life, by the leadings of God's holy spirit and so walk and live with him therein for ever.

O that thou couldst have a true sense of my love, and of what I write to thee, and from whence it comes: for I have often felt thy state and thy soul's great danger, even in the sight of God, and in the sense and demonstration which is from him, though I have not found clearness before him often either to write or speak to thee. I remain,

Thy true friend, in true and tender love and in earnest desires after thy eternal peace and welfare with the Lord.
18th of 12 month 1668. I. P.

One thing more now comes into my mind, which was in my heart to thee sometime since, and I came to thy house on purpose to express it to thee but thou wast not then at home: it is thus:

O friend, Lean not to thy own understanding, but pray to God to deliver thee from thy own understanding, and to give thee the understanding which is of him. O learn of God to become a fool in thyself, that thou mayst be wise in him [1 Cor 3:18] and mayst rightly distinguish between the knowledge, wisdom, understanding and reasonings which are not of him, and that which is of him: so that by which is of him thou mayst come into him (abide in him and be found in him) who is the only life of the soul, who is the Lord Jesus Christ, our Saviour; who is now revealed in spirit and known in spirit, as really and comfortably as ever he was known in flesh, in the days of his flesh.

For that life, which was then manifested in flesh, is now manifested in spirit (even now, after the long night of darkness: the fullness of time being come for the day to spring again) and is soon felt, heard, tasted and handled [1 Jn 1:1, Ps 34:8], by those whom God gathers thither, who are in the life which is eternal, and from the quickenings, presence and power of life, testify of it to others. Also, whosoever the Lord God of life circumciseth and hath opened, heareth and cannot but get his soul thereto, to God's glory, even to the glory of the riches of his grace and mercy, which were to be shown forth in the ages to come, which ages are come, blessed be his name, whose love abounds, whose power is arisen, whose life is revealed, whose Spirit is received and dwelt in, by those who have travelled out of and forsaken the spirit and ways of this world, by the leadings, and in the virtue and strength which they have obtained of his holy spirit, who is come to live, dwell and reign in his people, and to bring down and lay flat all rule and authority in them, but his own.

This is the true and faithful testimony, both of the holy spirit of God and of the Bride the Lamb's wife which both say, "Come to the well of life which is now opened, to the waters of life", which now freely and abundantly flow forth to those which were once parched for thirst: so that the wilderness is become a fruitful field, and that which was once a fruitful field is now counted a forest [Rev 21:9, 22:1–2].

Dissident Quakers at the village of Horton[2] continued to give trouble. Isaac wrote on a number of occasions to two of the leaders, Edward Board and Robert Hall.

To Edward Board, 4 March 1669 (JP 1.146)

Friend,
When thou wast last with me at Aylesbury with R[obert] H[all] there was tenderness in my heart towards thee. Though there was a mixture in thee and somewhat did start from thee which was to be judged by the life and power of God: yet my eye was to the good, and to the owning and cherishing of that in thee. But for R.H. I felt him for the sword, being wholly in and speaking from a wrong spirit, of which in true and tender love I gave both him and thee faithful warning. And now Friends have you not (O that you could consider seriously and in true weightiness) since gone on in that spirit and (by the righteous judgment of the Lord upon you) stumbled yet more and more?

The Lord knoweth how earnestly I have desired and still desire the life and peace of your souls. O that your eyes might be opened by the Lord and you led by him in the way which leadeth thereunto: and your ears opened to hear the sound and testimony of God's spirit, which they have hitherto been stopped against. Indeed you have deeply erred, not being taught and able by the anointing to judge of, but have mistaken both concerning principles and spirit, and so have called evil good and good evil. In the great day of the Lord upon you, you shall set your seals to this testimony. I have seen and know it in the spirit of truth

---

2. See pp. 50–52.

Part I The Life of Isaac Penington

which erreth not, nor suffereth to err those that are guided by it.

Ah my Friend (my love makes me call you so, which bursts forth still towards you), O that you were delivered from the spirit of Antichrist, and knew the spirit of Christ truly and spiritually. For of a truth you are not in the sight of God, what you take yourselves to be, but are very deeply in the fairsaying and perishing estate. The Lord God break in upon you by his power and redeem you out of it.

This is in true friendship, great love and tenderness whatever it may appear to you, from him who is

A true and faithful Friend to your souls, and your Friend most in that which is most unwelcome and seems harshest to you

4 of 1 month 6$\frac{8}{9}$ [i.e. 4 March 1669]

There is that in you (even much of it) that is for the slaughter [condemnation by God]: O that it were slain by the two-edged sword of God's holy spirit, that your souls may come truly to live to him.

Another letter to Bridget Atley, undated, is placed here as it is in the same manuscript group (JP 1.145–1.148) as the last, and mentions Robert Hall. There is an unusual metaphor near the end of the second paragraph, that learning the will of God is like coming to know, and being subject to, a small child. Isaac probably had in mind a combination of Mark 10:15, receiving the kingdom of heaven as a little child, with the heavenly man-child of Revelation 12:5.

To Bridget Atley, [Spring 1669] (JP 1.148.2, *Works* II.507)

The version in Works *omits a section relating to the dispute at Horton.*

My dear Friend,
If thine heart come to feel the seed of God, and to wait upon him in the measure of his life, he will be tender of thee as a Father of his child, and his love will be naturally breaking forth towards thee. This is the end [aim] of his dealings with thee, to bring thee hither, to make thee fit and capable of entering and abiding here. And he hath

changed and doth change thy spirit daily, though it is as the shooting up of the corn, whose growth cannot be discerned at present by the most observing eye: but it is very manifest afterwards that it hath grown. My heart is refreshed for thy sake, rejoicing in the Lord's goodness towards thee, and that the blackness of darkness begins to scatter from thee, though the enemy be still striving the same way to enter and distress thee again. But wait to feel the relieving measure of life, and heed not distressing thoughts when they rise ever so strongly in thee, nay though they have entered thee, fear them not, but be still a while, not believing in the power which thou feelest they have over thee, and it will fall on a sudden. When thou hast such a thing simply in thy heart as to have sent R[obert] H[all]'s letter to me, thou shouldst have abode in the simplicity [straightforward impulse from God] thereof, and have done it: for the enemy will be opposing all the paths as well as the nature of the simplicity.

Qfp § 2.48

After thy last letter there passed somewhat in my spirit before the Lord towards that people, which was sweetly refreshing to me, which I committed to the Lord in the faith and was at rest. As for R[obert] H[all] he hath many wounds and strokes from the Lord (which is the Lord's mercy and tenderness to him) O that he would wait for healing from the same hand, and could distinguish voices within him, that knowing the voice of the witness of God from the voice of his own spirit and enemy in the reasoning spirit, he might see and shun the deceit wherein he is at present entangled. He must come down, he must lie low, he must become a fool [1 Cor 3:18], he must see that he is so far from being able to teach, that he yet knows not how to learn, and must be taught of God even how to learn or he cannot. He hath let in some of the notion of truth into his mind and understanding, but that hath but hurt him and got him farther off. That he must lose again, with the ability that received it and begin in sense, and fear to feel somewhat of God witnessing, striving, checking, etc., that he may come to know a little child, and in the denial of all his wisdom learn subjection to that little child: and this he will find very hard to him, yet there is no other way for him: and let him bless God for the judgments and strokes that bring him down and prepare his heart in any measure for this.

Qfp § 2.48

As for thee, it is good for thy spirit and greatly to thy advantage, to be much and variously exercised by the Lord. Thou dost not know what the Lord hath already done, and what he is yet doing for thee therein. Ah! how precious it is to be poor, weak, low, empty, naked, distressed for Christ's sake, that way may be made for the power and glory of his life in the heart. And O, learn daily more and more to trust him and hope in him, and not to be affrighted at any amazement [1 Pet 3:6], nor to be taken up with the sight of the present thing, but, wait for the shutting of thine eye upon every occasion, and for the opening of the eye of God in thee and the sight of things therewith as they are from him.

It is no matter what the enemy strives to do in thy heart, nor how distressed thy condition is, but what the Lord will do for thee, which is with patience to be waited for at his season in every condition. And though sin overtake, yet let not that bow down, nor let the eye open in thee, which stands poring [worrying] at that, but wait for the healing through the chastisement, and know there is an Advocate, who in that hour hath an office of love and a faithful heart towards thee [1 Jn 2:1]. Yea though thou canst not believe, yet be not dismayed thereat: thy Advocate who undertakes thy cause hath faith to give, only [provided that] thou sink into or at least pant after the hidden measure of life, which is not in that which distresseth, disturbeth, and filleth thee with thoughts, fears, troubles, anguish, darknesses, terrors, and the like. No, no, but in that which inclines to the patience, to the stillness, to the hope, to the waiting, to the silence before the Father, which is the same in nature with the most refreshing and glorious visiting life, though not the same in appearance: and if thy heart be turned to it, not minding but overlooking the other, thou wilt find some of the same virtue springing up in thy heart and soul, at least to stay thee.

And in and through these things thou wilt become deeply acquainted with the nature of God, and know the

wonderful riches and virtue of his life, and the mightiness of
his power, and the preciousness of his love, and tenderness
of his mercy, and infiniteness of his wisdom, and the glory
and exactness of his righteousness etc., wilt be made large
in spirit to receive and drink in abundantly of them, and
the snares of the enemy will be so known to thee and
discerned, and the way of help so manifest and easy, as their
strength will be broken, and the poor entangled bird will
fly away singing, from the nets and entanglements of the
fowler [Ps 91:3], and praises will spring up and great love in
thy heart to the forgiver and redeemer. O wait, hope, trust,
look up to thy God, look over that which stands between,
come into his bowels, let in the faith which openeth the
way of life, which will shut out the distrusting and doubting
mind, and close up the wrong eye, that letteth in reasonings
and temptations, the wrong sense and death with them,
that thou mayst witness, in and through thy redeemer, the
abundance of his life and peace.
   I. P.

The following letter may have been connected with the same dispute. Shocking as it is in the twenty-first century, one must remember that Isaac was, inevitably, a man of his times, and that Katharine Skippon would not have been shocked or surprised. But compare the letter to Sarah Elgar in the next chapter. In the intervening period, the Peningtons themselves lost a child.[3]

To Katharine Skippon, 5 April 1669 (JP 1.62)

Ah K.S. whom I have dearly loved and in faithfulness testified
to in the pure life of God. There is at this time the sense in
my heart (though not only at this time) that thy son and
thy daughter were both taken from thee in the displeasure
and righteous judgment of the Lord upon thee, for turning
thy back up on his truth, and despising his love in the many
precious visits which he hath been pleased to give thee. And
truly Katharine it is deep upon my heart, that the judgment
of the Lord will not end here, but unless thou bow to the

---

3. See p. 89.

Lord, and be acquainted with his living truth, and become subject and obedient thereto, thy soul will also perish, and not partake of the precious redemption and power of life, which those that abide in and are faithful to the truth are witnesses of.

This is in the tenderness of love, for thy soul's good (O that thy ear might be opened by the Lord to know and receive what comes from him) from

Thy soul's true Friend, I.P.

5 of 2 month 1669

Some new Quakers were meeting at the house of the Peningtons' friend Thomas Zachary in Beaconsfield. This letter to them is an example of Isaac's use of the Bible. "Young", as in the address, usually means young in Quaker experience rather than in years.

For the young and tender ones at T. Zachary's, 10 August 1669 (JP 1.158)

Friends,

There came into my mind some scriptures this morning, the remembrance whereof was sweet and refreshing to me, and indeed it was with me in the single and tender love of my heart unto you, to lay them before you.

The first was, that promise of wisdom, Proverbs 1:23, "I will pour out my spirit unto you". This wisdom which here speaks is Christ who is the wisdom and power of God, 1 Corinthians 1:24. Now mark, upon what terms Christ the wisdom of God pours out his spirit unto the sons of men. The terms are expressed just before, in the foregoing words, "Turn you at my reproof". O therefore wait to know the reproofs of wisdom in your heart and to turn thereat from what wisdom reproves you for, that ye may be made partakers of this sweet, precious and glorious promise. And when the spirit of wisdom is poured out unto you and rests upon you, then ye will easily know true wisdom's voice and words inwardly, from the voice and words of the other wisdom and so come to witness that scripture fulfilled in you. His sheep hear and know his voice (John 10:3–4) who is the shepherd and bishop of the soul, 1 Peter 2:25. Now the pure fear of the Lord is the beginning of wisdom's instruction, Proverbs 1:7, 9:10, and indeed is of the nature of the wisdom which teacheth it, yea it is true and pure wisdom itself in the seed or beginning of it, according to the testimony of that scripture Job 28:28, "Behold the fear of the Lord, that is wisdom, and to depart from evil is understanding". This is it which the true child (the birth of God's spirit) which enters into the kingdom learns; he learns this wisdom of his heavenly Father and mother, even to choose the good and refuse the evil [Isa 7:14–16].

The next scripture was at Revelation 3:20–22. Read the scripture and wait on the Lord, that ye may know in yourselves the door at which Christ knocks, and may hear his voice (which he that hears, though he was dead, yet shall he live: for his voice gives life. "Hear and your souls shall live", Isaiah 55:3) and may open the door, and witness him to come in and to sup with you and to give you to sup with him. Shall ye not then partake of the feast of fat things [Isa 25:6], and drink of the wine of the kingdom fresh and new in the kingdom [Lk 22:16]? And mind the overcoming (by the power of Christ) what is contrary to Christ's nature and spirit in you: for he was to overcome before he sat on the throne [Rev 17:14 with 21:5], and they that are his, must follow his steps.

Another scripture was at Matthew 11:19, "Wisdom is justified of her children". O that ye might feel the spirit of life begetting and bringing you forth alive unto God, from the womb of the pure heavenly wisdom, that so ye may know and justify every voice of wisdom in your own hearts, and walk in her living path out of all the ways of death!

Another scripture was at Isaiah 25:7. O mind that precious promise, and wait to know that mountain where the face of the covering is destroyed and the veil taken away: for no man can see into the mystery of life and redemption, but as the veil and covering which hinders him (standing between him and his sight of the glory of the gospel) is removed. Now mind: the veil is done away in Christ (2 Corinthians 3:14) there is no darkness, no covering in him. Therefore wait so to know Christ, and so to be brought into union with him, as that ye may feel the veil, which covers and hinders from the sight of the pure glory, removed by him.

The last scripture is at Proverbs 4:18, "The path of the just is as the shining light, that shineth more and more unto the perfect day". O wait to feel in your hearts the renewing spirit, the regenerating spirit, that by it your hearts may be renewed and regenerated, and that then ye may know the path wherein the just walk, and wherein they witness life and preservation. For this is the true resemblance of it, as it hath been in all ages, it is like a shining light, which light is the beginning of the everlasting day of God, in the heart in which it shines, 2 Corinthians 4:6, and this is the way or manner of its path, its holy light, its holy stirring increases in the just, shining more and more in them unto the perfect day. Now this is the great work ye are to mind, even to find your minds turned from the darkness to the light (which the holy measure of the gospel was sent by Christ to turn men to, Acts 26:18, and 1 John 1:5) and then that ye travel out of the darkness into the light, and be changed by the light and become light in the Lord, Ephesians 5:8 (for the light of life is powerful, and leavens into its own nature) and so dwell and walk in the light, as God is in the Light, 1 John 1:7: and in this light ye will truly, certainly and satisfactorily know the blood of Christ which cleanseth from all sin, and feel it cleansing your hearts therefrom, and so ye will come out of the miserable state, out of the cursed state into the holy and blessed state: and feel the God of peace and blessings treading down Satan under your feet [Ps 8:6; Rom 8:20], and blessing you with all spiritual blessings and mercies in Christ Jesus, who is the son of his love, and the Lord and King of all the living. This is from one who is,

Your real Friend desiring your eternal peace and happiness with the Lord for ever, and also your welfare in this world.

10 of 6 month 1669 IP

The year 1670 brought a return of persecution with the passing of the Second Conventicle Act, which offered rewards to persons informing against Quaker meetings. The gaols were again filled with Quakers, and Isaac was arrested in Reading when paying a visit to imprisoned Friends, and committed to Abingdon assizes in July. A little notebook was sent to him containing an account of his imprisonments. Isaac corrected it and added a request for a record to be kept of "the true deeds and names of the witnesses thereto, and those set down in a little black book in the shelf in my closet". He also wanted "one pair of white gloves that I left in the basket in my closet" (Gibson MSS II.45).

He was held for some 21 months.[4] Like many Quakers at the time, he was ordered to take the Oath of Allegiance, the refusal of which could incur the penalty known as praemunire, by which the guilty person forfeited his estate to the crown, and was outlawed and imprisoned for life. Isaac's estate had already been lost, but Mary became aware of the court's intention to use the praemunire as a weapon against her own estate, which could not be forfeited but could be frozen during Isaac's lifetime and the income from it confiscated. She therefore "sent to London, and had the arrears and rents, that hereafter should be due (for the estate itself they could detain no longer than my husband lived) made over to a friend of mine, for the use of me and my children" (Penington, John 1682, 10–13). This was quite legal.

Soon after Isaac had been imprisoned, the Peningtons suffered a personal tragedy in the death of their second son Isaac. He had been sent on a voyage to gain experience to prepare him for a career as a merchant, and was lost overboard during the return voyage. It may be that Isaac was given compassionate leave from prison, as Ellwood recorded that he visited Isaac and Mary at home during September (Ellwood, 161–4).

Widow Hemmings and her family were among Isaac's major correspondents. Among the Penington manuscripts there are seventeen letters and papers addressed to her, and others to her daughters Ruth

---

4. Ellwood's "Testimony" states that Penington remained in prison for 21 months. There are letters addressed from Reading Gaol from July 1670 to 29 May 1671, then several from other addresses from 25 April to 7 October 1672, then a single letter from Reading Gaol dated 30 November 1672. Since prisoners were released following Charles II's Declaration of Indulgence in March 1672, it is probable that the November letter is incorrectly dated. Isaac was apparently at liberty in December 1670, if a letter sent from Catsgrove (location unknown at present) has the correct date.

Palmer and Elizabeth Stonar and her son-in-law Nathaniel Stonar, all dated 1670–76. Some of these letters have a considerable theological content. Note the opening to this letter; Isaac often mentioned that he was writing out ideas that came to him soon after he woke up. The part omitted consists of seven theological queries, a short paper on baptism, and another set of seven queries. Written queries were a common device in theological argument at the time, normally being intended to catch out one's opponent, but Isaac says that this is not his intention.[5]

To Widow Hemmings, 9 November 1670 (JP 1.48.2)

Dear Friend,

When I awaked this morning, (which was very early as it is usually with me) my heart was whirled to the Lord; and immediately I felt his life spring in me, and my spirit fed thereon and was refreshed and bowed to the Lord my God, and worshipped him in spirit and truth. As it was then thus with me the sense of thee came upon me, and some queries sprang in my heart to propose to thee, not to perplex thy mind, or set thy thoughts and reasonings on work: but to affect thine heart, and to bring that and to bring thee into weightiness of spirit and true sensibleness before the Lord, that thou mightest so wait upon him, as that thou mightest receive from him the virtue and power of life and of his holy spirit, which subjected to, is able and will not fail to mould thee into the image of his son [Rom 8:29]. There arose also in my heart something concerning baptism, and of breaking of bread, and [taking] wine in remembrance of Christ's death which because it sprang and in relation to thee, I shall also mention, though otherwise I should rather forbear, and put thee upon the inward sense of the seed of life, and to wait to feel that operation of that in thy heart, and the discerning which is from and in that.

The time is but short and we must all appear before the judgment seat of Christ [Rom 14:10], to give account of all things done in the body: of all our words; of all our thoughts and of all our worships etc.; blessed will he be,

---

5. For other letters to Widow Hemmings, see Part II, pp. 194 and 208.

4. From Aylesbury Gaol to Reading Gaol, 1667–1672

whose works will then abide the fire and the trial of God's unerring impartial balance. That which will bear the trial of the seed and holy anointing now, shall not need to fear the trial of that day. And because we are redeemed and found in the Son's life and righteousness and find God justifying us [making us right with God] and the works of his son in us, by the light of his own holy spirit, bearing witness with our spirit [Rom 8:16]; therefore we have boldness before the throne now [Heb 10:19], being now assured, that what is now justified by God's holy spirit shall never be condemned. The sincere desire of my heart for thee is, that God may try thy heart and ways, and bring thee out of all paths of error, deceit and doubt, into the way everlasting, that thou mayest perform all thou dost to God, on the assurance of faith, and in the assurance of true understanding.

[…]

> Thy friend in true and faithful love and service of truth
> Reading Gaol 9 of 7 month 1670. IP

We place here one of a group of letters to unknown recipients whose median date is around 1670. Especially in the second paragraph, note Isaac's criticism of the intellectual approach to religion, which had failed him. The term "inward Jew" in the final paragraph derives from Romans 2:29 and means "one who obeys the spiritual law".[6]

Unknown recipient and date (JP II.278.2, *Works* III.458)

Friend, Hearken to a word of advice, which is in my heart to thee, it may be of great use to thee, if the Lord open thy spirit, and cause it to sink in. It is this. Wait on the Lord, that thou mayst from him feel the right limit to the mind in reading the Scriptures, for the mind of man is busy and active, willing to be running beyond its bounds, guessing at the meaning of God's Spirit and imagining of itself, unless the Lord limit it. Therefore read in fear, and wait understandingly to distinguish between God's opening to thee words concerning the kingdom and the things of the kingdom to thee, and thy own apprehensions about them:

---
6. See the letter to Elizabeth Walmsley in ch 5, p. 114.

Part I The Life of Isaac Penington

that the one may be always cast by, and the other always embraced by thee.

And always wait God's season: do not, do not presume to understand a thing, before he give thee the understanding of it: and know also, that he alone is able to preserve the true sense and knowledge in thee, that thou mayst live dependently upon him for thy knowledge, and never lean to thy own understanding. Little dost thou know what it hath cost us, to have our own understanding and wisdom broken down, and how demonstratively by this Spirit the Lord opens scriptures to us (yea, the things themselves which the Scriptures speak of), since he hath taught us to deny our understanding, and to lean upon his Spirit and Wisdom.

The Lord guide thee by his certain infallible Spirit into the certain, infallible, everlasting way of life, that by the shinings of his light, Spirit, and power in thee, thou mayst see light, and enjoy life. For if thou didst certainly and infallibly understand all the words (testimonies and descriptions) concerning the thing, yet it is another matter to understand, know, enjoy, possess, and live in that which the words relate to, describe, and bear witness of.

And Friend, if thou wilt be an inward Jew, and know and understand the laws of life, the laws of the new covenant, thou must read them in those tables, where God writes them, in and by the new covenant. Indeed, by reading in the letter, thou mayst read testimony concerning the Spirit and his ministration: but thou must read in the Spirit, *Qfp* § if ever thou come rightly to understand the letter. And the 27.27 end [goal] of words is to bring men to the knowledge of things, beyond what words can utter. So learn of the Lord to make a right use of the Scriptures, which is by esteeming them in their place, and prizing that above them, which is above them. The eternal life, the Spirit, the power, the fountain of living waters, the everlasting pure well is above the words concerning it. This, the believer is to witness in himself, and to draw water with joy out of it.

I. P.

In the following letter, Isaac makes a strong plea for his release:

To the Justices of the Peace for the County of Berkshire
[1671, date from context] (JP III.544.2)

I have suffered now above a year's imprisonment, coming in these parts as a stranger, and not giving any offence. My cause was twice cleared at this very place (the last sessions here) by two Justices on the Bench, and the Court was desired both times to take notice if my cause was justified and cleared, to which no reply was made but the Court silent, nor was any accusation laid to my charge, nor one word contradicted which I spake in my own defence.

If ye believe me to be innocent, and yet still condemn me, consider what all just men will think thereof, and how ye will answer it to God, when ye shall give an account to him of the exercise of your authority and power.

Let honour and justice move you not to suffer the innocent to be oppressed, but rather to defend him: for such carriages as these do not at all advantage the King, nor make the government lovely in the people's eyes, whose hearts are his strength.

This is from one, who fears God and loves his country, and wisheth well to the King (and hath earnestly desired the establishment of his throne in truth and righteousness) who though a stranger here, yet in his own country [district] is generally known to be a man of an innocent and peaceable behaviour, who heartily wisheth well to you.

I.P.

Isaac was finally released following Charles II's Declaration of Indulgence of March 1672, by which the penal laws against "whatsoever sort of nonconformists or recusants" were suspended. Charles II regularly tried to ease the incidence of the laws against Dissent, maybe from a genuine inclination to toleration as well as from a wish to reduce the pressure on Catholics, but he was dependent on Parliament for money, and Parliament feared the increase of Catholic influence. Parliament, at its next meeting in January 1673, insisted that the Declaration should be cancelled, but in the meantime Quakers and other Dissenters enjoyed a short breathing-space.

CHAPTER 5

Domesticity and Controversy: The Last Years, 1672–1679

Soon after his release, Isaac Penington took part in a major pamphlet war between Quakers and Baptists.[1] He was then briefly to the fore in Quaker internal politics, when one William Mucklow stirred up the hat controversy by publishing a number of letters and papers that had been written during the height of the dispute, including a set of queries by Penington (Mucklow 1673, 63–5, reproducing Harvey MSS XIII.3). Penington admitted his authorship but said he had changed his mind. Otherwise, the Peningtons were occupied with their own affairs for the next few years. Guli was married to William Penn, and Isaac and Mary did not feel settled in Berrie House. Mary's estates, their sole source of income, were in Kent, but Isaac did not wish to live there. They thought of moving to Waltham Cross to be near their children's school, but they then heard of a suitable property nearby in Amersham, called Woodside, and Mary took the initiative to sell one of her own farms and purchase it.

The house, probably on the site of the present Community and Leisure Centre, was in a ruinous condition and had to be extensively rebuilt. Probably Isaac's health was failing after his long imprisonments, and Mary handled the household affairs and sheltered her husband from bother as much as possible. She was a practical woman, and from her own account could manage very well so long as he did not interfere. She became rather worried at one point during the building operations, when Isaac made some plans which, she

---

1. See Appendix A on *The Flesh and Blood of Christ*.

thought, were too costly, but in the end all went well. The work took less than four years, and they were settled in Woodside by the early autumn of 1676 (*Experiences* 53–62).[2]

Isaac visited London during the autumn of 1675, and the next letter shows him in controversy with John Pennyman, who had joined with Friends around 1658 and had a love-hate relationship with them for the rest of his long life.[3] He was an associate of William Penington, and Isaac noted that one of Pennyman's letters was delivered "by the hand of my brother" (JP 1.155, November 1675). The second paragraph and postscript to this letter suggest that Pennyman had been instrumental in influencing Isaac in favour of John Perrot.

To John Pennyman, 29 June 1675 (JP 1.154)

J. Pennyman,

Upon seeing thee last 4th day at our meeting I was greatly exercised in my spirit towards the Lord for thee, earnestly breathing unto him, that if it might stand with his holy pleasure, thou mightest (for thy own good) be stopped from speaking that day, as also that thou mightest have some sense of the living power and presence of our God among us that day. And was it so with thee? O that thou couldst say yea! Why should my life have a testimony against thee, whom I love and most sincerely wish well unto? O that thou sawest thy state and habitation, as the eye of his life seeth it! Surely thou wouldst not abide any longer there, nor any longer to be subject to that spirit and power, which having been let in by thee hath great power to blind, darken, harden and bewitch thee, and engage thee (even in thy heart, through the deep and great deceit he hath brought in thither) against the holy, pure, living spirit and power of the Lord, revealed and dwelling in, and manifesting itself through his people.

---

2. Some authorities have suggested another site, or have dated the building of Woodside between 1668–9 and 1672–3, following Mary's account in *Experiences*, which suggests that the building was started fairly soon after the the children had gone to school. However, the last letter from Berrie House is JP 1.56, dated 20 March 1676, and the first from Woodside is JP 4.141, of 21 September 1676. Mary, *Experiences* 58, says that they first went to view the property in "my son Penn's coach", which suggests a time after Penn's marriage to Guli in April 1672.
3. See p. 40 and note.

I have suffered very greatly by once hearkening to thee, and receiving a wrong sense and testimony from thee. (O the great sorrow my soul hath undergone, and the great danger I was in thereby!) O that thou couldst hearken unto me for thy good as I once hearkened unto thee for my hurt! Indeed John, my life, the holy birth of life in me, hath a testimony from my God against thy present spirit and state, as true, as full, as certain a testimony against thee, as against the most manifest idolaters and transgressors of his holy law: and I see you, in and through his holy light, to be in the same nature, spirit and ground of iniquity. O that thou (whom it so much concerns) mightest see it also! O that thy mind might be turned unto that which gives the sight of it! ... I.P.

POSTSCRIPT.

Indeed, John, this is the same spirit thou wast entangled in before, and whereby thou didst entangle me also, I letting in the seriousness of thy words too far upon my spirit (O the woe upon woe, and misery and distress of soul, which I came to feel thereby! O what a separation between me and the God of my life did ensue and I was taught the contrary to what thou speakest to me, by the briars and thorns of the wilderness!) But O that I might be a means to disentangle thee! though thou hast travelled very far with that spirit, and hast sold thyself unto it, and lost the true understanding, sense and judgment, and provoked the Lord exceedingly against thee, by trusting to lying vanities and forsaking the tender mercies wherewith he visited thee (even as he had done my soul, and the souls of others) and began to open thy eyes, and tender thy heart towards himself his truth and people.

29 of 3m 1675

The following year, Isaac heard that his younger brother Arthur was becoming a Catholic. By now such a conversion was less dangerous and shocking than it would have been thirty years earlier, for the Court was known to favour this faith. Nevertheless, it was still a bold move, for Catholics were deeply unpopular in the country and were subject to penal laws (until 1829). Near the end of the letter, Isaac refers to the radical Protestant and Seeker belief, which Quakers shared, that the church had been in a state of apostasy from early times.[4]

To his brother Arthur, 20 September 1676 (JP III.366, *Works* III.514)

Dear Brother,
I have been a traveller after the Lord from my childhood, and great misery have I undergone for want of him. That which I wanted was his Spirit, life, virtue, and redeeming power, to be revealed in my own heart. O, blessed be the Lord! beyond my expectation, he hath directed me where to wait for this within, and hath revealed it in me, and now I can say in truth of heart, and in the sense of that birth which God hath begotten in me, Lo this is my God whom I so wanted and waited for, and I find him stronger in my heart, than the strong man which possessed it before he cast him out from thence, and made a spoil of his goods [Mt 12:29].

And now, dear Brother, how can I hold my peace, and not testify of the love, mercy, and good-will of the Lord towards me, and invite others to the redeeming power, which the Lord in his goodness hath made me a partaker of. And now, brother, a few words respecting thy return to what I sent thee; not for contention's sake, the Lord knows my dwelling is in that life and peace which shuts them out, but in the tender love and care of my heart concerning the eternal welfare of thy soul, which I would not have by any means or device of the enemy eternally deceived.

All sides may agree in notions about the regenerating power; but all do not receive the regenerating power, nor are truly regenerating in the sight of God; nor come to witness the head of the serpent inwardly crushed [Gen 3:15], and his works destroyed and kingdom laid waste inwardly, by this power; which must needs be, before a man be translated out of the kingdom of darkness into the kingdom of the dear Son. There is an inward kingdom of darkness in which the unbelieving and disobedient to God's Spirit and power dwell; and there is an inward kingdom of light, wherein the

---

4. See p. 158.

children of light dwell with God, and walk in the light, as he is in the light.

But that the work of regeneration is only begun in this life, and not finished till the other life, that is a great mistake. For the Scriptures testify that salvation is to be wrought out here, and not hereafter. Christ had all power in Heaven and Earth, and he sent out his Spirit and power to work out the work here, and his sanctifying Spirit and power is able to sanctify throughout in soul, body and spirit, and the gifts of the ministry is for perfecting the Saints, till they all come to the unity of the faith, to a perfect man, that they may be presented to God perfect in Christ Jesus. . . .

And blessed be the Lord, who hath brought many wanderers and distressed ones to the sight of the true Church, and to delightful obedience to her; whose voice is not different from Christ's, but one with it; and such are in fellowship with the Father and Son, and with the saints who dwell in the light, and are clothed with the Lamb's innocency and righteousness, and do not dwell in darkness, nor in sin, having crucified the old man with his affections and lusts, and put off the body of the sins of the flesh, by the circumcision of Christ, and put on the new man which is preached in Christ Jesus in the righteousness and holiness of truth [Col 3:9–10, the "old man" is Adam, or unregenerate nature]. They that are here dwell not in fancies, nor feed on fancies, but on eternal life, in the pure pastures of life, where the shepherd of the inward and spiritual Israel feeds his holy flock day by day.

As for the Romish Church, or any other church built up in the Apostasy [time of wilful separation] from the spirit and life of the apostles: the Lord hath given me to see through them, to that which was before them, and will be after them: and O dear Brother, if thou couldst but rightly wait for and meet with the holy, regenerating, purifying power, which in tender love I testified to thee of, that would lead thee to that which is the true church indeed, which hath been persecuted by the Dragon and false church, and the blood of her seed drunk by the bloody dragonish church for many ages [Rev 12].

The Lord hath made me thy brother in the line of nature; oh that thou wert my brother in that truth, which lives and abides for ever: O that thou knewest the Church of the firstborn [Heb 12:23], whose names are written in Heaven, the Jerusalem which is above which is free [Gal 4:26], which is the mother of us all who are born of the regenerating virtue and power.

I. P.

20th of Seventh Month, 1676

To Joseph Wright, [1676] (JP III.367, Works IV [supp]. 39)

Immediately after the letter to Arthur Penington in the manuscript.

I entreat thy son to acquaint my brother Arthur, that I took very kindly, and was very glad of his affectionate expressions towards me; having been somewhat jealous that though my religion had enlarged my love towards him, yet, his religion might have diminished his to me. I bless the Lord on his behalf, that he enjoys his health so well: and for myself, though I have been exceeding weakly formerly, yet the inward life and comfort, which the Lord daily pleaseth to administer to me, increaseth the health and strength of my natural man, beyond my expectation, blessed be my tender and merciful Father, who hath visited one so distressed, miserable and helpless as I was for so many years.

And, whereas he saith he is like me in speech, but most unlike me in opinion, I pray tell him from me, that my religion doth not lie in opinion, but in that which puts an end to opinion. I was weary and sick at heart of opinions, and had not the Lord brought that to my hand which my soul wanted, I had never meddled with religion more. But as I felt that in my heart which was evil and not of God, so the Lord God of my life pointed me to that of him in my heart which was of another nature, teaching me to wait for and know his appearance there; in subjection whereto, I experience him stronger than the strong man [devil] that was there before: and, by his power he hath separated me from that within, which separated me from him before: and, that being separated, truly I feel union with him, and his blessed presence every day, which what it is unto me my tongue cannot utter.

I could be glad if the Lord saw good, that I might see my brother before I die; and, if I did see him, I should not be quarrelling with him about his religion, but embrace him in brotherly love, and in the fear of the Lord. As for his being a Papist or an ArchPapist [particularly enthusiastic], that doth not damp my tender affection to him. If he be a papist I had rather have him be a serious than a loose papist. If he hath met with any thing of that which brings forth an holy conversation [way of life] in him, he hath so far met with somewhat of my religion, which teacheth to order the conversation aright, in the light, and by the Spirit and power of the Lord Jesus. My religion is not a new thing, though newly revealed more fully, than in many foregoing ages; but consists in that which was long before Popery was, and will be when Popery shall be no more. And he that would rightly know the true church must know the living stones whereof the true church is built, against which church the gates of Hell cannot possibly prevail [1 Pet 2:4, Mt 16:18]. O the daily joy of my heart in feeling my living membership in this Church, where the true gold, the white raiment, the pure eye-salve [Rev 3:18], (with which the eye being anointed sees aright) is received and enjoyed inwardly (by such as the world knows not but despiseth) blessed be the name of the Lord.

I desire my sincere, entire affection as in God's sight, may be remembered to my dear brother.

I. P.

Much of Isaac's correspondence was now concerned with a major Quaker internal dispute.[5] Fox's administrative reforms were not universally liked, and the dissatisfaction focused on his introduction, during the 1670s, of women's business meetings. It was Quaker

---

5. This is the "Wilkinson-Story separation", named after the two original protagonists, John Wilkinson and John Story. See Braithwaite *Second Period of Quakerism* 290–323, 469–81. There is no full scale modern study of this dispute, but see Clare J. L. Martin, "Tradition versus Innovation: the Hat, Wilkinson-Story and Keithian Controversies" in *Quaker Studies* vol. 8/1, September 2003, 5–22.

practice that, before giving permission for a couple to marry, monthly meetings would assure themselves that the couple were clear of previous "entanglements", and had made provision for any existing commitments. Many men strongly objected to having their marriage intentions made subject to the women's monthly meeting as well as to the men's.

One of the leaders of the opposition was a Quaker minister named John Story. Fox described him as being a "forward, bold lad" in his youth, on an occasion when he had offered Fox tobacco, but since that time he had had a long career as a Quaker minister, and was well respected among Friends (Fox, *Journal* 110). Isaac wrote to him as follows:

To John Story, 21 September 1676 (JP IV.141)

Some pages have been excised from the manuscript, including the start of this letter

... I have been often with the brethren in their concerns and debates about thee, and have seen their love and tenderness and deep fears and sense and testimonies of life, and have felt life spring in my heart, and a bright unity with their testimonies in the springing life. And this is the sense of our hearts, as in God's sight, that a wrong spirit had entered thee (O the cries in the hearts of many before the Lord because of it) and thou art sorely inwardly hurt and languishing, and also leavening many with this wrong spirit, whose ears are open to thee in the wisdom which is out of the life and not in the life. O dear J[ohn] S[tory], I am loath to part with thee eternally. Thou dost not know the living sense and dread that is upon me in relation to thee. How certainly doth the eye of life in me see many hurt by thee already! How often have I been discouraged in my heart from writing to thee! How can I hope (considering what I am) that my testimony should have any place with thee! Yet would I not spare being thy enemy, if at length thereby I might prove to be thy friend. They are not thy friends that stand by thee; yet err in vision concerning thee: but they that give life's testimony in plainness and uprightness to thee, they are thy friends. O my bowels, O the concern of my heart for thee! O that thy eye were opened, O that the dark wisdom were confounded in thee! Come, John, be a fool once again: let life arise. The Lord visit thee and strengthen that which is ready to die, and kill that which is now alive in thee. The wrong, hard, stiff, exalted, selfish wisdom is now alive in thee. Be not offended with me, that I thus nakedly and faithfully speak! I have ground for it in the inward feeling and testimony of life. And feel the cry of my heart to thee in one thing, for thine own sake, chiefly, though also for the truth's sake, O do not nourish any hard thoughts against dear George Fox whom the Lord hath honoured and is with and who faithfully goes on in the work of the Lord and is attended with the power of the Lord, and they that fight against him, or think hard things concerning him, and abide not in the thankfulness to the Lord for him cannot prosper. This is that which rose in me this morning, in the melting, breaking power of life in my heart, who never felt such a travel since I knew the truth (as I have very lately felt) for the preservation of the springing life in these parts and also wherever else it is witnessed) and for the crushing of the head of the contrary wisdom. O dear J[oh]n: pure love and desires after thy recovery spring so in me, that I could even lay down my life for it. The Lord grant that the dreadful fears of my heart (and of many more of the tender-hearted brethren, whose concern and travel with the Lord hath been exceeding great for thee) may not come to pass concerning thee!

   Amersham-Woodside
   21 of the 7 Month 1676
   This is from a deep mourner and traveller for
   thee, in true sense of heart, and with true
   breathings to the Lord.
   I.P.

To the Peningtons' distress, their Reading friends, Ann and Thomas Curtis took the dissident side. The trouble came to a head late in 1677, when Reading Friends split into two groups, so that for some years there were two monthly meetings in Reading.[6] Isaac

---

6. Some of the minutes of both Reading meetings have survived, held at Berkshire Records Office, and transcriptions are in Friends House Library.

wrote four times to the Curtises within two months, begging them not to follow the way of John Story and to respect George Fox, and Mary also wrote to them (JP IV.142–44, IV.158). This is the second letter from Isaac. Note the strong language that Isaac uses regarding the need to obey George Fox, and compare with his earlier views of diversity of practice.[7]

To Thomas Curtis, 13 December 1677 (JP IV.143.2)

Dear T[homas] C[urtis]
Since the meeting yesterday a great weight hath lain upon me, and under it a tender love to thee, and at length a request to thee rose in me, in the springings wherof the weight went off me. The request was thus in me, O my dear friend T[homas] C[urtis],

I beseech thee, in the bowels of the tender mercies which visited and relieved us in the day of our very sore and long distress, that thou take heed of letting in any thing against dear George Fox or oppose any thing that the Lord employs him in: for if thou do so indeed thou opposest not him, but the Lord, and must needs make an inward rent in thy heart from the life wherein he comes forth and wherein he is felt and owned. And so far thou knowst not nor canst keep to the anointing [right spirit], but another wisdom, sense and judgment gets up in thee which is not of the anointing. O that none may set up man instead of the Lord. That which sees not but opposeth the outgoings of the Lord that is man (man's eye, man's wisdom); from this arise the divisions and separations among us at this day which cannot but still rise higher and higher, as that eye sees and as that wisdom takes place in the heart. This is most manifest, there is a wrong eye, there is a wrong wisdom, there is an inward mistake about the anointing. The Lord make manifest where it is, that there may be a true gathering again to the anointing, to the pure life, wherein the true and pure unity hath been and still is. The Lord grant we may never be so unthankful to him as to find fault with or turn against any of his instruments, in anything

---
7. See Part II, pp. 158–165.

they bring unto us from him, and which his life in us would own them in, were there not somewhat got in to hinder.

I am not at unity with the anointing in my self, if it be not at unity with the same anointing in another.

13th of 10th Mon 1677

The lengthy fourth letter deals with Penington's relations with Story, harks back to his engagement with Perrot, and describes his subsequent troubles. Again, he emphasises the authority of Fox.

To Thomas Curtis, 25 February 1678 (JP IV.144)

If George Fox hath received from the Lord power and authority in his name to establish men's and women's meetings, among his gathered people, in such a way as the Lord hath shown him, and to which his witness in our heart answers: then that spirit and wisdom which opposes it, or sets up any thing else in the stead of it, is not of God.

Now I have been present when I have heard the voice of pure life springing in the hearts of many, sweetly owning it and testifying to it, and this more than once or twice in solemn meetings. Indeed I was, in my heart and judgment, somewhat against women's meetings when I was with you: yet I durst not conclude against them, but was still in my spirit before the Lord and waited. And I was never gained to the sense or owning of them from any reasoning or converse with any friends. But at a meeting, a glorious meeting indeed, when the power did mightily shine throughout the meeting, and I was filled and my heart opened exceedingly, the thing brightly opened in me, and I saw the Lord's hand, wisdom and will in it, and had the seal of life and of God's power upon my heart concerning it. And indeed, dear T.C., bear with me, for it just springs into my heart to say unto thee, the meeting of men and women together (set up since this to interrupt and break the force of this) is but an invention, and O that thou hast a sense of the wisdom and spirit from whence it came, I really believe such to be the honesty of thy heart towards the Lord, that thou wouldst fly from it as from a serpent. I was very unwilling to write thus much to thee (though I had much more on my heart this morning) but indeed I am constrained. I do not question thy coming to rights, but I am sensible it will be through sufferings: and therefore I would fain have thee feel a stop from God, that thy sufferings might be less. O my dear friend, I know this snare, yea my feet were once taken and held in it: and what the restoring and experience of deliverance cost me, none knows but the Lord. ...

(at this point Penington describes his experiences regarding Perrot)[8]

... O my friend, feel my tender love, feel the truth of my heart to thee, feel my single desires for thee. O the Lord make thee exceeding honourable and glorious in his truth, life and power. Anything that stops, the Lord discover to thee and remove from thee. I do not look upon myself as any way able to inform or help thee. Indeed, I have been often and much bowed down and filled with shame and confusion before the Lord, for my former being overtaken and erring: and if the Lord now preserve me, and let me see others taken in the same snare (as to the nature and substance of it) it doth not become me to fall foul upon them for it. To be made use of to help them, I look upon myself altogether unworthy and unfit: or to bear a broken, tender-hearted testimony for the Lord in the case. I must end.

    25th of 12th mon: 1677
In the close I have not freedom to say what I am unto thee, but O feel what I am towards thee in the sight of the Lord.
    I.P.

The dispute rumbled on for some years, but Isaac managed to find time for other concerns, including his sister Judith, probably a former friend of Samuel Pepys.[9] Isaac remembers her early sensitivity to faith, and hopes that it may return.

---

8. See p. 40.
9. See p. 5.

To his sister Judith, 26 March 1678 (JP III.544)
>
> Dear Sister,
> My heart is exceedingly at this time melted and broken before the Lord in consideration of his dealings with me: and I am filled with reverence and bowings of spirit to him, and breathings of his pure life are upon my heart, not only for my own soul, but for others also. And indeed thou wast particularly before my view, I remembering what a tender sense the Lord had begotten in thee, and how near thou wast then to the birth of life which the Lord had begotten in me, and which in some measure he kept alive, in the midst of the great darkness and captivity my soul met with in my desiring and seeking after the Lord.
>
> Now, O my dear Sister, there then lies the stress of the salvation, or of the utter undoing of thy soul. Without a new birth, without a new creation inwardly felt and abode in, thou canst not possibly be saved: and he that is not saved from sin, cannot but corrupt and perish inwardly, and be exposed in the dreadful wrath of the great God. O how many walls doth the enemy build in the mind, and how many taking notions and apprehensions doth he fill the mind with, that he might lull it asleep in the undone state, and fill it with a vain hope and belief until its condition be past remedy! O my dear Sister, it was not an imaginary thing, but a real misery I was in; and nothing could have helped me, but a real healing and salvation; but a real entering in at the strait gate into the narrow way [Mt 7:13–14] where no flesh or nature alienated from the life of God can walk. O my dwelling place is not now in darkness, nor my walking, blessed be the name of the Lord.
>
> Ah, that thou wert with me, even there where the Lord hath led me, and is with me! where the things of his spirit and kingdom are as manifest to the inward man, to the eye of the new birth, as the things of the outward creation are to the outward eye: O my dear Sister, I am sure God hath visited thee: O that thou didst remember and improve the laws of thy visitation, and wert inwardly separated in thy heart from all that is contrary to God there. O how terrible is destruction and separation from God inwardly:

(the Lord grant it may never be thy portion!) O how sweet
is salvation, union and communion with the Lord of life
and glory inwardly! O that thou mayest experience what
it is, while thou art here in this vale of tears, and it may
also be thy portion for ever! I have sent thee here enclosed
a little token of my love, and how glad would my heart
be, if it might be conducive and helpful in the Lord's hand
thereunto!

>   So with etc. I take my leave of thee, remaining
>   Thy affectionate brother with true and sincere love
>   I.P.

During July and August 1678, presumably because of Isaac's poor health, the Peningtons spent some time at a popular spa called Astrop Wells, near Kings Sutton in Northamptonshire. According to the traveller Celia Fiennes it was "much frequented by the gentry", and had "a fine Gravell Walke that is between 2 high Cutt hedges where is a Roome for the Musick and a Roome for ye Company besides ye Private walkes" (Fiennes, 23–4). Spas in the seventeenth century were places for an active social life and often debauchery, and Isaac attempted, in a series of letters and theological papers, to show his companions a better way (JP III.379.2–III.382, *Works* III.531–534).

While in that part of the country, he and Mary visited Armscote, then a strong Quaker centre, just over the border in a detached part of Worcestershire (later absorbed into Warwickshire). They both wrote letters to the newly appointed women's meeting. Note their contrasted styles and content.

Isaac's letter to Women Friends at Armscote, 7 September 1678 (JP IV.155, *Works* III.535)

Dear Friends,
In your meetings together to do service for the Lord, be
every one of you very careful and diligent in watching to his
power, that ye may have the sensible living feeling of it, each
of you in your own hearts, and in the hearts one of another;
and may keep within the limits of it, and not think, or speak,
or act beyond it. And know, O wait more and more to know
and keep the power's silence, that that in every one of you
may be kept silent, which the power would have silent.

O take heed of the forwardness of the flesh, the wisdom of the flesh, the will of the flesh, the talkativeness of the flesh; keep them back, O let them for ever be kept back in every one of you, by the presence and virtue of the power. The power is the authority and blessing of your meetings, and therein lies your ability to perform what God requires: be sure ye have it with you. Keep back to the life, keep low in the holy fear, and ye shall not miss of it.

You will find it easy to transgress, easy to set up self, easy to run into sudden apprehensions about things, and one to be of this mind and another of that: but feel the power to keep down all this, and to keep you out of all this, and every one watching to the life, when and where it will arise to help you, and that ye may be sensible of it when it doth arise, and not in a wrong wisdom oppose it, but be one with it, and if any thing should arise from the wrong wisdom in any, ye may be sensible of it, not defiled or entangled with it, but may abide in that which sees through it and judge it: that so life may reign in your hearts and in your meetings, over that which will be forward and perking over the life, if ye be not very watchful.

So, the Lord God of my life be with you, and season your hearts with his grace and truth, and daily keep you in the savour thereof, that ye may be blessed by him and a blessing in his hands, all that is evil and contrary to truth being kept down in your own hearts, and so ye will be fit to keep down evil in the minds and hearts of others, and so if any thing be unsavoury any where, it will be searched into, judged, cast out, and the recovery of the soul which hath let it in sought, that if possible it may be restored; and then ye will know the joy of seeking out and bringing back the lost sheep. And be tender to others in true bowels, as ye would be tendered by others, if ye were in their conditions.

There is that near you which will guide you, O wait for it, and be sure ye keep to it; that ye being innocent and faithful in following the Lord in the leadings of his power, his power may plead your cause in the hearts of all his tender people hereabouts, and they may see and acknowledge that your meetings are of God, and that ye are guided by him into that way of service, in his holy fear, which he himself by the movings of his holy spirit in your hearts, hath engaged you to and is with you in. So be not hasty either in conceiving any thing in your minds, or in speaking it forth, or in anything ye are to act; but feel him by his Spirit and life going along with you, and leading you into what he would have any of you or every one of you do. If ye be in the true feeling sense of what the Lord your God would have done, and join with what is of God as it riseth in any, or against any thing that is not of God, as it is made manifest among you, ye are all in your places and proper services, obeying the blessed will and doing the blessed work of the Lord your God.

I had somewhat upon me yesterday to you, but my weakness was great. This morning this lay as a weight upon my spirit to lay upon yours, that the weight may come upon you to weigh down anything that is light or chaffy in any of you, that the seed of Life may come up over it, and ye may be weighty before the Lord in the weighty seed of Life. The Lord make you rightly serviceable to him, and truly glorious in your Meetings and in your several places. Ye will find a great work to keep one part down, that that which is pure and living of God may come up in you, and ye act only in it and not exceeding the limits of it.

I.P.

Written at John Hawford's, 7th of 7th Month, 1678.

Mary's letter to Women Friends at Armscote, 7 September 1678 (JP IV.159.2)[10]

For those women friends that are dissatisfied at present with the women meeting distinct from the men, and having collections and several businesses apart.

Friends,

These following particulars I find freedom to lay before you, wherein women's meetings have been serviceable, where they have been gathered and established, and may be serviceable where they are now settling.

---

10. Previously published by H. Larry Ingle, ed., "A Quaker Woman on Women's Roles: Mary Penington to Friends, 1678", *Signs*, XVI (Spring 1991), 587–96.

First, to remove prejudice against them out of the way, I thus say, Our meeting apart from the men in point of business is both comely and advantageous, and that which we have found virtue in, and is honest, and of good report among those that have proved it, as to do those services that are more proper for us than for the men, and to do some other services that are mean, and of less concern than is convenient to engage the men in. Those more proper to the women are:

The having the marriages brought before them in the first place, it being more modest and comely, and more suitable to the bashfulness of a woman, to lay her intention before those of her own sex: for the laying it in the first place before the men puts a force on their bashfulness more then is right. Now to lay it before the women, and some grave woman or women to accompany the couple to the men, and recommend them to them, with some testimonies for them by such as know them, makes it more easy and soft to the woman, and sometimes to the man.

Then as to their entanglements [existing connections], women can better look in to those things, and it is more seemly for them to take notice of inconvenient familiarities, through the letting up the affectionate part. And women having thus brought it to the men, it is left to them to determine of, to set by or reject, or to give certificate or permit, as they feel, when the women have presented before them their right information, according to their diligent enquiry.

Now there are some services more mean, as above expressed, which are these:

The visiting the sick, ordering nurses and helpful necessaries for them, and looking into poor families to provide food and helpful necessaries, when poor children are without a mother, or have a weak mother, either in respect of understanding or weakness of body, and to put out girls either to trade or service, that these things to be discharged by collections among ourselves.

As for our disposing of money to several uses without the men, it is just: we have a right to a share of our husband's substance, and may dispose of it to lawful

5. Domesticity and Controversy: The Last Years, 1672–1679

and serviceable uses as well as they. But where any are contentious we have no such custom, that is, if the husband be not given up to serve the Lord with his substance, then we take none of his for such uses; but what such husbands give to us to lay out in superfluous things, either in the house or upon our bodies, we being moderate in all such things, give that money to the Lord's service. And we judge it not right to put such among us, upon contribution to those services, who are strait [miserly] in their minds, but leave them with the Lord to judge them for their straitness.

Our place in the creation is to bring forth and nurse up, to keep things orderly, sweet and clean in a family, to preserve from waste and putrefaction, and to provide things necessary for food and raiment; to whichever employment in the Church of God answers to bring forth and nurture, to cleanse out what is unsavoury and unclean, and to cast out evildoers out of the house of God to preserve and keep wholesome and orderly things in this house. The men need not grudge us this place in the body, wherein we are meet helps, and usurp not authority over them, and act as the inferior parts of the body, being members, though but a finger or a toe.

Now friends, I am willing to commend to you the manner of things, in the gathering whereunto I belong, and the Lord's owning of us. We meet in a holy, reverent manner; we come together and sit down solemnly to wait on the Lord to feel his savoury life to savour us and fit us for his service: and in this weighty frame, if prayer or praises arise in our hearts, we give up unto it, and if any words of exhortation or quickening, and to stir up the pure mind, or to encourage one another in the work we come about, be given to us, we in an humble manner give it forth in the quick and sensible life: but we do not find that it is our work and service there to spend our time in declaration one to another in an instructive way, as to make known truth, but only what is suitable to our present service. And in a weighty orderly manner one of us proposes a business, and the rest judge of the matter, speaking but one at a time; and then as we reject or approve, so we orderly manifest it in as few words as may be.

We apply ourselves between the meetings to enquire into several things, as the ground of affection, where we hear of any that have let it in [i.e., Friends showing signs of beginning a relationship], that they may not proceed so far as to bring it before the meeting, if they begin not orderly. We also enquire of disorderly walking in any kind, which some of us are ordered to reprove and to bring them to a sight of their evil, and take it in writing in such a manner as those that are without may see their repentance, if they have seen their transgression, and so not charge truth with it; but if reproof and tender admonition will not do, to lay it before the meeting, and so draw up a paper of denying them, that their going to our public meetings may not make their evils charged on Friends. These enquiries and reproofs and admonitions are only to those of our own sex.

And further this is the course of preventing backbiting and tale-bearing. If a report be made to the disadvantage of anyone, to put the reporter upon proof, by bringing forth the accuser; if they cannot or will not, then to let shame light on the reporter, and so judge them. By this they are discouraged, and whisperings and envyings shut out.

Thus in these our actions we have found acceptance with the Lord, and have been preserved in unity and a living sense, and many of those that simply stood off, and had not a root of bitterness in them (we keeping in the power and not judging them, but patiently waiting the Lord's season) were brought in, and our number is increased double, if not treble. And since their coming in they have given testimonies that they were kept back by having a slight sense [poor understanding] of the thing (which testimonies I may send hereafter) but when they come to prove these meetings, they never went away again, but confessed of a truth the Lord was with us, and that his mercy was great that he preserved some of us faithful, not withstanding our great discouragements.

Friends, seeing your discouragements hereaway, and having hope it is not in opposition, but in a fear of that ye know not, that makes you so shy of this kind of assembling yourselves together, do give you this account of my sense

of women's meetings, and also an account of the manner
of our gathering, who have found the Lord's presence with
us, by which we are so girded together, that we can bear
our testimony by suffering for the manner of assembling
ourselves, as in other things that we have been led to by the
Lord.
Armscote 7th of 7th month 1678

The Peningtons took the opportunity to visit several meetings in this area. During the next two days Isaac was at Radway near Edgehill, writing to Evesham Friends (JP 1.156, 1.157), and after that nearby at Brailes, where he again addressed Friends on the subject of women's meetings (JP IV.157.2), and wrote to one Thomas Bray, presumably the local Church of England minister:

To Thomas Bray 10 September 1678 (JP III.391)

Friend,
I remember the Apostle Paul wrote after this manner to
one of the Churches, "Say to Archippus take heed to thy
ministry which thou hast received of the Lord" [Col 4:17].
But this is on my heart to say to thee, Hast thou indeed
received the true ministry from the Lord? or dost thou
minister from that part that doth not receive the true
ministry, but ministers in a wisdom and from motions above
the true power of motions of life. This is of great concern
to thy own soul, and those thou ministrest to. I beseech thee
wait, that thou may'st have true and certain understanding
from the Lord in this matter, that thou may'st only do his
work and fulfill his will, in what thou undertakest to do in
this kind. I am
Thy Friend in this, perhaps beyond what thou canst
easily apprehend. I.P.
Brailes, 10 7 Month 1678

During these last years Isaac wrote several papers reflecting on his life and faith, and some were published after his death.[11] He continued to write letters throughout 1679, including one to Elizabeth Walmsley (now Widow Walmsley) and her meeting:

---
11. See General Introduction, p. x, and Appendix A.

To Widow Walmsley etc., 24 July 1679 (JP II.185)

'Etc.' is part of the heading, and indicates an address to a number of people.

This morning when I awaked, after some exercises of spirit upon me, ye were before me and I felt somewhat spring up in my heart towards you, which I was moved to write to you. And indeed it was with me (in a deep sense concerning you, and the many temptations and difficulties ye were like to meet with: for through much tribulation is the entrance into the kingdom) to beseech you, by the tender mercies of my heavenly Father to you, that ye prize the love and goodwill wherewith he hath visited you, and that ye express it in an upright and faithful minding of that precious principle of his life, to which he hath directed your minds. For, of a truth, the living testimony hath reached unto you, and there hath been an answer in your hearts thereto, from a living feeling of God's truth there, which hath opened and tendered you, before the Lord, in a true and precious measure.

Now watch and pray, that ye enter not into temptation [Mk 14:38]. Temptation ye will meet with: but take heed of entering into it. There's the danger. If ye watch with the Lord against the enemy and pray to him, who is able to preserve and deliver you from him; though he may and will tempt; yet ye shall not enter thereinto, but fly away as a bird from the snare of the fowler [Ps 91:3].

And O, know that your strength lies not in yourselves, nor in any thing ye can do of yourselves: but in God's living principle of truth, wherein he appears and whereby he works in your hearts. Therefore wait for the Lord's visiting and appearing to you there, and making your souls acquainted with him therein. The outward Jew was to know God by outward descriptions of him: but the inward Jew is to know him by the inward manifestations of his life in the heart [Rom 2:28].

[…]

The God of my life, my tender Father (who hath at length shown me mercy and comforted me with the living springs of the holy Comforter, after my many deep

distresses, sore travels and trials) give you to feel more and
more of his precious truth (teaching you how to wait and
to know the issuings of it) draw you more and more to his
Son (and from everything which hinders your union and
fellowship with him in his Son) engraft you more and more
into him the holy branch or tree of life, build you more and
more upon him the precious living foundation, and keep
your minds to his grace and spirit of truth; that ye may abide
in him, grow up in him, and bring forth fruit in him: till at
last ye arrive at the full stature in him, and the complete
experience and enjoyment of these things, and a firm and
unmoveable establishment therein, to the praise of the
riches of his grace, and the exalting of the name of our Lord
Jesus Christ in your hearts, Amen. I am most dearly

   Your Friend in the truth weightily therein concerned for
the everlasting welfare of your souls. I.P.

   From Amersham Woodside, 24 of 5 Month 1679

Later that summer the Peningtons visited Mary's estates near Canterbury in Kent, and there Isaac wrote his last few letters and papers. One, dated 25 August, was a meditation on the sweep of human history, "Concerning the Times and Seasons, both which have been and which are yet to be", ending with an assertion of a fundamental Quaker belief: "The gospel religion is very precious, being inwardly felt and experienced in the life and power of it; but a bare profession of it, out of the life and power of godliness, is of no value in the sight of God, nor is it of any profit or advantage to the soul" (*Works* IV.431). His last dated personal letter, which follows, was probably written about the same time. Compare this letter with that on the same subject to Katharine Skippon.[12] Perhaps the loss of his own son had led Isaac to think again about the meaning of the death of children.

To Sarah Elgar, August 1679 (JP III.391.3, *Works* IV [supp]. 8)

Nothing is known about the recipient

S[arah] E[lgar], The child which the Lord hath taken from
thee was his own. He hath done thee no wrong in calling
it from thee. Take heed of murmuring, take heed of

---

12. See p. 85.

> discontent, take heed of any grief, but what truth allows thee. Thou hast yet one child left. The Lord may call for that too, if he pleases; or he may continue and bless it to thee. O, mind a right frame of spirit towards the Lord in this thy great affliction. If thou mind God's truth in thy heart, and wait to feel the seasoning thereof, that will bring thee into and preserve thee in a right frame of spirit. The Lord will not condemn thy love and tenderness to thy child, or thy tender remembrance of him: but still in it be subject to the Lord, and let his will and disposal be bowed to by thee, and not the will of thy nature set above it. Retire out of the natural into the spiritual, where thou mayst feel the Lord, thy portion; and that now, in the needful time, thou mayst day by day receive and enjoy satisfaction therein. O wait to feel the Lord making thy heart what he would have it to be, in this thy deep and sore affliction.
>
>   I. P.
> Nonington, 6th Month, 1679.
>
> Now let the world see how thou prizest truth, and what truth can do for thee. Feed on it; do not feed on thy affliction; and the life of truth will arise in thee, and raise thee up over it, to the honour of the name of the Lord, and to the comfort of thy own soul.

The story of Isaac's last days come from the "Testimony" written by his son John (*Works* I [App. A]. 448). The Peningtons were staying on Mary's farm at Goodnestone when, the day before they intended to return home, Isaac was taken ill. He continued to write to the very end, and a set of Queries on the salvation of mankind is dated the day before his death (JP III.394) in the early morning of 8 October.

Mary survived her husband by less than three years, living long enough to put her affairs in order and make her will. Her youngest sons, William and Edward, were sent to school, and she completed the manuscripts known as her "Experiences". Elizabeth Walmsley wrote to her, referring to Mary's "great exercises and trials" and the illness that prevented her from attending meetings. It was the Lord's will, but the Lord would "bring thee forth yet as a mother in Israel" (JP IV.180.3). But it was not to be, and Mary died in 1682 at Warminghurst in Sussex, the house of William and Guli Penn. Isaac and Mary are buried in the Quaker cemetery at Jordans.

John inherited the bulk of Mary's estate, his mother requesting him to "entertain friends at this my house at Woodside and be helpful to Chalfont meeting and the meetings there away as his dear father used to do"(*Experiences* 111). He never married and remained a devoted and active Friend till his death in 1710. Mary junior married Daniel Warley, a Quaker, and they settled at The Grove, a property in Chalfont St. Peter which had long been a Quaker centre and which is now headquarters of a telecommunications company. She died in 1726. Young William became a druggist in London, dying in 1703. Edward emigrated to Pennsylvania where he became Surveyor-General. He died in 1701, relatively young, but he was the only son of Isaac and Mary to have male heirs, and he founded a family of American Peningtons whose descendants are still living.

It is probable that much of the preparation of the collected edition of Isaac's works, published in 1681, was undertaken by Thomas Ellwood with the help of John Penington. Many Friends, including national figures, family and friends, wrote testimonies in Isaac's memory. John then copied his father's personal letters and those papers which were not to be printed into four large manuscript books. They include an unpublished testimony by Elizabeth Walmsley, and an extract from it makes a fitting conclusion to the first part of this volume:

From the Testimony of Elizabeth Walmsley [1680]
(JP IV.112)[13]

> In this weighty work and service of the Lord's truth and people, dear Isaac Penington was called forth by the Lord, who gave him a double portion of his spirit [II Kings 2:9], the Light of God shined through his earthen vessel and reached the seed of life, which lay deep in many. ... He faithfully declared the everlasting gospel, and what he had testified, felt and handled of the eternal word of life he freely communicated to others [1 Jn 1:1]. ... Glory to the Lord,

---

13. The complete "Testimony of Elizabeth Walmsley", edited and introduced by Diana Morrison-Smith, is published in the *Journal of the Friends Historical Society*, vol. 60 no.2, 2004.

who gave him a deep sight of the way and work of the Lord in the hearts of the children of men, and also of the secret and subtle working of the enemy; for he having travelled through the great deeps and close exercises, the power of the Lord upholding him, he was enabled to speak a word in season to the weary traveller, that hungered and thirsted after the living God, and a secret hope hath been raised he that hath delivered can yet deliver; so that deep answered deep, the depth of mercy reached the depth of misery, glory to the Lord. He was tender in spirit to all, not willing to hurt any tender spirit yet could not daub with untempered mortar; for a close heart-searching ministry he had, and the prosperity of life of truth was greatly his concern, and his exhortations were to keep close to the Light, that life might have scope and all keep within the limits of life; for in this the work of the Lord would prosper, and the subtle enemy be made manifest, and that birth born which alone can serve the Lord, but cannot serve another. True and right judgment was near his habitation in the light, he was a diligent traveller in his day and time, in the work and service of the Lord that the stones might be squared and fitted for the spiritual building, and the top-stone raised, and Alleluyahs, living praises, glory and honour be given to the Lord, who is worthy, worthy of all for ever and for evermore [Rev 4:11].

And now dear Isaac Penington hath finished his travel, the work and service of his day, and having kept the faith, he is gone to rest in everlasting peace with the Lord, and a crown of glory rests on him. The memorial of the just shall be had in everlasting remembrance. Though he is taken hence, his life yet speaks, yea the life of truth speaks through many, glory to the Lord. The truth of our God abides for ever.

Part II

*The Spirituality and Thought
  of Isaac Penington*

R. Melvin Keiser

The way of Life and Death

Made manifest and set before men.

Whereby the many paths of Death are impleaded, and the one path of life propounded and pleaded for.

In some POSITIONS concerning the Apostacy from the Christian Spirit and Life.

With some PRINCIPLES guiding out of it.

As also in Answers to some Objections whereby the Simplicity in some may be entangled.

Held forth in tender good will both to *Papists* and *Protestants*, who have generally erred from the Faith for these many Generations, since the dayes of the Apostles; and with that which they have erred from are they comprehended.

By *Isaac Pennington* the younger.

LONDON,
Printed by *J. M.* for *Lodowick Lloyd* at the Castle in *Cornhil*, 1658.

INTRODUCTION
Reading Penington Today

Isaac Penington uses a multiplicity of metaphors for God and the spiritual life in diverse areas of our existence – religious, theological, historical, political, social, economic, ecclesiastical, philosophical, and moral. Throughout his Quaker writings the central theme is life: the life of the Spirit, the life of selves in the world, and the full presence or obstruction of that divine life in our life on earth. In this Introduction to Part II, I offer assistance in understanding why and how he uses metaphors, how his thought is theological and why it spreads into so many areas of existence, and what the theme of life means to him – and make a beginning in suggesting what such metaphors, complexity, and theme of life could mean for us today.

The problem for many of us in reading Penington is that his writings are metaphorical, biblical, theological, stylistically difficult, combative, and Christian.

Many metaphors pervade his writing – *life, light, seed, truth, presence, spring, fountain, breath, spirit*. The use of metaphors can be unsettling since their meaning radiates out in so many directions that we cannot arrive at one meaning that will stay fixed. They elicit one's own individual experience and thus hook people in different ways bestirring different and very personal meanings. They say what something is "like" rather than what it "is" so the desire to catch something in its complete meaning is left unsatisfied. When several are used, they interact with one another. Each provides a perspective on reality. For example, when "light" is used for God, it emphasises the luminosity and clarifying character of the divine; when "seed", the engendering character; when "spirit", the animating energy of divinity. When these are used together, we may find ourselves experiencing God through these perspectives. This can be disconcerting if we expect "God" to have a fixed meaning that we can embrace – or attack.

Moreover, metaphors are evocative. They not only stir things in our memories but open in us a deeper sense of reality underlying our everyday existence. To be opened to such depths can be scary because we are changed, if only because we glimpse places in ourselves of which we have been unaware. More profoundly, what we discover may begin to pervade our consciousness. Then it begins to connect with other parts of ourselves, working unanticipated integrations. For example, Jesus' story of the woman taken in adultery may function as a metaphor through which we may glimpse our own judgmental attitude and the harm it has done and find our whole approach to others challenged and reshaped. Or the metaphor of light in John's Gospel may cleave us open to an uncontrollable energy and creativity within us, whether we call it "God" or not, that we yearn towards, desiring this creative intensity in all our encounters with reality.

Quakerism from its inception has depended upon such powerful metaphors to bring people into and sustain them within the Quaker movement, to transform them from self-directed to Spirit-led individuals, to connect them with each other and the larger world, to elicit social action, making them members of the world, and to fill them with abundant life and power. If we will open ourselves to Penington's metaphors, however strange or shocking, they can work upon us today in these same ways.

Penington is supported in his extensive use of metaphors by the Bible's irrepressible use of them. A second problem for many today is that Penington's writings are laced with biblical quotations and allusions. Quakers and others have recognised oppressive elements in the Bible, and how it has been used for the purposes of dominating others. Patriarchal subordination of women, acceptance of slavery, the Christian anti-Judaism which lent support to the holocaust, confront the ethically concerned modern reader. Some come to reject the Bible. Yet most of us find value in our culture even though it has the same oppressive elements embedded in it. Can we not approach the Bible and find worth in it? From where else historically in the west has come the insistence on establishing peace and justice, overcoming "the system of domination" (Walter Wink), but from the Bible? Since the Bible has shaped irrevocably the nature of Quakerism, it is better to be aware of and own this positive shaping, even while maintaining a critical perspective.

Many voices, many spirits speak in the Bible. If we attempt to discern the Spirit in our world and everyday lives to discover what we ought to do and how to be, we can also seek among the spirits, including the oppressive ones, in the Bible for a holy spirit that can touch us, change us, and guide us. The Bible is many things – stories, poems, laws, gospels, letters, parables, apocalypses, history, myth. Among these it has been for Quakers, Christians, and Jews throughout the centuries a deep well of metaphor and wisdom that has sustained, enriched, and transformed their lives.

A third problem is the complexity of Penington's thought. His spiritual wisdom is expressed in a conceptually intricate and archaic seventeenth-century idiom. But most especially it is irrepressibly theological. His theological rendering is difficult since he uses ideas and doctrines foreign to us. We find alien, if not seditious, terms familiar to the tradition of Christian theology such as apostasy, sin, justification, regeneration. He is unequivocally committed to the Protestant language of mid-seventeenth century England. This is the very language that many have fled today, feeling its oppressiveness as forms of belief and practice that require conformity rather than creativity, exclusiveness rather than openness, abstract thought rather than immediate experience, social irrelevance rather than the transformation of society, and distance rather than intimacy.

Many of us now avoid theological language to express what is important and turn rather to languages of psychology, politics, history, economics. This is in part because we feel that theological words are abstract dead forms. So does Penington. While Penington does use traditional ideas, he handles them differently. He acutely criticises his fellow Christians – Puritans and Anglicans – because he sees them mistakenly using theological language as objects in themselves which are true and in need of defence against attack. Yet he does not discard that language but seeks to use it differently: to express experience – to evoke a sense of the divine in our lives, to discern the stirrings of the Spirit and our own obstructions to it within, and to impel social transformation. Ironically, it is this very difference which contributes now to Quakers insisting upon the primacy of the spiritual life over doctrinal belief, for he insists on the meaningfulness of theological words only if inward experience underlies and is expressed through them. His theological language does not seek to establish objective forms to which our thought and lives are to conform; rather he uses it to engender life – life in us that is in the Life, that is expressive of the Life, that contributes to life and Life in others.

If we who are Quakers believe that all theology obstructs authentic engagement with the life of the spirit, we would do well to wait – a Quaker virtue in all other areas – for meaning to emerge, for the Spirit to speak. As we wait in meeting for worship, in business meeting, and in our personal lives for the Spirit to lead us into understanding and new ways of seeing things, so in approaching Penington, we could wait in the Spirit with his ideas, metaphors, and biblical references long enough to receive their spiritual significance for us today. The advices and queries of Yearly Meetings, read from time to time in meetings to challenge and inspire, urge us to receptive listening, to hear meaning beneath words' outer shell (*Qfp* §1.02:12). We need to follow such advice in the reading of seventeenth-century Friends. The result can be that our familiar discourse becomes defamiliarised so as to open us to new insight. What after all do we mean by "Inner Light", which we use with all too much ease? Quakers may think it an impertinent question since it should be obvious by what our lives speak. To read Penington's different way of using our familiar terms, as well as ones strange or offensive to us, can carry us beneath our conventional talk to a deeper grasp of reinvigorated meaning.

Theological language was the coin of the realm in Penington's day in which issues personal and social, psychological and political, economic and communal were discussed. Today with the elaboration of each of these areas into distinct disciplines, as if to separate compartments, we have relegated religious thinking to personal spiritual development and we have lost the useful process of theological exploration for spiritual maturing. To read Penington's essays is, however, to encounter a person both alive to spiritual growth in response to the ongoing presence of the divine in his life and engaged in serious thought about the nature of self and God within the social and natural world. To read Penington is to be drawn into this wholemaking process. He is difficult, but anybody who is trying to live and articulate a spiritually awakened life in wholeness today knows similar difficulties. We may find in Penington a way to regain the lost inte-

Introduction: Reading Penington Today

grative activity of *religare* (Latin etymology of religion: to bind back) to re-bind the parts of our life together into a whole, and reflect on the underlying ligatures that connect the seemingly disparate areas of thought. Penington did not separate the life of the spirit from the life of the mind, but carried his spirituality into the intellectual, socio-economic, and political issues of the day.

Penington's writing has caught the interest and nurtured the spirit of Quakers from his time to ours, but if we draw from his entire work and make a more comprehensive selection than was made in the twentieth century, we come upon language that obstructs our grasp of his meaning and its intended transformative effect. While Penington urges a simplicity of thought, his sentences are long, his vocabulary archaic, and often his thinking seems to wander. His logic is associative: one thing inspires another – seemingly whatever comes into his head. His writing overall is like what he says of God: "there is no straitness in the Fountain. God is fullness" (*"To Fds of Both Chalfonts"*, II.495). Like a fountain, spraying off in many directions, amidst the streams there are crystalline drops of beautiful and profound insights, unsurpassed by his Quaker contemporaries.

Why does Penington write this way? He was university educated, like Barclay and Penn, and yet they both write in a much more structured and conceptually coherent manner. We do not know what he thought of Barclay's and Penn's more rational discourse, but they had not experienced reason as an obstruction to the life reaching to their hearts through Quakers' words or silence. I believe that Penington's stress on daily "getting low" to open to the presence leads to his style. Only inspiration of the moment should be written, and the Spirit inspires in this wandering way, as the scripture says, like the wind blowing where it will (Jn 3:8). Writing from what he feels of the Spirit in non-linear ways, he is reassured it is language of the Spirit rather than the logic of natural understanding's captivity.

While he is non-linear, he is not presenting a stream of consciousness. He is thinking with ideas as he seeks to grasp and convey his experience. He not only creates crystals of insight but also spends much time answering Protestant critics, writing with a theological acumen equal to Robert Barclay's, William Penn's, and Elizabeth Bathurst's. But he does not write like them in an essay form, with a beginning, middle, and end; nor does he write systematically moving through a progression of logically connected ideas. I would not recommend his prose style as a model for us today. But I do recommend his method of sinking into the depths. To allow our words to originate from the place where we are stirred by the life can give us, as it did him, the power of spiritual creativity – to respond to the Spirit and to speak to the S/spirit in others.

Penington's characteristically seventeenth-century manner of address is, however, confrontational. While he is admired as "the most mystical" of early Friends, while he articulates a wisdom and evokes deep feeling, he is, nevertheless, sometimes combative (like Fox), judgmental, preachy. Even present-day Quakers can be quite direct and critical both of each other and of the larger society – "speaking truth to power" – but typically our style is much more conciliatory. We recognise that verbal attack raises defensiveness, defeating effective communication, and we acknowledge truth in a diversity of viewpoints and practices. Regardless of whether we are exhibiting greater humility, or simply uncertainty, Penington's aggressiveness can grate on our sensibilities – even though he is one of the least combative of early Friends.

To be reached by his meaning, we have to tolerate his confrontational approach, recognising that verbal aggressiveness is characteristic of the period. He is dramatic, speaking of breakings and shakings in himself and in Britain. He is self-assured, having found what others are looking for and claim to have found, but about which he believed them in reality to be self-deceived. It is possible that we might learn something if we take his attacks to heart. Recognising self-deception in himself, he was constantly vigilant against his sharp intellect separating him from the feeling sense of spiritual presence. Are there any seeds of self-deception in us? Have we created dead forms in our individual and communal lives? Are silent Quaker meetings open to the creativity of the Spirit, or do we prohibit anything out of the ordinary? Do we use Quaker words so that their deeper meaning is not lived but obstructed? We may quote early Friends, such as Fox saying "be examples" (*Journal*, 263; *Qfp* §19.32) but do we live it? As we pride ourselves on our historic achievements for example of sexual and racial equality, are we aware of how we are currently implicated in sexism and racism?

Finally, Penington uses unequivocal Christian language. Many liberal Quakers may find the talk of Christ problematic. Others may find shocking what he actually says about Christ's relations to his followers. Christian language is rejected by many convinced Friends because they identify it with the dogmatic narrowness in other Christian denominations they have fled, and by many "birthright" Friends who believe it incompatible with their universalism. From the point of view of both these groups, Christian theology is anathema because it seems to necessitate belief rather than experience, right or wrong thinking rather than ambiguity or uncertainty, a dominating supreme entity rather than an intimate and engendering divine presence, and an ethical focus on individual salvation rather than on peace and justice.

While Penington is emphatically Christian in his writing, he uses Christian language in ways very different from these objections. Christian language is the form in which he speaks, but he makes it clear that it is the underlying Spirit that matters more. It is the function of Christian words to bring one to the end of words – to the indwelling reality of the Spirit. Words become, therefore, vehicles into experience of the ultimate mystery rather than standards for belief and judgment. Those alienated from Christian talk may discover through Penington that it can become the means of deeper religious experience. Those appreciative of Christian talk may find themselves being moved into a strange new territory of religious life as the words take them beyond conventional meanings to unimaginable, mystically sensed divine presence.

For Penington the Spirit is, no doubt, understood in Christian terms, but defining its ultimate reality as beyond words opens up the possibility, which some liberal Friends have taken, of seeking non-Christian words that more effectively, they believe, will bring them to the God beyond words – or to "the God beyond God" (Paul Tillich), to make us "honest to God" (Bishop J.A.T. Robinson).

Venturing forth with one of early Quakerism's great leaders into this archaic medium and style – metaphorical, biblical, theological, and Christian – we may open ourselves, not without difficulty, to vast resources for "knowing the mystery of life within" ("Reply [Concerning ... New Covenant]", IV.191).

The essays that follow are grouped under twelve concepts to show the range of Penington's Quaker thought. The chapters deal with his life-engendering spirituality; community and political life; philosophical insights into how we know; what freedom and virtue are; the nature of religion; experience of prayer; and theological orientation in doctrine and the nature of God. To provide easy reference to the *Works* each category has been organised chronologically as sequenced through the four volumes.

Penington's spiritual and intellectual perspective is the same as other early Quaker writers, with differences in style and emphasis. He shares with George Fox, Margaret Fell, Robert Barclay and Elizabeth Bathurst the spiritual vocabulary of *life, light, seed, power* and *truth*. His special contribution is his central development of this theme of *life*. It relates to so many current Quaker concerns about the oppression of life (racism, sexism, militarism, classism, homophobia) and degradation of our biological and inanimate environment. We care about the quality of our own spiritual lives. "God" is problematic conceived traditionally as a dominating supreme entity, but to image divinity as Life brings God into the centre of our life and hopes. "Life" then is a fruitful way to think about self, world, and God as an interrelated whole.

Because life is central to Penington and because it stands out among our needs, I have presented this focus here in Part II. Nevertheless, he can make other contributions to our day, all connected with the theme of life. He humanises our *knowing*, making it a personal achievement, rather than an objective mechanism, that draws on unconscious and pre-rational dimensions of self, as creative discovery. He deepens *spirituality* by presenting it as a daily return to these unconscious and pre-rational depths of silence, sensing, feeling in which we can learn to pray without ceasing. By seeking to discern Life in Bible and doctrine, his approach can open for us a treasury of resources for spiritual growth and community among Quakers, the Christian church, and beyond. Finally, our understanding of *religion* and *God* may benefit from locating religion in depths of feeling within conscience, and speaking of God as mystery present in these depths transforming self and world. Now if your interest is whetted and your courage strengthened let us enter upon this strange and complex world which is one locus of the spiritual origins from which Friends have come.

CHAPTER I

The Way of Life and Death (1658): Penington's First Quaker Writing

Isaac Penington begins his career as a Quaker writer with a 100 page essay on the life engendered in us by divine presence and the way of death that resists it. He moves back and forth between the political, prophetic, and autobiographical, speaking of the Civil War, its "turning the world upside-down" (1.80, alluding to Acts 17:6 RSV; cf. Christopher Hill's *The World Turned Upside Down*), and its inadequate results, and of his own failure to discern the Spirit at work in his life until his convincement. He then lays out themes that will be important throughout his Quaker writings: prayer, Christian life, and doctrines – all as expressions of inward religious experience.

The brief excerpts presented here are about the rule for a Christian – prayer pervading every moment of our lives, and God's battering grace transforming us to attain humble attentiveness. The rule is not belief in some image or doctrine of Christ nor performance of a certain practice, but the life that was in Jesus. His rule was the fullness of divine life within himself. Ours is some measure of that same life within ourselves, for we come out of the same spring of life as Jesus. The rule is thus the life of a transformed self, "the new creature".

Penington and early Friends experienced a dramatic change in their lives as they embraced this rule, this Life within. He expresses it in violent imagery of hammer, sword, and fire that break down our intellectual defences to open us to feeling that Life. In our modern religious lives we may not imagine such struggle. It is only in the therapist's office that we discover such knotted resistance in ourselves; yet

Part II The Spirituality and Thought of Isaac Penington

such an experience is spiritual as well as psychological. The result for Penington of letting go of our cramped grip on our defences is "to get low". This means letting go of our controlling ideas so as to sense and feel the presence and guidance of the divine; moreover, it breeds an attentiveness to "the day of small things" (1.89; from Zech 4:10; cf. pp. 52, 131, 152, 155, 229), to the small concrete matters in our lives "in its lowest knock" (1.89; cf. Rev 3:20) within which God whispers to us. God meets us, not in grand heroic events of spiritual triumph, but in the everydayness of our ordinary lives in the simple moments of breaking an egg, the foaming up of raspberries when making jam, touching deep places with friends or new acquaintances, or the sudden nearness of absent ones. Within this dailiness Penington urges us to pray continually within every act and word. Using metaphors of birth, growth, and artistry, he sees such prayer contributing to the formation of our spiritual life and to "finishing" God's creation. Since the creation is unfinished (a tradition in Christianity opposed to the mainstream view that God finished the creation in the beginning; see John Hick, *Evil and the God of Love*), we are drawn in to participate in God's ongoing creativity.

The Way of Life and Death (1658)

1.26–27   A Christian is to be a follower of Christ, and consequently must have the same rule to walk by as Christ had.
A Christian proceeds from Christ, hath the same life in him, and needs the same rule. Christ had the fullness of life, and of his fullness we all receive a measure of the same life. "We are members of his body, of his flesh, and of his bones". Ephes 5:30. Yea, we came out of the same spring of life from whence he came: "For both he that sanctifieth, and they who are sanctified, are all of one; for which cause he is not ashamed to call them brethren". Heb 2:11. Now what was his rule? Was it not the fullness of life which he received? And what is their rule? Is it not the measure of life which they receive?... This was Paul's rule, after which he walked, "The law of the spirit of life in Christ Jesus". Rom 8:1–2. This made him "free from the law of sin and death".... The spirit forms the heart anew, forms Christ in the heart, begets a new creature there, which cannot sin "(He that is born of God sins not)"

[1 Jn 3:9]. And this is the rule of righteousness, the new creature, or the spirit of life in the new creature. Gal. 6:15–16.

I.34–36   The true worship of God in the gospel is in the Spirit. ... There is a continual praying unto God ... in eating, or drinking, or whatever else is done, ... in every thought, in every word, in every action, though it be in worldly things and occasions; yet the Spirit of the Lord is seen there. ... When the creation of God is finished; when the child is formed in the light, and the life breathed into him; then God brings him forth into his holy land. ...

I.87–88   There was a spirit, soul, or image of God brought forth, and standing in his life, before the fall.
    This soul was brought into death, under the burthen and bondage of corruption, out of its proper centre and resting-place, by the fall.

I.89–90   ... Therefore, if you will live, come to that hammer, that sword, that fire which flesh dreads, and let the flesh be delivered up to it: and do not despise the day of small things [Zech 4:10], waiting for some great appearance; but know it in its lowest knock: for its power of redemption is as truly there, as in its greatest appearance. ...
    For though I had a true taste of life and power from God; yet not knowing the foundation, there could be no true building with it; and so the spirit was quenched. ... But at length it pleased life to move in a low way in the midst of the powers of darkness in my heart; and by sinking low out of the wisdom, out of the reason, out of all high imaginations, and trusting myself to it; though dreadful strokes and oppositions were felt from the powers of darkness; yet at length there was some appearance of the deliverer, in such a poor, low, weak, despicable way, as could never have been welcomed, had not the soul been first brought to distress, and the loftiness of the imaginary part [i.e. imagination] brought down. And then coming out of that into the feeling, in another

part, there was a seed sprung up into a child; and as the child grows, and feeds on the milk of the immortal Word, I live, and am strengthened in him, and daily weakened in that part which lived before.

1.93 Now our work in the world is to hold forth the virtues of him that hath called us; to live like God; ... all our words, all our conversation, yea, every thought in us, is to become new. Whatever comes from us, is to come from the new principle of life in us, and to answer that in others....

1.94 We are also to be witnesses for God, and to propagate his life in the world; to be instruments in his hand, to bring others out of death and captivity into true life and liberty. We are to fight against the powers of darkness everywhere, as the Lord calleth us forth. And this we are to do in his wisdom, according to his will, in his power, and in his love, sweetness, and meekness.

CHAPTER 2

The Life

The metaphor of life weaves together the multiple metaphors of Penington's thought. He takes it from the Gospel of John where it is presented as a divine characteristic. Jesus says: "I am the way; I am the truth and I am life" (⅛N 14:6; NEB). Yet "life" at the same time means being fully human, as when Jesus says: "I have come that men may have life, and may have it in all its fullness" (Jn 10:10). Likewise, Penington uses "life" in the same way as either divine or human, or as simultaneously both. Often it is confusing; you cannot tell which he means. This is intentional. It underscores a different view of God from the mainstream Protestant one. Divinity and humanity are not separate realities but are intimately involved with one another. God is not simply outside us but dwells deep in our self. At that depth we cannot distinguish the mystery that is God from the mystery that I am, that we are.

Life is both spiritual and earthly. That is what using it as a metaphor does: it is both literal vitality – biological and bodily – and "like" a living organism yet different, as the "vitality" of heart, mind, soul, and spirit in individual selves and community. Western culture, since Plato and Aristotle, separates and opposes body and spirit. Penington holds them together so that our spiritual existence is lived out in our bodies and our bodies are sacred space (temples of the living God; see 1 Cor 3:16–17, 2 Cor 6:16).

While the metaphor of life is taken from John's Gospel, Penington develops it through several pairs taken from Paul's letters: inward and outward (Rom 2:28–29), spirit and letter (2 Cor 3:6), power and form

Part II The Spirituality and Thought of Isaac Penington

(2 Tim 3:5). These terms are not central to modern Quaker thought, but they were central, not only to Penington, but to early Friends. Is there possibly wisdom embedded in them from which we can benefit? They are complex. Before following an Ariadnic thread through this labyrinth, consider what we know generally about early Friends. They followed the Spirit and they attacked the rituals and practices of their fellow Christians. Not only baptism, eucharist, prepared liturgies and sermons, but also clothes that flaunted one's class, speech that supported staying in one's niche in the social hierarchy, and tithes that undergirded the state church and kept people poor – all were rejected. They saw these as death-dealing rather than life-giving forms. Did this mean that all forms are dead? If not, what makes a form vital or deadening?

Forms in themselves, the forms of our bodily existence in the world – such as what we wear, our social roles, the jobs we do, the committees we have set up, the way we worship – are not dead. They are in fact life-giving if the Spirit's Life originates, energises, pervades, and guides them. But those are deadening which are not begun by the Spirit but by our own spirit or mind. Penington uses many words for the natural self which controls its life according to its untransformed self-centred values, closed off from rather than open to the Spirit's guidance: natural understanding, will, or wisdom, old nature, dead spirit, flesh, veiled heart, veiled seed. Forms begun by what I will call a "veiled self" do not have the Life in them because the self is closed off to this deeper reality. Or they become destructive if, once initiated in the Spirit, they are no longer sustained by and expressive of the Spirit's life. We set up a committee or take a job that will make life better for others and ourselves. But over time we come to work at the committee or job for its own sake. We have lost the Life/life that led us into these roles and are now captive to maintaining the form itself. In Penington's words the form – committee or job – is "out of the life," no longer "in the life". Penington experienced traditional worship as harmful because it obstructed experience of the Life as the church sought to perpetuate its forms for their own sake.

Any form can, therefore, become a vehicle for or an obstruction to the divine life. It is not just that the empty forms lack the Spirit. They become vehicles for other spirits or harmful energies: of domination, oppression, ego-gratification, and destruction of life. So for Penington it is less a question of what a form is than how it is used.

The "spirit" is how we are oriented when we use a form: whether we are open to the energy and creativity emerging from the divine depths within or get fixated on the form, defending it and using it to control others, and ourselves.

Now perhaps we can wend our way through the meaning of Penington's pairs taken from Paul. Throughout his Quaker writings Penington speaks of inward and outward. Inward means personal, experiential, existential; outward means structures that are political, social, economic, ecclesiastical. The structures of outwardness are always forms but inwardness too has its forms, such as ideas, decisions, beliefs. All forms, whether outward or inward, are expressions of some kind of spirit: the spirit of divine life or the spirit of domination of others and oneself by the veiled self. Outward is not, therefore, opposed to inward, but emerges from it. The crucial distinction which Penington construes from his experience is whether the outward or inward form has arisen from the "inward light" rather than from the veiled self: "The outward which is right in God's sight, must come from the inward, but not from the inward will or wisdom of the flesh, but from the inward light and Spirit of God; but it is a great matter to receive singly [Mt. 6:22] and go along with the inward light, and avoid the inward, deceitful appearance of things" (*To K[atharine] Pordage* [1671], III.484).

So also with scripture. It presents many forms, both outward and inward, of the ways Jews and Christians have lived their lives and worshipped God. Through these many forms various spirits speak. We hear voices of ego-gratification, domination, and oppression. On the other hand, becoming open to the light, we find throughout the Bible a holy spirit that speaks of inclusive non-judgmental love of neighbour, the goodness of creation, the divine presence in our lives, and opening to and following the Spirit through whatever transformations of self and society – to whatever end it will lead.

I will say more about Penington's understanding and use of scripture later in chapter 10, "Interpreting the Bible", but Paul's distinction between letter and spirit as Penington uses it calls our attention to discerning the Holy Spirit in the text, rather than fastening upon its apparent literal meaning. We must be filled by the Spirit as readers, open to this loving, creative, transformative presence, in order to understand the scriptural meaning aright. We can get captured by the biblical forms either of belief or practice and seek to perpetuate them for their own sake "out of the life". This is a misreading of the Bible even when quoting it extensively because we have missed the divine life in it and are caught up in the spirit of control and construction or destruction by the veiled self. We have engaged in the activity of conforming to a form rather than responding creatively, spontaneously to the divine life acting on and within us.

To observe this distinction between inward and outward, spirit and letter, is to affirm different levels of consciousness. The inward and spirit are beneath what appears on the surface. The structures of outward practice and behaviour are visible to anyone. The structures of inward thoughts and beliefs are visible as we express them, whether directly or indirectly. But beneath these there is a depth that shades into mystery at the roots of our being, which contains the greatest meaning in our lives but is least accessible to others and to ourselves. That is why Quakers worship in silence, to become open to such depths. "Inward" refers to such deep levels of existing where consciousness shades into the tacit or unconscious dimension of our lives.

To centre the spiritual life in these inward depths of life, distinguished from forms (both outward and inward), is to stress the immediacy of the present moment, the vitality of our way of being, and creativity. The reality of spirit and life is not one form among many other forms but is itself formless. It is energy that can issue in forms but is not itself a form. The way we are aware of it is not through ideas which are themselves inward forms that may or may not be filled with the life. We are aware of the life by sensing it, feeling it, abiding in it, being transformed by it. Such awareness is beneath conceiving, although it can be drawn into thought. But expressing such a thought gives no guarantee of life's continued presence in it.

Life acts on us immediately beneath the ideas we think. Vital in its formless fecundity and freshness, the life is creative, filling us with a sense of deep meaning, emerging into new forms of thought and action, and reinvigorating or reorienting old forms. God acts on us and leads us in creative, not routinised ways, and elicits creativity not conformity in response. That Friends do not live under conventional controls is one of the things that scared people about Quakers early on and that makes them suspicious of us today. We ourselves may want to slip away from the intensity of the immediate presence of the divine to the shelter of modern forms that keep our lives under objective control. The spiritual way of life for Penington is, therefore, focused on a dimension in our personal and social existence beneath the thoughts our minds construct; there we are touched by spiritual energies, drawn forth, challenged, transformed, and brought into the peace and fullness of being. It is this Life that we seek and that we know in the depths of silence and the words emerging from them.

To describe this whole spirituality "in the life", Penington uses many traditional images, but also untraditional ones. He uses metaphors of hammer and fire to insist on the self being shaken from its control in order to gain access to the divine life within. He speaks of us becoming nothing, of continually taking up our cross, of daily getting low (that is, becoming humbly attentive to divine leading). He says there is no "straitness" (narrowness, severity, stinginess) in the divine fountain. He speaks often negatively of the self as "natural", referring to the untransformed self closed off to the divine within and attached to forms of domination by the veiled self. But sometimes he speaks positively of the self as "natural" as it becomes natural to live in the Life and its virtue.

If such language is troublesome, realise that Penington experienced his veiled self-led life, dominated by his natural intelligence, will, and desire, as a great captivity from which he could not extricate himself. He realised that he was often too smart for his own good. Before he became a Friend his head ruled his life rather than his heart. Once convinced, he sought to live from the sense and feeling of his heart rather than controlling his life by thought. Every day he struggled to get low. This may resonate more with us than Fox's seeming certitude and perfected righteousness. We might learn something from Penington, moreover, since we too are capable of using our own critical thoughts about Christ and the Bible to protect us from immersing ourselves in the feeling and sense of the treasures of Christianity, however much hidden in earthen vessels (2 Cor 4:7).

Our spiritual task is to become open to the Life at work in the depths of our life. It draws us into expressiveness on all levels of our being so the forms we create emerge from the motions of Life and are maintained in the present filled with Life. Penington challenges us to be alert to our own self-deceptions, to wait through the nights of spiritual darkness for divine awakening, to create vital structures of existence, and to be open to joy, love, and glory of the fullness of being.

Part II The Spirituality and Thought of Isaac Penington

The Scattered Sheep Sought After (1659)

1.106 The deep sense of this hath afflicted my soul from my tender years; the eternal witness awakening in me, and the eternal light manifesting the darkness all along unto me; though I knew not that it was the light, but went about to measure its appearances in me by words which itself had formerly spoken to others, and so set up my own understanding and comprehension as the measure, although I did not then perceive or think that I did so. Thus continually, through ignorance, I slew the life, and sold myself for a thing of nothing, even for such an appearance of life as my understanding part could judge most agreeable to scriptures. This the Lord blew upon, though its comeliness was unutterable (the life still feeding my spirit underneath, from whence sprang an inward beauty and freshness). Then such a day, or rather night, of darkness and distress [Amos 5:8–9, 18] overtook me, as would make the hardest heart melt to hear the relation of; yet the Lord was in that darkness, and he preserved me, and was forming of me to himself; and the taste I had then of him was far beyond whatever I had known in the purest strain of my religion formerly.

1.107–08 But the tempter did also set himself on work again to entangle Israel. For this end he brings forth likenesses of that which Israel desired, and was seeking after. He brings forth several forms of worship, to allure some with; several sorts of notions, to allure others with; several fresh appearances of life, of love, of liberty, to tempt the people of God aside from following that spirit which rose up to deliver. Thus comes he forth and prevails; he divides in Jacob, and scatters in Israel [Gen 49:7]; drawing one part to this form; another part toward that form; one to this notion, and another to that notion; one to this inward image, another to that spiritual idol; and all from the life, all from the power, all from the Saviour, all from the deliverer, and so the work stops. It stops in the nation, and it stops in people's spirits; and men generally wheel about and enter again, and apply themselves to make images like the images they had destroyed: and so the captivity returns; Israel is turned back into his bonds, and the spirit which oppressed him before, crusheth him again, and rules over him.

I.111 ... wait to know the nature of things, that ye may not be deceived with the highest, choicest, and most powerful appearances of death in the exactest image of life, nor stumble at the true life in its lowest and weakest appearance. And this ye can only attain to by a birth of, and growth up in, the true wisdom, which slays that spirit which lives on the same things in the comprehension, and gathers a stock of knowledge and experiences in its own understanding part. These are words of tender love, and they will also be words of true life. ...

Babylon the Great Described (1659)

I.185–87 And having tasted, having seen, having felt, having handled [1 Jn 1:1], I cannot but commend the life; and dissuade all men from all knowledge, all worship, all religion, all ways, and practices (though ever so taking, pleasant, and promising), out of the life. And this is to know Christ; namely, to know the life: and this is to obey Christ, to obey the life: and this is the kingdom of Christ which is to come, to have the life reign in power and great glory. But the knowing or believing of a history concerning Christ, this is not the knowledge or the faith. ...

... When the life is at any time lost, the only way of recovery is by retiring to the invisible, and keeping there, and growing up there; and not coming forth in the visible further than the life leads, nor staying there any longer than the life stays.

Now this is the mistake of persons generally; they look for the finding the invisible life in visibles. They run to corrupted ordinances and ways of devotion, and think to find God there: but do not wait to feel him in their hearts, and to be led by him into what he pleaseth. ...

Part II The Spirituality and Thought of Isaac Penington

The Axe Laid to the Root of the Old Corrunpt Tree (1659)

1.256–57   . . . Therefore rest not in opening of prophecies, or true meanings of these things (though this kind of knowledge is very excellent, and hath been very rare), but wait to feel the thing itself which the words speak of, and to be united by the living Spirit to that, and then thou hast a knowledge from the nature of the thing itself; and this is more deep and inward than all the knowledge that can be had from words concerning the thing.

. . . When thou feelest things, then seek their preservation in the proper spring of their own life. Let the root bear thee, and all thy knowledge, with all that is freely given thee of God. When thou feelest thyself leavened [yeasted] with the life, and become a branch shot out of the life, then learn how to abide in the life, and to keep all that is given thee there; and have nothing which thou mayest call thine own any more; but to be lost in thyself, and found in him. Know the land of the living [Ps 52:5], wherein all the things of life live, and can live nowhere else.

A Warning of Love from the Bowels of Life (1660)

1.410   Now, who will be wise? Let him become a fool in the flesh. Who will be strong? Let him become weak in the man's part. Who will be saved by the eternal power? Let him cease from the man in himself. Whoever would be able, in the life, to do all things, let him sink into that in himself which is not, that it may bring to nought all things in him that are; that so it alone may be: and he by it being brought to nothing, will easily become all in it. This is the true way of restoration, of redemption; first to be lost, to be overcome, to be drowned, to be made nothing by that which is not; that that may come to BE in him, and he be quickened, raised up, and perfected in that, and so become possessor of the fullness.

Where is the Wise? Where is the Scribe? (1660)

1.415   . . . The true light springs from the life; and it must be held in the life, in the vessel which the life forms, in the new bottle, in the new understanding; not in the fleshly part, nay, not in the natural part: for as the natural man cannot receive the things of the Spirit, 1 Cor. 2:14, so neither can he retain them.

Some Directions to the Panting Soul (1661)

II.205–06 ...Know what it is that is to walk in the path of life. ...
Qfp § Give over thine own willing; give over thine own running;
26.70 give over thine own desiring to know or to be any thing, and sink down to the seed which God sows in the heart, and let that grow in thee, and be in thee, and breathe in thee, and act in thee, and thou shalt find by sweet experience that the Lord knows that, and loves and owns that, and will lead it to the inheritance of life, which is his portion. And as thou takest up the cross to thyself, and sufferest that to overspread and become a yoke over thee, thou shalt become renewed, and enjoy life, and the everlasting inheritance in that.

...Know in what light it is to walk, which is in the light of the Spirit...[which] shineth fresh in the renewed spirit every day, and so is daily gathering it more and more inward into itself, comprehending it in itself, and preserving it in its own purity, clearness, and brightness. O! this is it hath undone many, even catching at light from the Spirit, transplanting the image of divine things into the earthly principle, and there holding of them in the earthly part, growing wise by them there, and making use of them from thence as man sees good, and not seeing a necessity of depending on the Spirit for fresh light and life every day to every spiritual motion.

II.208–09 ...When God begets life in the heart, there is a savour of it in thy vessel, and a secret, living warmth and virtue, which the heart in some measure feels, whereby it is known. Lie low in the fear of the Most High, that this leaven may grow and increase in thee. This is the leaven of the kingdom [Mt 13:33, Lk 13:21]; this is it which must change thy heart and nature, and make thy vessel (which perhaps hath been long and much corrupted) fit to receive the treasure of the kingdom. Now while the savour is upon thee, while the virtue of the life is fresh in thee, thou findest some strength towards God, with some little taste and discerning of the things of his kingdom. Know thy weakness, and go not beyond the measure; but in what thou hast received bow before the fullness, worship God in that, and be patient in what he exercises thee withal, waiting for more from him. And when the night comes upon thee, and thou perhaps art at a loss, missing the savour and presence of the life, and not knowing how to come by it again, be patient and still, and thou wilt find breathings after a fresh visitation, and a meek, humble, broken spirit before the Lord. Thou wilt see thou canst do nothing to recover his presence again; nay, thou canst not so much as wait for him, or breathe after him, without his help;...but in the night of distress, feel after somewhat which may quiet and stay thy heart till the next springing of the day....in the day of thy weakness his grace will be sufficient for thee [2 Cor 12:9];...and he will be teaching thee to live, and to speak, and to move and act from the principle, and within the compass of his light and life eternal.

Some Questions and Answers for the Opening of the Eyes of the Jews Natural (1661)

II.219 Several things hath the life, begotten by the eternal virtue, breathed in me towards my Father for, in relation both to myself and others, from my childhood. As touching myself; first, that I might be a vessel for him; that I might be freed from the bondage of corruption, and brought forth in the image of his life. Secondly, that I might be filled with his life; that I might be satisfied in the presence, and with the fullness of the spring of my life; even that I might have enough of my God in my heart continually. Thirdly, that he would, of his own mere goodness, both preserve the vessel, and dwell in it for ever; that so my tenure and possession of him, and fitness for him, might be of his grace, of his love, of his goodwill, of his own nature, depending wholly and altogether on him, and not at all on any thing that can be expected from the creaturehood in its pure state. And likewise, that if he please to use me in any service, it might be of him, and for him, and to him. ...

II.251 *Quest.* Why doth God thus exercise his Israel? Why doth he lead them in such a knotty, and not in a more easy and ready way to the everlasting possession, and to the fullness thereof?
Ans. Because their estate and condition require it. They could not be so purified and fitted for the life; their vessels would not be so enlarged to receive it in, nor they so safely enjoy it, were it not for this course of wisdom, wherein God exercises and trieth every cranny of their spirits, until he hath perfected them, and stopped up the entrance of death everywhere.

II.252 ... It prepares for a clearer entrance into, and safer enjoyment of, the fullness. As the soul is more emptied of the strength and riches it received from God; so it is more prepared to enter into, and live in, the Pure Being itself. For nothing can live there which veils. In the life God was, and is, and is to be all in all for ever.

"To Friends in Truth, in and about the Two Chalfonts" (20 June 1666)

IV.399
JP 1.87
And, dear friends! watch, that life may be always fresh and savoury in you, to the seasoning of all your thoughts, words, conversations, and actions, that ye may feel the name of God written upon you, and his precious presence in you, and with you.

"To Friends of Both the Chalfonts" (2 and 3 August 1667)

II.494
JP 1.27.3
O the treasures of wisdom and knowledge, the riches of love, mercy, life, power and grace of our God which are treasured up for the soul in the Lord Jesus, and are freely dispensed and given out by him to them that come unto him, wait upon him, abide in him and give up faithfully to the law of his life, whose delight it is to be found in subjection and obedience to the light and requirings of his spirit! Feel my Friends, O feel your portion, and feel

that and abide in that wherein the inheritance is known, received and enjoyed. For thus it is. There is no knowing Christ truly and sensibly, but by a measure of his life felt in the heart, whereby it is made capable of understanding the things of the kingdom. The soul without him is dead; by the quickenings of his spirit it comes to a sense and capacity of understanding the things of God. Life gives it a feeling, a light, a tasting, an hearing, a smelling of the heavenly things, by which senses it is able to discern and distinguish them from the earthly. And from this Measure of Life the capacity increaseth, the senses grow stronger: it sees more, feels more, tastes more, hears more, smells more. Now when the senses are grown up to strength ...doubtings and disputes in the mind fly away and the soul lives in the certain demonstration and fresh sense and power of life.

II.495–96 ...For Friends, There is no straitness in the fountain. God is fullness: and it is his delight to empty himself into the hearts of his children, and he doth empty himself according as he makes way in them, and as they are able to drink in of his living virtue. Therefore where the soul is enlarged, where the senses are grown strong, where the mouth is opened wide: the Lord God standing ready to pour out of his riches, what should hinder it from being filled? And being filled, how natural is it to run over, and break forth inwardly in admiration and deep sense of spirit concerning what it cannot utter, saying, O the fullness, O the depth, height, breadth and length of the love [Eph 3:18]. ...now he extends peace like a river, now he puts the soul forth out of the pit into the green pastures [Ps 23:2], now it feeds on the freshness of life and is satisfied, and drinks of the river of God's pleasure and is delighted. ...

Now my dear Friends, you know somewhat of this, and you know the way to it. O be faithful, be faithful, travel on, travel on; let nothing stop you: but wait for and daily follow the sensible leadings of that measure of life which God hath placed in you, which is one with the fullness, and into which the fullness runs daily and fills it, that it may run into you and fill you. O that ye were enlarged in your own hearts, as the bowels of the Lord are enlarged towards you. It is the day of love, of mercy, of kindness, of the working of the tender hand, of the wisdom power and goodness of God, manifested richly in Jesus Christ.

II.496–99 *Postscript* Be not discouraged because of your souls' enemies. Are ye troubled with thoughts, fears, doubts, imaginations, reasonings, etc? yea, do ye see yet much in you unsubdued to the power of life? O do not fear it; do not look at it, so as to be discouraged by it; but look to him. ... So be still before him, and in stillness believe in his Name; yea, enter not into the hurryings of the enemy (though they fill the soul) for there is yet somewhat to which they cannot enter, from whence patience and faith and hope will spring up in you in the midst of all that they can do. So into this sink, in this lie hid in the evil hour, and the temptations will pass away, and the tempter's strength be broken and the arm of the Lord (which brake him) be revealed. ...

Now, Friends, in a sensible waiting and giving up to the Lord in the daily exercise, by the daily cross to that in you which is not of the life, this work will daily go on, and ye will feel from the Lord that which will help, relieve, refresh and satisfy which neither tongue nor words can utter. And in that the Lord God breathe upon you, preserve and fill you with his life and holy Spirit to the growth and rejoicing of your souls in him. ...

And then, as to what may befall us outwardly, in this confused state of things, shall we not trust our tender Father, and rest satisfied in his will? ... And he that provides inward food for the inward man, inward clothing, inward refreshment, shall he not provide also sufficient for the outward? Yea, shall he not bear up the mind, and be our strength, portion, armour, rock, peace, joy and full satisfaction in every condition? For it is not the condition makes happy or miserable, but he or the want of him in the condition. He is the substance of all, the virtue of all, life of all, the power of all: he nourishes, he preserves, he upholds with the creatures or without the creatures as it pleases him. And he that has him, he that is with him, he that is in him, cannot want. Has the spirit of this world content in all that it enjoys? No it is restless, it is unsatisfied. But can tribulation, distress, persecution, famine, nakedness, peril or sword come between the love of the Father to the child [Rom 8:35], or the child's rest, content, and delight in his love? And does not the love, the peace, the joy, the rest felt, swallow up all the bitterness and sorrow of the outward condition?...

So my dear Friends, let us retire, and dwell in the peace which God breathes, and lie down in the lamb's patience and stillness night and day, which nothing can wear out or disturb. And so the preservation of the poor and needy shall be felt to be in his name, and Glory sung to his name over all. ...

CHAPTER 3

Process of the Spiritual Life

The spiritual life for Penington is a process of personal growth, not a faithful adherence to belief nor dutiful repetition of ritual practice. Growth begins in inwardness by being touched in the heart, the centre of our being, and drawn forth by the divine life within. Growth comes by opening to the life, waiting upon its stirrings in the depths of self, feeling that divine presence, and following its leadings. We can know opening to the life in the silence of meeting for worship, feeling that we have descended beneath ordinary concerns into a deep space of stillness and peace, loving connectedness with others and with the natural world, illumination of our condition and that of the world, and a sense of Presence that touches, sustains, reassures, terrifies, and changes us. Such moments of descent into depth may also occur throughout our ordinary day. Then, if faithful, we are drawn into attentiveness to it, seek to be fully present in it, and move with it as led. The stirrings that come within such a sacred place in daily life are often so apparently insignificant. Penington calls them "little weak stirrings" (*To All Such ... Power* [1661], II.289).

The glint of soft summer light on green leaf might bring back the childhood experience of marvel at the beauty of nature and the mystery of being, and find us in touch now with that same wonder. We sense that there is more in this light on leaf than can be grasped intellectually which somehow opens out into "the more" of being that holds ultimate meaning. Or an irritation with partner or friend, seemingly so insignificant that it is not worth mentioning, if expressed, may make us conscious of a big conflict that when faced can become a growing place, drawing us deep into closer ties and maturity beyond our capacity and imagining. We usually do not think of such almost imperceptible flickerings in daily living as the workings of the Holy Spirit, yet that is what Penington directs us to. Perhaps more clearly, we know the Spirit's working in meeting for worship when a concern comes into focus, an act beckons to be done, a problem is suddenly seen from a different and liberating angle. In either daily life or worship we know in such moments, if we are open to see and feel, that God is present in us and the situation, affecting and enabling us beyond our control and understanding.

It is not just to moments of sudden realisation of divine presence in the concrete texture of everydayness that Penington directs us. Spiritual life grows through such moments into daily dependence upon God. He uses the metaphor of divine breathing. Think, he urges, of our breathing as also God's breathing through us. Breath is one of the first metaphors for God's action in the Bible. In Genesis the breath of God moves over the face of the waters (Gen 1:2; the Hebrew *ruach* means breath, wind, and spirit, but is usually translated as spirit). By such divine breathings we are inspired (in-breathed) to speak with our own breath in meeting, speak truth to power, or write about spirituality. But Penington calls us closer to the ordinariness of our lives, to our breathing, in which we can be aware of God's breathing in us – upholding us in life. As we grow in awareness of this deeper level in us of God's ongoing presence and learn to attend to it and live from it as we go about our daily round, we come, Penington says, into a sense of fullness. In his long spiritual search Penington sought neither religious knowledge nor religious experiences for themselves but the pervasive quality of freshness and fullness of the life as lived from moment to moment.

Life does not breathe through our lives without initial struggle to break loose from captivity to our own will, reasonings, imaginings, and desires – our veiled self. While he calls for the death of all our natural understanding and desiring, desire and understanding are central for Penington to the spiritual life. He rejects desire and understanding that are "out of the life", that issue from the veiled self and are subject to its control. He affirms desire and understanding that arise from and are filled with the divine life. Such desirings, breathings, understandings will, he says, become natural to those filled with life. Even though he demands a constant vigilance against deceptions, especially self-deceptions, that lead us back to a life of control by the veiled self under the guise of the religious life, Penington is a far distance from mainstream Protestant assertion that we are constant sinners in whom there is no natural health.

The spiritual life begins in and grows from almost imperceptible stirrings – the "small things" – of life, not from grand displays of religious practice, intellectual understanding, or moral deeds. Its end is to abide in the life and be content in whatever situation we find ourselves (Phil 4:11). He speaks of his incarceration in noisome prisons which became places of pleasure as God comforted him and filled him with love for his captors. In biblical language this transcending of the veiled self, not focusing on the pain but looking beyond it to the Life within, he calls waiting under the "yoke" and "daily cross". Every moment, regardless of circumstance, can and should be filled with the Life, even eating and drinking: "in eating and drinking, and whatever we do, our heart is retired to the Lord, and we wait to feel every thing sanctified by his presence and blessing…" ("Life and Immortality", IV.74). In going deep and letting go of the veiled self our lives receive a divine ordering by the inward teacher: "the Lord will teach you… ordering every thing for you, and ordering your hearts in every thing…" ("To My… Fds in Scotland", III.514).

To describe spiritual growth Penington will use traditional theological categories. He speaks of initial growth as "conversion" in which we turn from darkness to light through the divine assistance of Light in our conscience that keeps us "pliable" as we resist control by the veiled self. "Faith" is not adherence to belief but trust in this Life streaming through us. Penington often speaks of "obedience". It is not, however, an active conforming to rules but a waiting on the Light, relocating the level of consciousness at which we relate to God from assertion of will – "I will obey the King's command" – to receptive attentiveness – "I am ready to be drawn into creativity by the Spirit's leading". "Redemption" is an ongoing process of creativity, not conformity, in relation to God who is not an outside judge and rule-giver but an intimate presence with whom we are united ("engrafted"). Penington speaks of "Christ", meaning this intimate presence and this drawing into creativity, but he makes it clear that Christ is the symbol for him of the Life, not the object of biblical knowledge and belief; that would belong to the veiled self.

The use of biblical theological words by Penington does not

eviscerate the self of all meaning and worth, relegating it to a passive and corrupt thing, but seeks to evoke the deeper place in ourself beneath the veiled self where we give up our own judging, controlling, our spiritual life "to savour this little which ariseth from God" (*To Widow Hemmings* (28/9), III.452) and "feel leadings and drawings from the life, suitable to thy state" (*Concerning God's...Israel*, II.395).

Penington's understanding of the process of the spiritual life highlights the difference between the life of the dead spirit of the veiled self and the life of Spirit. He usually articulates this difference in oppositional, even combative, terms. Recognising this difference, we can be enriched by grace and by our own responsiveness, growing into virtue and wisdom. But there are alternative ways to relate to it other than combat. As we love a wayward child, embracing it as it struggles towards maturity, so also we can love our own self. Its desires and capacities are integral to us being fully human. The problem is when the veiled self usurps leadership, denying and rejecting leadership from the unveiled mysterious depths. We have been taught in modernity that such depths are untrustworthy, that only reason is dependable. Yet we have seen such reasonableness carry people, ungrounded in the divine presence, into war and systems of domination. To be sure, the depths can take over people in destructive ways. It is the holy, not destructive, spirit we seek to be led by, that which affirms and engenders life. While Penington's earlier experience is expressed through the combative metaphor of captivity, self-deception, slaying and breaking, we do find alternatives in Penington when he speaks of our lives becoming "natural" (*Warning of Love*, I.403; *Where is the Wise?*, I.416; *Concerning Persecution*, II.193; *Some of the Mysteries*, II.343; "To Fds of Both Chalfonts", II.495; *Some Things...Royal Society*, III.107; "To _____" (27 Nov 1670), III.449; "Seed of God", IV.343); "pliable" (*Concerning the Worship*, II.215); "flexible" (*Concerning Persecution*, II.195); the natural senses "grow[ing] stronger" and being "enlarged" ("To Fds of Both Chalfonts", II.494–495); and dwelling humbly in the mystery of God (*Some Things of Gt Weight*, III.15; *Flesh and Blood*, III.357–358, 369; "Reply [Concerning...New Covenant]", IV.176, 191; "Reply to...Gospel-Baptism", IV.396). We can benefit, therefore, from Penington's finely honed distinguishing between the veiled self of natural understanding and the life, while choosing to articulate it through metaphors of growth rather than combat.

"Short Catechism", in *The Scattered Sheep Sought After* (1659)

1.122–23   Q. How may I come by that heart?
A. As thou, being touched with the enemy, didst let him in, and didst not thrust him by, with the power of that life which was stronger than he, and nearer to thee; even so now, when thou art touched and drawn by thy friend (who is nigh), and thereby findest the beginning of virtue entering into thee, give up in and by that life and virtue, and wait for more; and still as thou feelest that following, calling, and growing upon thee, follow on in it, and it will lead thee in a wonderful way out of the land of death and darkness, where thy soul hath been a captive, into the land of life and perfect liberty.

The Axe Laid to the Root of the Old Corrupt Tree (1659)

1.256–57   ...When thou feelest things, then seek their preservation in the proper spring of their own life. Let the root bear thee, and all thy knowledge, with all that is freely given thee of God. When thou feelest thyself leavened with the life, and become a branch shot out of the life, then learn how to abide in the life, and to keep all that is given thee there; and have nothing which thou mayest call thine own any more; but to be lost in thyself, and found in him. Know the land of the living, wherein all the things of life live, and can live nowhere else.

Where is the Wise? Where is the Scribe? (1660)

1.416–17   ...O! how doth the soul that is begotten of the divine breath, that is born of the living power and virtue, depend upon God for his continual breathings! There is nothing that hath so much from God, and yet nothing is so little able to live without him. ...The thing that I wanted in my great misery, it was not outward knowledge, it was not experience of God's mercy and goodness; but this I wanted, the issuings-forth of his fresh life, and livingly to know where to wait for it, and livingly to know it when it appeared: for it was still near me all the time of my darkness, and did preserve me, and appear unto me; but I livingly knew it not, but thought I would be wiser than others: for I saw many deceived, and so I would not own it in such a way as it then appeared in me, lest I also should be deceived like others; but waited for such an appearance as could not be questioned by the fleshly wisdom. And he that waits for that, and so despises the day of small things [Zech 4:10], cannot but refuse the little seed; and so, not being received into his earth, it can never grow up in him into a great tree. ...

The New Covenant of the Gospel distinguished from the the Old Covenant of the Law (1660)

II.74–75 ... By the stirring of life in the soul, desires after life are kindled. He in whom the desires are kindled, and who feeleth the eternal virtue, ... the spring stirring, the soul cannot but move towards its centre; and as it entereth into and fixeth in its centre, it partaketh of the rest. Now to know the leadings of the Spirit forward and backward into these, into desires, ... here is the safety and sweet progress of the renewed spirit. That man who is born of the Spirit is to wait for the movings, breathings, and kindlings of the Spirit in him: ... to wait under the yoke [Mt 11:29–30], under the daily cross [Lk 9:23] to that part which is to be brought and kept under, till all the bonds of captivity be broken through by the life, and the veil of flesh rent from the top to the bottom [Mt 27:51] (the remaining of which is that which stops the free current of life), and then shall the soul enter into the holy of holies. ...

Concerning the Worship of the Living God (n.d.; ca. 1661)

II.214–16 *Quest.* What is the way of conversion?
Ans. To turn men from darkness unto light. ...
Quest. How is man converted?
Ans. By the operation of the light and power of God upon his conscience. ...
Quest. What doth God make it in his working upon it?
Ans. Gentle and tender, fit to receive the impressions of his Spirit. By the influence and power of his Spirit on the conscience, he openeth the ear to hearken to his voice, and prepareth the heart to follow him in his leadings.

Quest. How doth God carry on his work in the converted soul?
Ans. By keeping it low and tender, out of the self-wisdom and hardening reasonings of the human understanding: by this means he keeps it pliable to the light and power of his Spirit.

Some Questions and Answers for the Opening of the Eyes of the Jews Natural (1661)

II.240–41 *Quest.* How is faith and obedience here exercised?
Ans. In waiting on the light for the leadings in the law of life, and then in subjecting to the leader, being content with all his dispensations therein; with the time he chooseth for standing still, and with the time he chooseth for travelling on; with the proportion of light and leading that he judgeth fit, with the food and clothing which he prepares and preserves; with the enemies which he sees fit to have avoided or encountered with. Hereby the own wisdom, the own will, the own strength, the own desires, the own delights, with all the murmurings, weariness, and discontents, which arise from the earthly part, are by degrees worn out, and a pure vessel prepared for the pure birth to spring up and appear in.

Some Questions and Answers Showing Man His Duty (1662)

II.268 But oh, how sweet is the stream of life in the sensible manifestation of the promise! He who feels the covenant in Christ, and life streaming into his heart through the covenant, and the seal of eternal peace to his soul, and that he shall never be left nor forsaken by the fountain of mercy, but all that ever befalls him shall conduce towards the working out of the perfect redemption and salvation of his soul; this is a precious state indeed; and this is the state which the feeling of the faith, and the living obedience in the Spirit leads to. Happy are they that walk in the path thereof, who content not themselves with man's knowledge of Christ, with man's belief of the things written concerning him, with man's obedience to the precepts left on record by the apostles, but whose living soul cannot be satisfied without the feeling and pressing after Christ, the life, and without a true engrafting into him in spirit, through the living Word, or testimony of life, received into, and believed on in the heart.

To All Such as Complain that They Want Power (1661)

II.287–89 ... being touched, being quickened by the eternal power, being turned by a secret virtue and stirring of the life in his heart, then he can turn towards that which turneth him. Being drawn by the life, by the power; he can follow after the life, and after the power. Finding the sweetness of the living vine [Jn 15:1–8], and his soul made alive by the sap of the vine, his heart can now cleave to, and abide in, the vine, and bring forth the fruit of the living faith and obedience to the husbandman, who daily dresseth the heart, that waiteth in the living principle for further life from the fountain, that it may bring forth the fruits of life more and more. ...

    I confess the power doth not so flow forth to man, as man expects it; but the power of life works man out of death in a mystery, and begins in him as weakness. There is all the strength, all the power of the enemy, against the work of God in the heart. There is but a little thing (like a grain of mustard-seed [Mk 4:30–32]), a weak thing, a foolish thing, even that which is not (to man's eye), to overcome all this; and yet in this is the power. And here is the great deceit of man; he looks for a great, manifest power in or upon him to begin with, and doth not see how the power is in the little weak stirrings of life in the heart, in the rising up of somewhat against the mighty strength of corruption in him; which he returning towards, cleaving to, and waiting upon the Lord in, the strength of the Lord will be made manifest in its season, and he will be drawn nearer and nearer to the Lord, and his enemies be overcome and fall he knows not how. But he that waits for such a mighty appearance of power at first, looking so to begin, and after that manner to be preserved and carried on, can never in this capacity so much as walk in the path eternal: nor is not in the way of

> *3. Process of the Spiritual Life*

> receiving the power, which springs up as weakness, and leads on and overcomes enemies in a mysterious way of working, and not in such a manifest and direct way of conquest, as man's wisdom expects.

II.296–97 Thou must come down, thou must become nothing by degrees, thou must lie at the foot of the reprovings of that light, which thou thinkest thou hast gone far beyond, and be glad of a little help now and then in the lowliness and humility of thy heart, which must not choose what appearance and manifestation it will have from God, before it will begin to follow him, but be glad of ever so little, that the infinite wisdom sees good to give forth by the hand of his mercy.

Whoever have been high, and are still waiting and expecting in the heights of their own wisdom and observations concerning the kingdom, let them take heed of despising the day of small things [Zech 4:10], and know that their proper beginning (yea the very path of eternal life itself) lies in the lowness, in the humility, even in that nothingness which bows before the least light of the day, and with gladness of heart enters into, and walks in it. For this I certainly know; the wise, the observing eye, the vast comprehending heart, which waits for such an extraordinary power, judging it cannot begin following the light, which daily appears to check and reprove, without some great manifest appearance of power; this cannot see the low little path of life, which is proper for it to walk in, and to the end whereof it must travel, if ever it come to sit down in the kingdom, or to inherit the power of the endless life.

Concerning God's Seeking out His Israel (1663)

II.395–96 … watch to feel the savour of life in thy heart day by day, and therein to feel leadings and drawings from the life, suitable to thy state; for in this savour, and in these drawings, rises the true light, which leads into the way of life. And then watch against the reasonings and disputations which the enemy will raise in thy mind, who will strive to make thee a judge over these drawings; whereas the light, which ariseth in the savour and in the drawings, is thy King (though in this low appearance), and not to be judged by the mind, thoughts, and reasonings, but to judge them all down, and be bowed unto and obeyed by thee.

Three Queries Propounded to the King and Parliament (n.d.; ca.1663–1664)

II.317–18 . . . I have had experience myself of the Lord's goodness and preservation of me, in my suffering with them for the testimony of his truth, who made my bonds pleasant to me, and my noisome prison (enough to have destroyed my weakly and tender-educated nature) a place of pleasure and delight, where I was comforted by my God night and day, and filled with prayers for his people; as also with love to, and prayers for, those who had been the means of outwardly afflicting me and others upon the Lord's account. . . .

Well: were it not in love to you, and in pity (in relation to what will certainly befall you, if you go on in this course), I could say in the joy of my heart, and in the sense of the good-will of my God to us, who suffereth these things to come to pass, Go on; try it out with the Spirit of the Lord; come forth with your laws, and prisons, and spoiling of our goods, and banishment, and death (if the Lord please), and see if ye can carry it. For we come not forth against you in our own wills, or in any enmity against your persons or government, or in any stubbornness or refractoriness of spirit; but with the Lamb-like nature which the Lord our God hath begotten in us, which is taught and enabled by him both to do his will, and to suffer for his name's sake. And if we cannot thus overcome you (even in patience of spirit, and in love to you), and if the Lord our God please not to appear for us, we are content to be overcome by you. So the will of the Lord be done, saith my soul.

"To The Lady Conway" (1679)

III.463–65
JP 2.183.3

O my friend, after it has pleased the Lord in tender mercy to visit us and turn our minds from the world and ourselves towards him, and to beget and nourish that which is pure and living of himself in us yet, notwithstanding this, there remains somewhat at first (yea and perhaps for a long time) which is to be searched out by the Light of the Lord, and brought down and subdued by his afflicting hand. When there is indeed somewhat of an holy will formed in the day of God's power; and the soul in some measure begotten and brought forth to live to God in and out of the womb of the heavenly wisdom; yet all the earthly will and wisdom is not thereby presently removed, but there are hidden things of the old nature and spirit still remaining, which perhaps appear not, but sink inward into their root, that they may save their life: which man cannot possibly find out in his own heart, but as the Lord reveals them to him. ... O ... that thou may wait to feel the pure seed or measure of life in thee, and die into the seed, feeling Death unto all that is not of the seed in thee; and that thou may feel life, healing, refreshment, support, and comfort from the God of thy life, in the seed. ... O the Lord guide thee daily, and keep thy mind to him, at least looking towards the holy place of the springing of his life and power in thy heart. ... O look not at thy pain or sorrow, how great soever, but look from them, look off of them, look beyond them to the Deliverer.

CHAPTER 4
Life in the Church

Jesus provides a model of how we should live in the church. Penington meditates at length on Mt 20:25–28 in which Matthew's Jesus says to the disciples that they are not to exercise the power of domination over one another, but be servants, ministering to one another, as he has done. The occasion for Penington's exegesis is the hanging of Quakers on Boston Commons in 1660 by English Puritans. In hopes that scripture understood aright will break through their self-righteous, exclusive and judgmental attitudes, he writes a long essay, addressed to the rulers and people of New England, in which he speaks of diversity and uniformity, and shows that Jesus' way with the disciples was not to dominate them, telling them what to believe or do. Rather he patiently "waited till their capacities were enlarged" (*Examination... Boston*, 1.380), embracing them meanwhile in their present degree of integrity. It is the wish for domination and greatness that destroys social order – says this son of Isaac Penington senior, Lord Mayor of London and judge over the King's life.

Jesus is not "Lord" in the sense of dominating authority. He is Lord in the sense of mentor and elder friend (see Jn 15:15 where John's Jesus says "I call you servants no longer;... I have called you friends"). Penington's scriptural interpretation here goes to the radical heart of the gospel, which the early church very quickly undid in becoming a great power of domination. This is what Penington means by "the apostasy" of the church. It lost the mutuality of people drawn together under the leadership of the Spirit, and set up a hierarchical structure. Where Jesus had sought to evoke the Light and Life in others, which filled him to the full, the church projected that authority in inwardness on to priests, bishops, and popes, emptying the self of divine intimacy, responsibility, and creativity. And it conceived that authority as certain, whereas for Penington "Paul may err, Apollos may err, Peter may err... and did err" (*Examination... Boston*, 1.387; 1 Cor 7:29–31, Acts 24:26, Mk 14:66–72). Only the Spirit's leadership is unerring, if we are able to discern it.

What Penington is advocating, what Jesus seems to be teaching, what early Friends attempted to put into practice, is a radical dependence on divinity within, rather than on human constructions according to our veiled self that invariably seeks domination. How shocking it must have been to Protestants and Catholics in mid-seventeenth century England to walk into a meeting for worship and find nobody in charge. How astonishing it is that what early Friends started has continued to this day, patterning both worship and business decisions on Jesus' advocacy of non-dominating ways of being. How easily do we forget how extraordinary this is, and where it comes from.

It has not been without difficulty, for we fail many times. Reading a Quaker from seventeenth-century England may awaken us to the remarkableness of what Friends are achieving, and to our failings too. And we can note Penington's own failure. In 1660 he wrote to Boston, affirming diversity, mutuality, and the responsiveness of each to the Spirit within, and in 1663 wrote recommending that Friends withhold judgment on John Perrot, waiting upon the Lord to correct anything that may be amiss. Yet by 1666 Penington advocated subjecting oneself to Fox's dominating authority, as he had come to feel revulsion for his support of Perrot (see Part I, chapter 3), confessing his own "interrupting... uniformity in the life" (*To Fds in England, etc.*, II.414).

Such failings, succumbing to pressure of Fox's domination – Fox's own failure – should keep us from idealising our founders; instead, we are thrown back upon the divine resources within. Our historic leaders cannot be the authority for us. Only the Spirit within can be, which demands constant alertness to distinguish between our natural understanding and the Life. Yet we can take from their words and lives, as we can take from the Bible and church history, whatever we can discern of the Life in them. That Penington failed in this matter does not deny his successes nor should it discourage our attempts.

Friends obviously need one another to assist in discernment, to grow in the Life. Penington defines such fellowship, the church, as "That gathering which is in the life and power" (*Some Qs...Man His Duty*, II.280). The responsibility of members of a meeting is not merely to be gathered and to gather others, but is to preserve and build up unity in the life, sharing daily in one another's personal struggles, "feel[ing] the wants, afflictions, and distresses of your fellow-members day by day" ("For Friends of Our Meeting", IV.408). The conscience is not to be constrained by outward conformity that limits how and where God self-reveals but by abiding in the life. Each must follow only as the Spirit has opened to him or her, but there is a greater fullness of divine revelation in the entire group. The mystery of truth and the kingdom is revealed in the full gathering, which stretches beyond our ken.

Within the larger church Penington insists on diversity. Writing to Boston during its persecution of Quakers, he argues that diverse forms of Christian belief and practice can express the same Spirit. He relishes the differences if in them he can feel the same Spirit. Although he is not opposed to sameness, spiritual unity does not consist in doing, thinking, and saying the same thing but in mutual participation in the Life. What destroys this inward unity is not different beliefs or practices but "judgment" by the veiled self which opposes differences, defending one side, seeking to impose it on the other, and persecuting them.

The Spirit is at work in a multiplicity of forms within Christianity, but also beyond. The true church does not limit the Spirit's activity to a Christian framework but "owneth God in whatever it reveals in any man upon the face of the earth". This means one should look for the Life in all forms of religious existence and not assume that God is present only in the Christian. No doubt this universalism is from Penington's Christian perspective, for the Life and Light he looks for in others is that which he sees in greatest measure in Jesus, and knows that it is revealed and grows "in the churches" ("Somewhat...Church Gov", IV.292). Nevertheless, stressing the life of the Spirit beneath belief and practice means that Christians have no control over God by using the "right language", no superiority of understanding God, and no privileged position from which to judge right and wrong between Christians' or others' perspectives.

Within our own Meetings when difference becomes conflict, Penington urges us to learn to distinguish the workings of the veiled self and Spirit. Such discernment is an intuitive thing; we sense it, feel it, more than reason about it. We should attend to the measure of Spirit we have as we feel the measure of Spirit in others, and accept both. We should be alert to our own failures in discernment if others do not feel our judgments are "in the life". The authority is the Life in the Meeting. When there is conflict, we must struggle together to discern the Spirit's truth. This takes profound humility, honesty, openness to new insight and new directions, and a flexibility ("pliableness") in reaching reconciliation and moving ahead together.

An Examination of the Grounds or Causes which are said to Induce the Court of Boston… (1660)

I.377,   In Matthew 20:25–28…Christ cuts off that power and authority which grows up in the corrupt nature of man, which was ever and anon springing up even in the disciples.

I.378   Such a kind of greatness as is in the world, is the destruction of the life of Christ; and such a kind of dominion and authority as is among the nations, is the direct overturning of the kingdom of Christ.…This spirit must be kept out from among you; this aspiring spirit, this lofty, ruling spirit, which loves to be great, which loves to have dominion, which would exalt itself, because of the gift it has received, and would bring others into subjection; this spirit must be subdued among Christ's disciples, or it will ruin all.

I.379   …Therefore if ever thou beest aspiring, if ever thou have a mind to rule, if ever thou think thyself fit to teach, because of what thou hast received, sink down, lie low, take up the cross to that proud spirit, make it bend and serve, let the life in every one rise over it, and trample upon it; and afterwards that in thee may arise which is fit to teach, yea, and to rule in the Lord.…

I.380   …Christ took not upon him this kind of greatness, nor did exercise this kind of authority; but he was a servant; he made use of the gift of the Spirit, of the power of life wherewith the Father filled him, to minister and serve with. He did never lord it over the consciences of any of his disciples; but did bear with them, and pity them in their infirmities. ... He did not hold forth to them whatever he knew to be truth, requiring them to believe it; but was content with them in their state, and waited till their capacities were enlarged, being still satisfied with the honesty and integrity of their hearts in their present state of weakness. Nor did he strive to reign over the world. ...

1.381 ... Is every one to do what he will, to be subject to his own fancies and imaginations, to the inventions of his own corrupt heart?

1.382 ... There are laws, there are governments, there are governors, there is ruling, and there is subjection: but all in the Spirit; ... that which is governed is the spirits of his people, and they are to be governed by his Spirit, and spiritually, and not after a fleshly manner.

... he that hath received a measure of the Spirit, in the same Spirit feeleth another's measure, and owneth it in its place and service, and knoweth its moving, and cannot quench it, but giveth way to it with joy and delight. When the Spirit moves in any one to speak, the same Spirit moves in the other to be subject and give way: and so every one keeping to his own measure in the Spirit, here can be no disorder, but true subjection of every spirit; and where this is wanting, it cannot be supplied by any outward rule or order, set up in the church by common consent: for that is fleshly, and lets in the flesh, and destroys the true order, rule, and subjection.

1.383 ... the great work of the minister of Christ is to keep the conscience open to Christ, and to preserve men from receiving any truths of Christ as from them further than the Spirit opens; or to imitate any of their practices further than the Spirit leads, guides, and persuades them. For persons are exceeding prone to receive things as truths from those whom they have a high opinion of, and to imitate their practices, and so hurt their own growth, and endanger their souls. For if I receive a truth before the Lord by his Spirit make it manifest to me, I lose my guide, and follow but the counsel of the flesh, which is exceeding greedy of receiving truths, and running into religious practices, without the Spirit.

1.384 "Let every man," saith the apostle, "be fully persuaded in his own mind" [Rom 14:5]; take heed of receiving things too soon, take heed of running into practices too soon, take heed of doing what ye see others do, but wait for your own particular guidance, and for a full persuasion from God, what is his will concerning you. Though I know this to be a truth, yet do not ye receive it, till God make it manifest to you. . . .

1.385 ... the apostle warns believers, to take heed of drawing one another on too fast, or of judging one another
Qfp § [Rom 14:5–15]. ... Even in the apostles' days, Christians
27.13 were too apt to strive after a wrong unity and uniformity in outward practices and observations, and to judge one another unrighteously in these things. And mark; it is not the different practice from one another that breaks the peace and unity, but the judging of one another because of different practices.

1.386–87 ... Men keeping close to God, the Lord will lead them on fast enough, and give them light fast enough; for he taketh care of such, and knoweth what light, and what practices are most proper for them; but for men to walk on faster than the Lord holds forth his light to them, this overturns them, raising up a wrong thing in them, and the true birth hereby comes to suffer, to shrink and be driven
Qfp § back. And oh! how sweet and pleasant is it to the truly
27.13 spiritual eye, to see several sorts of believers, several forms of Christians in the school of Christ, every one learning their own lesson, performing their own peculiar service, and knowing, owning, and loving one another in their several places, and different performances to their Master, to whom they are to give an account, and not to quarrel

Qfp §
27.74

with one another about their different practices! Rom. 14:4. For this is the true ground of love and unity, not that such a man walks and does just as I do, but because I feel the same Spirit and life in him, and in that he walks in his rank, in his own order, in his proper way and place of subjection to that. And this is far more pleasing to me, than if he walked just in that rank wherein I walk. ...this I can truly say concerning myself, I never found my spirit forward to draw any, either to any thing I believed to be true, or to any practice or way of worship I observed or walked in; but desired that the power and leadings of life might go before them, and was afraid lest men should receive things from my hand, and not from the Lord's. Yea, and this I very well remember, that when I walked in the way of Independency [Congregationalism]...I had more unity with, and more love towards, such as were single-hearted...than with divers of such...in whom a wrong thing...had caused them to swerve from the life. ...

1.387–88

...Care must be had that nothing govern in the church of Christ, but the spirit of Christ. ...Every minister in the church is to watch over his own spirit, that it intrude not into the work of God. ...every member is to wait in the measure of the Spirit which he hath received, to feel the goings-forth of the Spirit in him who teacheth and governeth; and so to subject not to man, but to the Lord. ...

...Care must be had that the conscience be kept tender, that nothing be received, but according to the light in the conscience. The conscience is the seat of faith; and if it be not kept close to the light which God lighteth there, faith is soon made shipwreck of.

1.388

...The great error of the ages of the apostasy hath been, to set up an outward order and uniformity, and to make men's consciences bend thereto, either by arguments of wisdom, or by force; but the property of the true church government is, to leave the conscience to its full liberty in the Lord, to preserve it single and entire for the Lord to exercise, and to seek unity in the light and in the Spirit, walking sweetly and harmoniously together in the midst of different practices. Yea, and he that hath faith, and can see beyond another, yet can have it to himself, and not disturb his brother with it, but can descend and walk with him according to his measure; and if his brother have any heavy burthen upon him, he can lend him his shoulder, and bear part of his burthen with him. O! how sweet and lovely is it to see brethren dwell together in unity [Ps 133:1], to see the true image of God raised in persons, and they knowing and loving one another in that image, and bearing with one another through love, and helping one another under their temptations and distresses of spirit, which every one must expect to meet with.

I.390 … uniformity is very lovely; and to be desired and waited for, as the Spirit of the Lord, which is one, leads and draws into one. But for the fleshly part (the wise reasoning part in man) by fleshly ways and means to strive to bring about fleshly uniformity, which ensnares and overbears the tender conscience; this is not lovely, nor spiritual, nor Christian. … the intent and work of the ministry (with the several ministrations of it) is to bring into the unity, Ephes. 4:13, as persons are able to follow: and not to force all men into one practice or way. … the unity being thus kept, all will come into one outwardly also at length, as the light grows in every one, and as every one grows into the light; but this must be patiently waited for from the hand of God … and not harshly … by the rough hand of man.

Some Deep Considerations Concerning the State of Israel (n.d.; ca. 1663)

II.385–86 *Quest.* 2. Wherein doth this unity consist?
Ans. In the life, in the nature, in the Spirit wherein they are all begotten, and of which they are formed, and where their meeting is. It consists not in any outward or inward thing of an inferior nature; but only keeps within the limits and bounds of the same nature. The doing the same

thing, the thinking the same thing, the speaking the same thing, this doth not unite here in this state, in this nature; but only the doing, or thinking, or speaking of it in the same life. Yea, though the doings, or thoughts, or words be divers; yet if they proceed from the same principle and nature, there is a true unity felt therein, where the life alone is judge.

Quest. 3. How is the unity preserved?

Ans. Only by abiding in the life; only by keeping to the power, and in the principle, from whence the unity sprang, and in which it stands. Here is a knitting of natures, and a fellowship in the same spiritual centre. Here the divers and different motions of several members in the body (thus coming from the life and Spirit of the body) are known to, and owned by, the same life, where it is fresh and sensible. It is not keeping up an outward knowledge (or belief concerning things) that unites, nor keeping up an outward conformity in actions, etc., for these may be held and done by another part in man, and in another nature; but it is by keeping and acting in that which did at first unite. In this there is neither matter nor room for division; and he that is within these limits, cannot but be found in the oneness.

Some Queries Concerning the Order and Government of the Church of Christ (n.d.; ca. 1665–1667)

II.368 ...in a case of doubt or difference, which shall be the judge; the measure of life within, or the testimony of others without?

II.369 ...Because we have had our begetting, birth, and teaching from the same life, the same Spirit. ... Now from this fountain, from this spring of life, never issueth any thing that is contrary to the life in any. Therefore if there appear a contrariety, there must be a waiting to feel who is erred from, or at least not yet fully gathered into, the measure of life. And such as are of an inferior stature and growth in the body, are (in an especial manner) to watch and wait in sobriety and fear, till the Lord clear up, and make things

4. Life in the Church

manifest; and likewise in the mean time to take heed of a hasty concluding, according to what riseth up in the understanding or judgment (though with ever so great a seeming clearness and satisfaction) as if it must needs be of and from the life in the vessel.

II.370 ...Let the measure of life judge freely in thee at any time concerning any thing, and that judgment will stand for ever. But be thou wary, wait on the Lord, that thou mayest be sure thou dost not mistake in thy own particular, calling that life which the Lord and his people know to be otherwise.

Naked Truth (1674)

III.288 ...the ministry of the gospel is in the light, Spirit, and power of the Most High, to turn people's minds to a proportion of the same light, Spirit, and power in themselves, and so to come to the manifestation and quickening of the same life in themselves, that so they may walk in the same light. For the life is the light; and he can never have light, or see light, who comes not first to feel some virtue from the quickening power.

The Flesh and Blood of Christ in the Mystery, and in the Outward (1675)

III.367 Now everlasting happiness and salvation depends upon true Christianity. Not upon having the name of a Christian only, or professing such or such Christian doctrines; but upon having the nature of Christianity, upon being renewed by the Spirit of Christ,...and bringing forth the fruits of the Spirit.

III.368 ...he lives, and believes, and obeys from a holy root of life, which causeth life to spring up in him, and love to spring up in him, and the Lamb's meekness and patience to spring up in him, and all grace to spring up in him....

III.369 ...they are experimentally known and felt among us, who are true Christians....Christianity is a mystery....

"Somewhat Relating to Church Government" (ca. 1675)

IV.292   ... The true church doth not limit God where he shall reveal, or not reveal; but owneth God in whatever it reveals in any man upon the face of the earth. For being in unity with God's Spirit, and born of the immortal life, they [i.e. "any" persons at any time] are in the feeling sense and knowledge of what came from the life in ages past, or in this present age, and are in unity with it; yet they know the Lord revealeth the mystery of his truth and kingdom in the churches. ...

"Some Misrepresentations of Me Concerning Church Government" (n.d.; ca. 1675–1679)

IV.329   ... as we have witnessed blessings in our first gathering, as we were gathered and joined to the light, Spirit, and power of the holy God in our own particulars, so we have witnessed blessings in our unity with the life in the body. O, how every motion of life is felt there! How the wisdom and power of God is revealed there! What help is administered to every member there! How the knitting in the life, and the flowing of the life and holy power from vessel to vessel, is daily experienced there! So that every one is quickened with the pure life; every one seasoned with the pure salt [Mk 9:50]. ...

CHAPTER 5

Life in the Nation

The political life is part of the spiritual life for Penington. He extends his inward–outward, form–life, or letter–spirit framework into the political arena. Events in history are outward forms motivated by and expressive of inward spirit. The visible events of Puritan revolution and Restoration that he witnessed have an inward dimension. A spirit of simplicity, life, and justice was stirring in the hearts of people in the revolution. But it soon got fixed in forms that squeezed out the life; out of this failure the King returned. This is what happens, he says, in all reformations: they begin in stirrings of life and hopes for better existence, and end in constructions of the veiled self, idols of domination.

Penington sees God at work in this history, establishing a republic and dissolving it in the Restoration. But the way of God's working is not as political or military leader making these things happen directly. By working in inwardness, in people's hearts, God stirs them to want life, simplicity, justice, and an end to oppression. The dramatic visible events are the result of such little imperceptible streams in people's hearts that become a confluence of raging waters as people come together in these wants and change things. While Friends today may have trouble with the notion that God works in history – because of its military triumphalism, or so much historical evidence to the contrary – we should remember the great changes in our time towards justice and life: the Civil Rights movement in America, the Berlin wall coming down, the end of the USSR and Cold War, the end of apartheid in South Africa. All of these had their origins in imperceptible stirrings in individuals' hearts.

God, for Penington, is the origin and sustainer of such stirrings. The "cause of God" is "the good of his people" feeling "their oppressions broken", establishing "just rights and liberties", achieving "integrity" (*Some Consids...London*, 1.286). Writing to Parliament Penington says God has "new created you, and given you a new being;...apply your selves faithfully to his work, without self-ends and interests" (*To the Parliament*, 1.280). God's work carries us beyond self to "seek the good of all" (*Some Qrs...Work of God*, II.94). All laws should embody "the principle of equity and righteousness" (*Somewhat...Weighty Qn*, II.164). While he agrees just laws are founded in "right reason", he is suspicious of reason being bent away from the good to favour one's selfish good. A change is needed in orientation to grasp that "The sum of law is love" (*Obs...Muggleton*, III.79). "Government is of God" but it should not be destructive: "government which destroyeth his work in any, is not of him" (*Some Obs...Scripture*, II.307). Punishments of offenders are necessary but love implies that "it were better and much safer to spare many evil men, than to punish one good man" (*Concerning Persecution*, II.193).

Government has a religious mandate, not to require conformity of belief and action, but to achieve justice and an end to oppression, and even more – quality of life for all. "The end of government is to bring men into...the fear of God, which is the spring of all goodness, righteousness and equity" (*Some Few Qrs...Cavaliers*, II.87). "Fear", coming from Hebraic wisdom, means awe and reverence for God (see Part II, ch. 7 on wisdom). For Penington the fear is the source of goodness and justice; it stirs the heart to humility and action that changes governments and societies.

The way of God's working is non-violent, and so also should ours be. God works in the heart. Our work too should speak to that of God in people's inwardness. Our weapons in the fight against oppression and injustice are spiritual because "carnal weapons...can reach only the carnal part; but the stronghold remains untouched by these" (*Examination...Boston*, 1.310). The stronghold is "the lusts" (*Somewhat...Weighty Qn*, II.153) ordered by the veiled self to dominate and defend our self-interests. Nevertheless, Penington is realistic about the nation's need for magistracy (police and criminal justice) and military defence, if "borne uprightly". Yet he believes there is a better way that nations are to move towards. Some people have already entered into this "better state", which is to trust in God as "defender" (*Somewhat... Weighty Qn*, II.157), for righteousness is "the strength of a nation and the seed of God the support of the earth" (*Somewhat...Weighty Qn*, II.153). Quakers, and any others drawn out from the veiled self's way of violence into the way of love and peace, become models of what nations are to become. They should not, therefore, be required by the government to fight, for their warfare is inward against the lusts out of which wars arise. To learn war no more and to trust in God does not weaken the defence of the nation but rather strengthens it, because the efforts at peace making and establishing righteousness remove contention from which violence comes and thus make the world a safer place. Truth will outlive all violence.

The question is how to wake the nation from "dreams" of domination and defence, so that it feels the presence of God in inwardness, and is open to being created anew so "this nation might become a paradise of God" (*To the Jews Natl & Spiritual*, III.390–91).

Babylon the Great Described (1659)

I.176–77   Now in this nation [England] the simplicity hath more stirred than in other nations; the seed of God in this land hath been exceeding precious and dear to him. And at the beginning of these late troubles, the stirring of the simplicity from the pure seed was more vigorous and lively than it had been in many ages before; and accordingly the answers of God to it were more fresh and sweet; and there was a taste of him, and fellowship with him, and sweet hopes and refreshments to the soul. ...

But this was it destroyed all; another thing got up under a cover, and the simplicity sunk; and so the life withdrew. ... Enter into your hearts, O ye backsliding children! is it not thus? You who had sweet tastes of God, is he not become a stranger to you? You that had sweet, fresh, lively breathings after God, are you not set down in a form, or under some pleasing notions, and have got a covering, but lost the simplicity of your life, and the sweet tastes of God, and refreshments from him? Thus it hath been in all reformations. There was commonly a pure, single, naked beginning; but an evil thing soon got dominion over it, slaying the pure, living stirring by the form which it raised up, under a pretence of preserving the life thereby, and of serving God more uniformly and acceptably therein. Ah! the precious seed that was sown at the beginning of these troubles! What is become of it? How is every one turned aside from the pure life, into some idol or other of his own heart!

Some Considerations Proposed to the City of London (n.d.; ca. 1659)

I.285 ... The Lord God Almighty, who made heaven and earth; who upholds them by the word of his power; whose they are, with all their inhabitants; he ruleth in the kingdoms of men; establishing or overturning laws, governments, and governors at his pleasure. Psal. 75:5. etc. Dan. 4:25, 35.

...If this late revolution was of God, and he saw it good to bring it about, for the further carrying on of his work, he will be able to maintain it; and those that oppose him therein shall not be able to stand before him.

I.286 ... The Lord did not throw down the former greatness of the nobility, for you to rise up in their places; but ye should have lain low, and remained little, and have let the Lord been great; and it is your true interest to descend and become little again. And if it were once manifest that ye did not seek yourselves, but the cause of God, the good of his people, and of the nation, that every part and sort of men might feel their oppressions broken, and their just rights and liberties recovered and preserved for them; this would draw the hearts of all the honest-hearted people to you as one man; and those which have been scattered would be again united; and our very enemies (seeing our integrity and righteousness and true reformation by the wisdom and guidance of God) would magnify that work of God, which, as yet, cannot but be a reproach.

Some Few Queries and Considerations Proposed to the Cavaliers (1660)

II.87 ... The end of government is to bring men into, and encourage and preserve them in the fear of God, which is the spring of all goodness, righteousness and equity (not to bring men into a formal way of worship, that the Lord always loathed; but to encourage in the true fear, which teacheth that worship of him in heart and spirit which his soul ever loved).

Some Queries Concerning the Work of God in the World (1660)

II.94–5, 98 Come, O nation of England, be bound! O powers of this nation, take the Lord's yoke upon you; seek righteousness, seek meekness, seek the good of all; not in words and pretences, but in truth and uprightness. Seek out that which is of God in every one of your hearts, and let that govern for God. Do not smite any for obedience to the living God, but come ye also under his yoke, that what is not of God in yourselves, but an enemy to your souls, may be yoked down; and let all laws be formed, directed, and managed, to reach the unrighteous, that the rod of the wicked may not always lie upon the lot of the righteous, Ps 125:3, nor oppression and self-will sit in the seat of judgment, and pass (because of its power and authority) for righteousness. Eccl 3:16 and 4:1.

...But if you will call them to account for any thing, let it be for being unfaithful to God and the people of this nation, to whom they made large promises, but performed little. And that which God required of them (and the nation had reason to expect from them) do ye now perform. Give all men the liberty of their consciences towards God; let them follow him out of the fashions, customs, and worships of the world without interruption; and let there also be a narrow search after what is unjust, unrighteous, and oppressive in any kind; and as fast as it is discovered let it be removed, that the nation may grow out of vanity, out of unrighteousness, into solidity and righteousness; and that the fear of offending man may not affright any from fearing, obeying, and worshipping of God in Spirit and truth, as he requireth; and then God will bless this nation and the powers of it. For the Lord God taketh not pleasure in overturning of nations, or breaking in pieces the powers thereof: yet if they will by no means hearken, but harden their hearts, and stand in the way of his counsel and design, he cannot spare them. Isa 27:4.

Somewhat Spoken to a Weighty Question Concerning the Magistrate's Protection of the Innocent (1661)

II.153

Qfp §
24.21

... Fighting is not suitable to a gospel Spirit; but to the spirit of the world, and the children thereof. The fighting in the gospel is turned inward against the lusts, and not outward against the creatures. There is to be a time, when "nation shall not lift up sword against nation, neither shall they learn war any more" [Isa 2:4]. When the power of the gospel spreads over the whole earth, thus shall it be throughout the earth; and where the power of the Spirit takes hold of and overcomes any heart at present, thus will it be at present with that heart. This blessed state, which shall be brought forth in the general in God's season, must begin in particulars; and they therein are not prejudicial to the world, nor would be so looked upon, if the right eye in man were but open to see with, but emblems of that blessed state which the God of glory hath promised to set up in the world in the days of the gospel. And though by this means there may seem to be a weakening of the strength of the magistrate, and of the defence of that nation wherein God causeth the virtue and power of his truth to spread in the hearts of his people; yet in truth it is not so, but a great strengthening. For if righteousness be the strength of a nation, and the seed of God the support of the earth, then where righteousness is brought forth, and where the seed of God springs up and flourisheth, that nation grows strong; and instead of the arms and strength of man, the eternal strength overspreads that nation, and that wisdom springs up in the spirits of men, which is better than weapons of war; and the wisdom which is from above is pure and peaceable, and teacheth to make peace, and to remove the cause of contention and wars, and uniteth the heart to the Lord, in waiting upon him for counsel, strength, and preservation in this state, who brought into it. Now is not this much better and safer than the present estate of things in the world. ...

5. Life in the Nation

II.157 … It is not for a nation, coming into the gospel life and principle, to take care before-hand how they shall be preserved; but the gospel will teach a nation (if they hearken to it) as well as a particular person, to trust the Lord, and to wait on him for preservation. Israel of old stood not by their strength and wisdom, and preparations against their enemies; but in quietness and confidence, and waiting on the Lord for direction, Isa. 30:15, and shall not such now, who are true Israelites, and have indeed attained to the true gospel state, follow the Lord in the peaceable life and Spirit of the gospel, unless they see by rational demonstration before-hand how they shall be preserved therein? I speak not this against any magistrates' or people's defending themselves against foreign invasions, or making use of the sword to suppress the violent and evil-doers within their borders (for this the present estate of things may and doth require, and a great blessing will attend the sword where it is borne uprightly to that end, and its use will be honourable; and while there is need of a sword, the Lord will not suffer that government, or those governors, to want fitting instruments under them for the managing thereof, to wait on him in his fear to have the edge of it rightly directed); but yet there is a better state, which the Lord hath already brought some into, and which nations are to expect and travel towards. Yea, it is far better to know the Lord to be the defender, and to wait on him daily, and see the need of his strength, wisdom, and preservation, than to be ever so strong and skilful in weapons of war.

Qfp § 24.21

II. 164 … That no laws formerly made, contrary to the principle of equity and righteousness in man, may remain in force; nor no new ones be made, but what are manifestly agreeable thereunto. All just laws, say the lawyers, have their foundation in right reason, and must agree with, and proceed from it, if they be properly good for, and rightly serviceable to, mankind. Now man hath a corrupt and carnal reason, which sways him aside from integrity and righteousness, towards the favouring of himself and his

175

own party: and whatever party is uppermost, they are apt to make such new laws as they frame, and also the interpretation of the old ones, bend towards the favour of their own party. Therefore we would have every man in authority wait, in the fear of God, to have that principle of God raised up in him, which is for righteousness, and not selfish; and watch to be guided by that in all he does, either in making laws for government, or in governing by laws already made.

Concerning Persecution (1661)

II.193 … It were far better in itself, safer for governors, more agreeable to equity and righteous government, and more pleasing to God and good men, rather to suffer some, by their craft and false covers, to escape due punishment, than to punish those who, by the goodness, innocency, and righteousness which God hath planted in them, are exempted from punishment. Yea, it were better and much safer to spare many evil men, than to punish one good man: for mercy and sparing, even of offenders, is natural to that which is good; but severity and punishments are unnatural and but for necessity's sake.

"Some Queries Concerning Compulsion in Religion" (1670)

IV.416 … For that which is of man, if it were not held up by man, would fall; but the truth will grow and increase, and that which is of God will stand and out-live all the violence and oppositions of men.

To the Jews Natural and to the Jews Spiritual (1677)

III.390–91 … O, how nigh is God inwardly, to the inward people, in this our day! O! the pure glory is broke forth. But alas! men are in their several sorts of dreams, and take no notice of it. What shall the Lord do to awaken this nation? In what way shall his power appear, to bring down unrighteousness, and to bring up righteousness, in the spirits of people? Do ye not think the Lord hath been at work? How could deceit be so wasted inwardly, and truth so grown inwardly, and overspread more and more, and gain ground in the nation, if the hand and power of the Lord were not with it, blessing it. O! take notice of the handiwork of the Lord, ye children of men, and wait to feel truth near, and to partake of the living virtue and power of it, that ye may feel your hearts creating anew, and the old heavens and earth may inwardly pass away, wherein dwells unrighteousness; and the new heavens and the new earth may be inwardly witnessed, wherein dwells righteousness. O that this nation might become a paradise of God! O that every one might be sensible of his presence and power and kingdom and righteous government inwardly in the heart, from the king that sits on the throne, to the beggar on the dunghill! Surely man was not made for himself! Surely he was not made such a creature as now he is! but in the holy image of God, with love in his heart to God above all, and to his neighbour as to himself. O, what are the religions and professions of several sorts where this love is not found! The Lord is restoring his image, and bringing forth the true, pure religion again.

CHAPTER 6

Knowing, Sensing, Feeling, Believing

The conception of the self as knowing through sensing and feeling rather than through believing is central to Quakerism not only in the seventeenth century but throughout its history. For Friends the self is an experiential being, whose knowing, even scientific reasoning, is personal. What this experiential knowing is aware of is not an object that an idea defines but something inward, out of sight of reason. Since Penington is focused on knowing God, not on knowing in general, what is felt and sensed in inwardness is the Life. If our experience of life is not of or through an idea, then what is "life"? We have said earlier that life is not a form but what can fill or be absent from forms (see commentary in Part II ch. 2, "The Life"). It is the energy he calls "spirit". We are back at this same point now in presenting his view of knowing. He uses another word for life and spirit: in excerpts below Penington makes it clear that life is "mystery" – "That which God hath given us the experience of ... is the mystery, the hidden life" (*Flesh and Blood*, III.357–58). What does this mean? It means at least that the reality we know, God in this case, is beyond our conceiving. Implicit here is the affirmation of God's transcendence, that God is not subject to our control, particularly to our intellectual control. While we invariably use ideas to understand God, they only catch an aspect of God. Yet the idea we have of God is not the divine reality. We easily forget this as we cling to the idea. While God's reality as mystery extends beyond all our ideas, we, nevertheless, can "know" the divine reality by feeling it, having a sense of it.

Penington's contributions to philosophy have been overlooked understandably because they are embedded in his spiritual, theological discourse amidst a people of great social activism. You might not think to look for philosophical innovation among activists, nor in someone always talking about how we know and what the self is in relation to God, sin, salvation, and spiritual growth. While Penington does use the word "Being," he never cuts it adrift from God. While he does talk about how we know God, he never uses philosophical jargon about justifying one's claims. In fact he and other early Friends are writing in the era when modern philosophy is being invented, following the rationalism of Descartes (1596–1650). They go in a very different direction which looks unphilosophical to modernity (the dualistic mindset, whether empiricist or rationalist, from Descartes to the present) as it develops. Only now as major efforts are being made to get beyond the modern mindset does Friends' experiential basis of knowing look important, and perhaps even useful.

What is this different direction? While Descartes, the founder of modern philosophy, grounds true knowing in reason, Penington grounds it in feeling and sense. For modernity, "feeling" is merely subjective emotions, and "sense" means physical sensations, stimuli received from the outer world through the receptors of our five senses. In recent Anglo-American modern philosophy "sense" is used along with "reference" to mean "meaning" – what sense does it make – along with how does it relate to the empirical world. For Penington, however, sensing is an intuitive, non-rational, feel for something. And feeling is a way of relating to something that affects us, moves us emotionally. "Feeling" and "sensing" are, therefore, synonymous. Both are ways of relating to a reality that involve an emotional awareness. They are a conscious awareness that does not use ideas, although we can get an idea about what we are feeling or sensing. But the idea is not the feeling, though it be filled with the feeling. Idea is erected upon sense and feeling as their clarification through intellectual content. Different from modern philosophers, then, Penington affirms that we know realities through conscious awareness that is not conceptual. Feeling and sensing make it clear that knowing is experiential and not merely having an idea. This would be nonsense to many modern thinkers but it is startling in its relevance today as some philosophers (existential, phenomenological, feminist, postcritical) turn to experience as their starting point and way of knowing.

Another word Penington uses for sensing and feeling is "tasting". Compare having the idea of honey and actually tasting it. These two kinds of knowing are very different. Having the idea means we have control over the situation, we know what the known is, what its properties are, what it is good for, how to use it in discourse. Tasting it, on the other hand, affects the quality of our experience and connects us intimately with the reality we are ingesting. We gain a sense, not an idea, of what honey is because it is in us. To talk about it we use ideas but we know the ideas do not quite catch the real taste. Here poets are useful because their metaphoric language, rather than giving an idea of honey, can evoke a sense of its taste, and move us to eat it. Using the word "taste" Penington allies himself with the biblical poets: "Taste, then, and see that the Lord is good" (Ps 34:8); and such medieval writers as Bernard of Clairvaux: "This intimacy moves man to taste and discover how sweet the Lord is" (*On Loving God*, IX.26).

Now, honey is an object, physical stuff, but God is not. That God is mystery means as well, then, that God is not physical stuff, nor an idea, nor an object that an idea identifies. Where modernity has divided reality into two kinds – objects (things, including our bodies) and subjects (the rational mind) – Penington presents a third, and more important kind of reality: mystery. Consider our experiences of mystery. While some phenomenon may be mysterious, the mystery we experience is not the thing itself through which we experience it: such things as, say, the night sky, sunrise, the self that I am (that I am here, that I will die, that there is that about me which I do not and cannot ever know), or the fact that I am loved by another, or that people are so terrible to one another. God for Penington is not something experienced yet mysterious like the sunrise. Rather God is mystery itself, mystery we experience in life, the mystery of human life, the mystery of the divine Life that touches, transforms, and wants to indwell us in fullness. Mircea Eliade, the recent great historian of religion, calls it "the sacred", that which is really real, that which is known in experience as ultimate meaning and as that which saturates us with being.

Penington is understandably not thought of as a philosopher because his view is not drawn out into a general theory of knowing. Yet it could be. All our knowing, then, like our knowing of God, would involve a pre-conceptual level of awareness that connects us with phenomena. They always transcend our knowing since we only

6. Knowing, Sensing, Feeling, Believing

grasp aspects through sensing and feeling, and subsequent thinking based on these. There is a mystery about everything since the reality of each thing eludes our comprehensive grasp. Yet through sensing realities we are aware of them by being connected with them, like the taster with honey. In fact, we "know" them "ere we were aware" ("Treatise", IV.259). The Spirit is at work in what we call today the unconscious. Penington refers to such stirrings of the life, which were happening in his experience throughout his growing into manhood, yet of which he was not aware consciously so as to be able to name them and think about them. But all this is going on beneath ideas. Where then? In our bodily awareness of sensing, feeling, tasting.

Rather than sight or hearing, Penington and other early Friends stress the non-conceptualising physical senses: "then by degrees...I felt, I tasted, I handled" (*Babylon the Great*, 1.137). While sight and hearing always function at a distance from the self, these senses of tasting, touching, and smelling (*Axe Laid to the Root*, 1.241; *Where is the Wise?*; 1.416; *Some Obs...Scripture*, II.305; "To Fds of Both Chalfonts", II.494) involve the intimacy of contact. While there are no doubt puritanical elements in Penington, nevertheless, his spiritual orientation affirms the body. God dwells in our bodies beneath consciousness which we first become aware of through sensing and feeling divine stirrings, which later we can talk and think about.

He understood these physical senses, not just literally, but metaphorically. When transformed in convincement he says that all five senses are new made:

> Life gives it a feeling, a light, a tasting, an hearing, a smelling, of the heavenly things, by which senses it is able to discern and distinguish them from the earthly. And from this Measure of Life the capacity increaseth, the senses grow stronger: it sees more, feels more, tastes more, hears more, smells more. Now when the senses are grown up to strength, ...doubtings and disputes in the mind fly away and the soul lives in the certain demonstration and fresh sense and power of life ("To Fds of Both Chalfonts", II.494).

Knowing God and knowing the world in its spiritual dimension is *like* knowing a phenomenon through literal seeing, hearing, tasting, touching, smelling. This likeness is metaphor not analogy, not mere similarity of different things. Through the literal senses we sense something *more*, something spiritual, in our daily living in the sensuous world. Even when withdrawn into silent meditation, what we become aware of arises from our bodily unconscious, like tasting or handling something physically. Opening to the Life activates spiritual sensitivities through our physical sensibilities: so we discern the Life in reading scripture, listening to persons talk about their lives, watching a group being gathered in worship or decision making. Keeping the body involved in spirituality, rather than splitting body and spirit apart as modernity does, Penington speaks metaphorically of sensitising our physical senses. When the spiritual senses grow through the literal senses, a freshness and confidence is felt in our lives.

Knowing for Penington is not only sensing and feeling (preconceptual) and metaphoric, it is symbolic as well. He does not have the vocabulary of metaphor or symbol so it takes alertness to see what he is doing. Symbol is defined in our day by Paul Ricoeur as a "region of double meaning" in word or thing in which "another meaning is both given and hidden in an immediate meaning" (*Freud and Philosophy*, 7). Hence a national flag is an ordinary piece of cloth that identifies a particular nation, but has deeper meanings of the aspirations and destiny of a people. A crucifix indicates the building or person is Christian, but deeper it carries the meaning of redemption.

When Penington speaks of mystery, he is speaking symbolically. Take for example his criticism of many believers in Christ. They believe in the things Jesus is reported in the Gospels to have done, "but the mystery they miss…in the midst of their literal owning…these things". There is a depth of mystery in the life of Jesus and its narratives which is hidden, yet shows itself. It takes a symbolic approach to become aware of this hidden reality in what is known on the surface. Penington then speaks metaphorically through this symbolic talk:

> The knowledge of these, without the knowledge of the mystery, is not sufficient to bring them unto God. …My meaning is, they have a notion of Christ to be the rock, a notion of him to be the foundation-stone; but never come livingly to feel him the rock, to feel him the foundation-stone, inwardly laid in their hearts, and themselves made living stones in him, and build upon him, the main and

fundamental stone. Where is this to be felt but within? (*Flesh and Blood*, III.358).

Believers think of Christ as the rock, but this is a mere notion. Understanding this symbolically connects us with the hidden mystery of divine support which we know through the feel of it. And we metaphorically become like stones, are changed as selves, as we participate symbolically (and therefore really) in these hidden depths of supportive mystery.

But the experience of mystery is not fixed like stones. It is evanescent. We experience mystery and then it is gone: "it is hard retaining it, nay, impossible rightly so to do, but in the spirit which gave it" ("Reply [Concerning... New Covenant]", IV.176). It will come again if we stay open in our inwardness to the hidden depths of Spirit. Its coming is not a thing seen but an event occurring – "the inward and spiritual appearance of our Lord" (*Flesh and Blood*, III.358). It is an event of appearing, revelation, a mystery unveiled showing itself. In knowing the life metaphorically and symbolically, the stress falls on the present: it is in the present that we experience the mystery of life.

How do we discern the life? Penington gives a detailed description (below) of the false appearance of life constructed by the veiled self. He believes scripture, is instructed by philosophy, undergoes visible changes in affections, will, and understanding. He works very hard doing all that he is supposed to – reading scripture, praying, meditating, denying self, acknowledging he can do nothing without the Spirit, receiving past revelation, waiting for further revelation, and living in hope he has the Spirit and is safe in eternal salvation.

Since this description of a changed life dependent on God sounds very much like the life Penington advocates, how does he distinguish them? He answers that it is not easy and takes a discipline of much waiting and exercising sense and feeling. But when you have waited, he says, you can tell with confidence. True life is given, not constructed by us. It springs up in inwardness from below the threshold of consciousness – what he calls "immediacy" (that is, unmediated by idea, word, or feeling). While there may be a waiting for it, when it comes, it comes more quickly than words or thoughts. As it crosses that threshold, it is powerful in a way that false life is not.

While the affections are changed in both, it is not merely the exciting ("boiling") of emotions that matters. There is simplicity rather than "gaudy" display, creativity rather than conformity, focusing on the divine reality rather than the means to it. Where the veiled self's life becomes defensive, hasty, and judgmental, projecting onto others faults of one's own, the received life is humble and patient. Discernment is discovery, not applying known principles. The discovery comes in "sinking down into the principle of his own life" (*Some Qs... Man His Duty*, II.270). This principle of our "own life" lies deeper than natural understanding. It is the life and "light within" (*Jew Outward*, 1.223) that we are united with because it is what fulfils us and connects us with the whole of being encompassed by God.

What we discern then in the true life is power – the power that enabled early Friends to change their lifestyle in spite of enormous social pressures, to endure imprisonment and beatings, and to work for social and economic justice, religious tolerance, and the overcoming of oppression. It involves dwelling in depth and responding creatively to what arises beneath consciousness. It involves humility and simplicity. And it involves feeling and being united with the divine life, which is the principle of our own being: to abide "in the nature of God" (*Axe Laid to the Root*, 1.239), in the Whole of which we are part. All that he says here is suggestive rather than definitive. Discerning God-based life in its difference from veiled-self-based life is like the taste of honey. It is discovery, savouring mystery. As we can learn to distinguish honey by taste so we can, Penington says, learn the feel of mystery and dwell in it, whether in the silence of worship or the talk of everyday.

While modernity following Descartes has sought an intellectual certainty in all that we know, Penington rejects this. But we may be shocked by his affirmation of infallibility. It is not ours; it belongs to the Spirit and Light. We never have the intellectual certitude Descartes sought, but we can receive a confidence by participating in the Spirit, a confidence not in the absolute truth of what we say or the unequivocal rightness of what we do, but that we dwell in the life and its mystery – and that this matters most "in the central of our being" (Wallace Stevens, *Collected Poems*, 380) and in all that we do; "...in minding this and being faithful in this," Penington concludes, "we mind our peculiar work and are faithful in that which God hath peculiarly called us". That is what we are doing in silent meeting for worship and business, and in our social action arising out of silence. Friends' peculiar work is "minding this... mystery" (*Flesh and Blood* III.358).

6. Knowing, Sensing, Feeling, Believing

The Axe Laid to the Root of the Old Corrupt Tree (1659)

1.233 There is a faith which is of a man's self; and a faith which is the gift of God: or a power of believing, which is found in the nature of fallen man; and a power of believing, which is given from above. As there are two births, the first and the second, so they have each their faith; and each believes with his faith, and seems to lay hold on the same thing for life.

1.235 ...A man may believe the history of the Scriptures; yea, and all the doctrines of them, so far as he can reach them with his understanding...[and] receive doctrines of instruction out of philosophers' books. ...

1.235–36 ...This being believed from the relation of the history of these things, it naturally sets all the powers of man at work (kindling the understanding, will, and affections) towards the avoiding of misery, and the attaining of happiness. What would not a man do to avoid perpetual extremity of misery on soul and body for ever, and to obtain a crown of everlasting blessedness? This boils the affections to an height, and sets the understanding on work to the utmost, to gather all the rules of scripture, and to practise all the duties and ordinances therein mentioned. What can the Scriptures propose to be believed, that he will not believe? What can it propose to be done, that he will not do? Must he pray? He will pray. Must he hear? He will hear. Must he read? He will read. Must he meditate? He will meditate. Must he deny himself, and all his own righteousness and duties, and hope only for salvation in the merits of Christ? He will seem to do that too; and say, when he has done all he can, he is but an unprofitable servant [Lk 17:10]. Does the scripture say he can do nothing without the Spirit [Jn 15:5]? He will acknowledge that too, and hope he has the Spirit. God hath promised the Spirit to them that ask it; and he has asked long, and asks still, and therefore hopes he has it. Thus man, by a natural faith, grows up and spreads into a great tree, and is very confident and much pleased; not perceiving the defect in his root, and what all his growth here will come to.

...Now, how easy is it for a man to mistake here, and call this the truth! First, he mistakes this for the true faith; and then he mistakes in applying to this all that which belongs to the true faith: and thus entering into the spirit of error at first, he errs in the whole course of his religion, from the beginning to the end. He sees a change made by this in him; and this he accounts the true conversion and regeneration. This leads him to ask, and seek, and pray; and this he accounts the true praying, the true seeking, the true asking. This cleanseth (after its kind) his understanding, will, and affections; and this he takes for the true sanctification. The justification which is to the true believer, he also applies to this faith; and so he has a peace, a satisfaction, a rest here, and a hope of happiness hereafter. Thus he receives what is already revealed; and he waits for what may be further revealed, which he can embrace and conform to, turning still upon this centre, and growing up from this root. And he that does not come hither in religion, falls short of the improvement of man's nature, and of the faith that grows there (which naturally leads all the powers of nature hither, and fixes them here), which is but dead. And now this man is safe; he is a believer; he is a worshipper of God; he is a Christian; he is an observer of the commands of Christ: when the overflowing scourge comes, it shall not touch him. ...

1.237–38 Thus far this faith can go: but then there is somewhat it is shut out of at the very first: there is somewhat this faith cannot receive, believe, or enter into. What is that? It is the life, the power, the inward part of this. Though it may seem to have unity with all the scriptures in the letter; yet it cannot have unity with one scripture in the life: for its nature is shut out of the nature of the things there witnessed. As for instance: it may have a literal knowledge of Christ, according as the scripture relates; of his birth, preaching, miracles, death, resurrection, ascension, intercession, etc. Yea, but the thing spoken of it knoweth not. The nature of Christ (which is the Christ) is hidden from that eye. So it may have a literal knowledge of the blood of Christ, and of justification; but the life of the blood which livingly justifieth, that birth cannot feel; but can only talk of it, according to the relation it reads in the scripture. So it may have a literal knowledge of sanctification; but the thing that sanctifieth, it cannot receive into itself. So for redemption, peace, joy, hope, love, etc., it may get into the outward part of all these; but the inward part, the life, the spirit of them, it is shut out of, and cannot touch or come near; nor can it witness that change which is felt and known here. And here is the great contention in the world between these two births; the one contending for its knowledge in the letter, and the other contending for its knowledge in the life: the one setting up its faith from the natural part, calling it spiritual; and the other, which has felt the stroke of God upon this (and thereby come to know the difference), setting up the faith of the true heir: which faith hath a different beginning, and a different growth from the other, and will be welcomed into the land and kingdom of life. ...

Quest. What then is that faith which is the gift of God? And which is distinct from this?

Ans. It is that power of believing which springs out of the seed of eternal life; and leavens the heart, not with notions of knowledge, but with the powers of life. The other faith is drawn out of man's nature, by considerations which affect the natural part, and is kept alive by natural exercises of reading, hearing, praying, studying, meditating in that part; but this springs out of a seed of life given, and grows up in the life of that seed, and feeds on nothing but the flesh and blood of Christ; in which is the living virtue, and immortal nourishment of that which is immortal. This faith, at its first entrance, strikes that part dead in which the other faith did grow, and by its growth perfects that death, and raiseth up a life which is of another nature than ever entered into the heart of man to conceive. And by the death of this part in us, we come to know and enjoy life; and by the life we have received, know, and enjoy, we come to see that which other men call life (and which we ourselves were apt to call life formerly) to be but death.

1.241 ...Indeed the proper use of all means, is to bring to the immediate voice, life, and power; and till this be done, till the soul come to that, to hear that, to feel that, to be rooted there, there is nothing done that will stand; but men stick by the way, crying up the means, and never knowing, tasting, or enjoying the thing which the means point to. But he that knows God comes into the immediate presence; and he that daily lives in God, lives in the immediate life; and the true faith leads to this, giving the soul such a touch and taste of it at first, as makes unsatisfiable without it.

1.255 ...Do not graft any of the fruit of the tree of life upon the tree of knowledge; for it will not grow there: an appearance, a likeness of the true fruit may grow there; but the true fruit itself will not. My meaning is, do not make a treasury of knowledge in the understanding part, which is to perish; but know the true treasury of all the things of life, which is in the life itself; and in that understanding which is formed, kept, and lives in the life.

1.269 ...The truth is a plain, simple thing; it is not gaudy in appearance; its excellency lies in its nature: but the appearances of truth which Satan paints are very gaudy, very glorious, seemingly very spiritual, very pure, very precious, very sweet; they many times even ravish that understanding and those affections that are out of the life.

An Examination of the Grounds or Causes which are said to Induce the Court of Boston... (1660)

1.313–14 ...the true trial of spirits is not by an assent to doctrines (which the hypocrite may assent to on the one hand, and the true believer may startle at on the other hand); but by feeling of them in the inward virtue of the light, in the spirit, and in the power.

I.354   ...Did not they set bounds to the truth, and bounds to the spirit of God, that thus far it should appear, and no further? Whereas God hath degrees of discovering and leading out of the antichristian darkness: and he that opposeth the next discovery of truth, the next step out of Babylon, is as real an enemy and persecutor, as he that opposed the foregoing.

Some Questions and Answers for the Opening of the Eyes of the Jews Natural (1661)

II.239–40   *Quest.* How is the voice of God known? Doth not the enemy speak inwardly also, and resemble his voice? How then is the voice of the redeemer distinguished from him who counterfeiteth the Shepherd and his voice?
Ans. By these two means:

First, The soul lying low, out of the wisdom in which the enemy appears and forms his likenesses; in the simplicity which the Lord hath begotten, the life opens to it, and the true light appears, which manifests the false light, and false appearances of the deceiver.

Secondly, In that which is begotten of God there is not a hastiness or suddenness to determine; but a silent waiting on the Lord in subjection, till the life speak, and make things manifest. Thus the knowledge and light of the child is held in the will of the Father, and received from his hand, and according to his pleasure. Thus what he will he hides, and what he will he makes manifest, and the child, which is born of his will, is content with his will; and lying down there, it keeps out of the enemy's territories, and of the reach of his temptations.

A Weighty Question Propounded to the King and Parliament (1663)

II.326   ...Whether the power of religion (and the true love) if it were raised up and restored again, would make the world happy, and set every thing in its proper place, both inwardly and outwardly? Is not sense an excellent thing in man, if it be guided by reason? And is not reason a much more excellent thing if it be guided by an inward principle of life? But sense left to itself, without the guidance of reason, how brutish is it! And reason left to itself, without the guidance of a principle of life, falls below sense. How cruel, how blind, how selfish, how unrighteous is man, that follows the dictates of his own corrupt reason, without knowing and becoming subject to that, which should enlighten it, and give him the right use thereof!

Concerning God's Seeking out His Israel (1663)

II.395–97 . . . That which God sows and brings up in thee is a sensible plant, not a knowing mind; and thy right judgment is only in the sensibleness of that plant, and not in the understanding or comprehension of thy mind; yea, that sensible plant (which thy wisdom will be very apt to despise and perk over) must batter down and bring to nothing thy understanding, and grow up in the stead of it, if ever thy soul be made a habitation for the life. Therefore sink into the feeling, and dwell in the feeling, and wait for the savour of the principle of life, and the touches and drawings of the savour, and walk along in it towards the land of life, parting with all, and leaving behind thee, whatever the savour of life disrelisheth; and entering into, and taking up, whatever the savour of life relisheth, that thou mayest be prepared for the Lord, and for the glorious appearance of his Spirit in thee.

Some Queries Concerning the Order and Government of the Church of Christ (n.d.; ca. 1665–1667)

II.368–70 Obj.5. But in a case of doubt or difference, which shall be the judge; the measure of life within, or the testimony of others without? Shall I judge as I feel the thing in the measure of my own life? Or shall I submit to others against my own sense and judgment, because I have an esteem of them, as being much above me in the growth, sense, and understanding of truth?

Ans. It is a great matter to judge aright, and to discern and know the measure of truth (the voice, motion, and judgment thereof) from all the enemy's false appearances, and from all the deceits of the heart. This is most certain; Jerusalem (the heavenly building, the church of the first-born) is at unity with itself. Truth is pure, eternal, unchangeable, always the same; the same in every member, in every vessel, throughout the whole body. ...

It is not an easy matter, in all cases, clearly and understandingly to discern the voice of the Shepherd, the motions of God's Spirit, and certainly to distinguish the measure of life from all other voices, motions, and appearances whatsoever. Through much growth in the truth, through much waiting on the Lord, through much fear and trembling, through much sobriety and meekness, through much exercise of the senses, this is at length given and obtained. And yet there is a preservation in the mean time to that which is lowly and submissive, looking up to the Lord continually, and not trusting to its own understanding, sense, and judgment. But that which is hasty and confident, and so ready to plead for its own sense and judgment, according to the measure of life, as it calls it; that is commonly out, entered into the erring spirit, pleading and contending for it knows not what, and is very apt to judge and condemn others in that very respect, wherein itself is most justly and righteously judged and condemned by the Lord, even by his pure life and Spirit in his people.

Concerning the Sum or Substance of our Religion (n.d.; ca. 1666)

II.454–55 ... How may the principle of truth be discerned?
Ans. By its piercing, quickening nature, which discovereth itself in its appearances and operations. For it appears and works, not like man's reason, or like motions of his mind which he takes into his understanding part; but it appears and works livingly, powerfully, and effectually in the heart.

... Now a man that is acquainted both with reason and with this light, he can distinguish the nature and operations of both. For there is a great difference between truth held in the reasoning part, and truth held in its own principle. It is very powerful in the one; it effecteth little in the other. In the pure quickenings of life this distinction is perceived, and also held. Therefore our advice is to all men, to retire from all mortality, that they may come to feel the spring of life in themselves, and something springing therefrom into them to quicken them, and to wait to have their understandings opened and kept open by that.

The Flesh and Blood of Christ in the Mystery, and in the Outward (1675)

III.357–59 ...Now whereas many are offended at us, because we do not more preach doctrinal points, or the history of Christ, as touching his death, resurrection, ascension, etc.; but our declaration and testimony is chiefly concerning a principle, to direct and guide men's minds thereto; to give a plain account of this...:

First, That which God hath given us the experience of (after our great loss in the literal knowledge of things), and that which he hath given us to testify of, is the mystery, the hidden life, the inward and spiritual appearance of our Lord and Saviour Jesus Christ, revealing his power inwardly, destroying enemies inwardly, and working his work inwardly in the heart.... So that in minding this, and being faithful in this respect, we mind our peculiar work and are faithful in that which God hath peculiarly called us to, and requireth of us.

Secondly, There is not that need of publishing the other as formerly was. The historical relation concerning Christ is generally believed and received by all sorts that pretend to Christianity. His death, his miracles, his rising, his ascending, his interceding, etc. is generally believed by all people; but the mystery they miss of, the hidden life they are not acquainted with, but alienated from the life of God, in the midst of their literal owning and acknowledging of these things.

Thirdly, The knowledge of these, without the knowledge of the mystery, is not sufficient to bring them unto God. ...My meaning is, they have a notion of Christ to be the rock, a notion of him to be the foundation-stone; but never come livingly to feel him the rock, to feel him the foundation-stone, inwardly laid in their hearts, and themselves made living stones in him, and build upon him, the main and fundamental stone. Where is this to be felt but within?...

Fourthly, The mystery, the hidden life, the appearance of Christ in Spirit, comprehends the other: and the other is not lost or denied, but found in it, and there discerned or acknowledged more clearly and abundantly. It was to be after it, and comprehends that which went before it. Paul did not lose any thing of the excellent knowledge of Christ, when he said, "Henceforth know we no man after the flesh; yea, though we have known Christ after the flesh, yet henceforth know we him no more" [2 Cor 5:16]. If he did not know Christ after the flesh, how did he know him? Why, as the Father inwardly revealed him. He knew him in his Spirit and power. He knew his death inwardly, he knew his resurrection inwardly, he knew the Spirit, the virtue, the power of it inwardly; he knew the thing in the mystery in his own heart. O, precious knowledge! O, the excellency of this knowledge of my Lord and Saviour Jesus Christ! What is the outwardly most exact literal knowledge without this? But what then? Do I now deny or slight the outward? No; I have it here, and I have the inward feeling of the Spirit of life, how it dwelt in him, how it wrought in him, and of what wonderful value all his actions and obedience were, in and through the virtue of this Spirit. ... For by the inward life and teachings of God's Spirit, am I taught and made able to value that glorious outward appearance and manifestation of the life and power of God in that heavenly flesh (as in my heart I have often called it), for the life so dwelt in it, that it was even one with it. Yet still it was a veil, and the mystery was the thing; and the eye of life looks through the veil into the mystery, and passes through it, as I may say, as to the outward, that it may behold its glory in the inward. And here the flesh of Christ, the veil, is not lost, but is found and known in its glory in the inward.

"Reply to Queries and Animadversions [Concerning the Rule of the New Covenant]" (1667/8)

IV.176   ... a man may apprehend his doctrinals to be right, as to the main substantials, when indeed they are not so. For the doctrines of the gospel are mysteries. Faith is a mystery; the love of God in the Spirit a mystery; obedience to the truth a mystery; the right confession of Christ in and through the Spirit a mystery; the worship of God in Spirit a mystery; justification, sanctification, and the peace and joy of the Spirit, mysteries of the kingdom, etc., and it is easy missing and misunderstanding these things, but hard to come to the true knowledge of them; and if any of the true, inward, spiritual knowledge of these things be received at any time, it is hard retaining it, nay, impossible rightly so to do, but in that which gave it. And, indeed, this is the great mystery of religion; to wit, to begin in the Spirit, and so to travel on in the pure light, life, and knowledge thereof, and not to entertain or mix with any thing of the flesh.

"To Widow Hemmings" (26 Eighth Month [Oct] 1670)

III.443–44
JP 1.77

... If thou come to know God's Spirit and to receive it, and feel it work in thee, and its pure light shine from the fountain and spring of life, thou wilt have a quicker sense and discerning therefrom, than can arise either from words written or from thoughts: that is, the Lord will show thee the way, whereof thou doubtest, quicker than a thought can arise in thee, and the Lord will show thee evil in a pure sense of the new nature, quicker than thou canst think or consider of anything.

"A Treatise Concerning God's Teachings, and Christ's Law" (1671)

IV.259,
Qfp
26.69

... we were directed to search for the least of all seeds, and to mind the lowest appearance thereof; which was its turning against sin and darkness; and so by minding and observing that in us which turned against sin and darkness, we came by degrees to find we had met with the pure, living, eternal Spirit; and by observing the movings, stirrings, guidings, directions, and law thereof, we found, ere we were aware, that we had met with the law of the new covenant, the law of the Spirit of life, which had life and virtue in it, to enable us to do the holy will.

"Some Experiences" (1679)

IV.430 I do not say that I, as a man, am infallible, or that any of us as men are infallible; but God's light, God's grace, God's truth, God's Spirit, God's wisdom and power, is infallible; and so far as we partake of that, are gathered into and abide in that, we partake of that which is infallible, and are gathering into and abide in that, which is infallible. And oh! let not men rest in, or be contented with, that knowledge which is fallible, but press after unity and fellowship with the Lord in his infallible spirit; there being no true union nor fellowship with him in any thing that is fallible.

CHAPTER 7

Freedom, Virtue, & Wisdom

Freedom of the will to do what we want and to be good was an issue seventeenth-century English Christianity inherited from the Reformation. The general Protestant view was that we were not good and could do nothing about becoming good on our own. Only God's grace could free us and move us towards righteousness. What freedom we had in this process and how far we were moved towards goodness depended on where one located on the Protestant spectrum: no freedom because God determines all by predestinating some for heaven and some for hell; no freedom but God forgives us through Christ's sacrifice; some freedom to accept salvation offered by God; and a little more freedom to live a disciplined life moving by grace towards righteousness. But only God could move us toward goodness, and no one arrived at the goal because each remained a sinner.

Today many Friends believe in an inherent goodness and assume they only need to work at it to be good. We might be instructed by what we have seen in Penington. He considered himself good in his pre-Quaker days because he had ideas of goodness which he was implementing, but came to understand himself to be self-deceived. He discovered he was captive not only to his own thoughts but to the way thinking dominated his life, obstructing the springs of life. In our own day we find ourselves captive to various things from which we cannot on our own extricate ourselves: consumer obsession, sexual images of the perfect body, the need to get ahead, the desire to have it our way in a marriage, social group, or business. Any one of these things can land us in a therapist's office seeking liberation from destructive patterns we are incapable of understanding, let alone free ourselves from. While Friends affirm the intrinsic goodness of our being, we should factor into our picture of humanity our own experience of captivity, the knots we get tied in, and the untying for which we need help.

Penington writes about the captivity he was in and his discovery day by day of God's liberation from a self-centred life. As God stirs life in our depths, we can respond and grow stronger as we allow the life to grow into maturity within. Our agency interacts with God's. Penington, like other early Friends, rejects predestination and affirms our freedom to accept or reject grace. Unlike the Reformers and Puritans, grace for Penington does not merely forgive and guarantee eternal life. Like radical Puritans – spiritual and mystical Protestants – grace for Penington transforms the self. Beyond them, however, this change of self for Penington engenders the originally created capacity in the self to live freely in response to God and fully in embodying God's presence. All that we are and can become issues from the intimacy of divine and human agency, a unity hidden in the mysterious depths of our being in the world. So we cannot untie our knots without God's help but neither does God untie them without our engagement. There is a constant interaction.

The result is genuine virtue. Where most Puritans believed virtue was imputed to us (God treated us as if we were good because we accepted Christ's sacrifice), and we could begin to live righteous lives while still sinners, Penington found in his experience that virtue became "natural" as we dwelt in the Life, issuing in the actual virtues of faith, hope, and love, as well as obedience, joy, and liberty. Hence he says: "the will which is created by God is mild and flexible, and easy to be led by the least child, in the line of goodness" (*Concerning Persecution*, II.195), and "the new understanding...is all in the natural" (*Where is the Wise?*, 1.415–16). Opening to the divine seed within, we partake of divine love, for the seed "makes it so natural to the children of God to love" ("Seed of God", IV.343). Penington's use of "natural" is confusing, since he often uses it negatively as identical with the life of "natural wisdom" or "the flesh". But here he is using it positively as the originally created way of willing, understanding, and loving, which through the divine presence at work in us we can recover. In this very different model from ordinary Christianity, virtue

Part II The Spirituality and Thought of Isaac Penington

for Penington is not a heroic exercise of the will, but the God-given capacity to accomplish hard things through a flexibility and responsiveness of spirit.

Living virtuously in the Life is wisdom. Penington defines wisdom as a life daily made fresh by feeling and following the invisible divine life within as it leads into visible forms of virtuous existence. He distinguishes two kinds of wisdom. Wisdom of the veiled self (what he calls "natural," "fleshly," and "earthly" wisdom) bends all things towards satisfying natural understanding, judging and grasping after everything in ego-centred terms, and attempting to retain what is acquired through fixing it in a form. Heavenly or divinely stirred wisdom is flexible, gentle, and patient as it is born daily from the womb of the Spirit. Each has its own way of judging and its own fear. As we have seen, Penington says that we should not judge and fear as the world does but find a hiding place in God's fear ("To Fds of Both Chalfonts", see pp. 145–46, II.498–99), and the end of government is to bring people into the fear of God (*Some Few Qrs...Cavaliers*, II.87, see pp. 172–73). He takes this fear from Hebraic Wisdom: "The fear of the Lord is the beginning of wisdom" (Prov 9:10). The world's fear is terror caused by dominating power or anxiety about protecting the veiled self. Wisdom's fear is awe and reverence inspired by ultimate mystery and transformative love. Judgment is then made not by natural understanding but from the life: "let the life itself be judge" (*Babylon the Great*, I.187).

Penington's interest in wisdom comes from the Bible. This interest anticipates present-day New Testament studies' view of the church's earliest understanding of Jesus, not as Son of God and saviour, but in terms of Hebraic Wisdom as the child and prophet of Sophia, who, as Wisdom, is the feminine personification of God (see Prov 8–9 and Elisabeth Schussler Fiorenza, *Jesus: Miriam's Child, Sophia's Prophet*). Like wisdom in the Hebrew Bible, Gospels, and Paul's letters, wisdom as Penington uses it refers to the individual life of virtue but also to that wisdom by which government should organise political life and the wisdom of God's order in all of creation. In freedom by grace we become virtuous and dwell in wisdom – personal, political, and cosmic (or "natural").

"Short Catechism", in *The Scattered Sheep Sought After* (1659)

I.123   Q. But can I do any thing toward my own salvation?
A. Of thyself thou canst not: but in the power of him that worketh both to will and to do, thou mayst do a little at first: and as that power grows in thee, thou wilt be able to will more, and to do more, even until nothing become too hard for thee. ... thou hast done nothing; but the eternal virtue, life, and power, hath wrought all in thee.

Babylon the Great Described (1659)

I.187   ... When the invisible life is felt and known, do not disdain to follow it into whatever visible thing it leads. Let not thy wisdom be judge what the life will lead into, or what the life is to be followed in; but let the life itself be judge: and let the child, which is born of the life, follow it singly.

Where is the Wise? Where is the Scribe? (1660)

I.415–16   To come yet closer. There is in every man, not thoroughly sanctified, that wisdom which is not of God; that wisdom from which God hides his precious truths; which wisdom lies ready to catch every discovery and revelation of truth to him, that it might improve it, and grow rich and wise by it. Now this wisdom cannot attain to the knowledge of any of the things of God: neither can this wisdom keep the true knowledge; but whatever this wisdom catcheth, it presently corrupts. The true wisdom, the true light, the true knowledge of Christ, is like the manna in the wilderness; it daily comes down from heaven, and must daily be gathered fresh [Ex 16:4]. ... the new understanding ... given by him that is true, 1 John 5:20, which new-forms and preserves, and is all in the natural. Sink out of the earthly part, and ... say within thyself, and concerning thyself, Where is the wise [1 Cor 1:20]?

The wise part, the knowing part, the reaching part in every man, will be putting forth its hand to gather of the tree of life; but what hath it ever been able to gather? ... notions ...; but who is able to come near the life, to touch the power, the truth, the everlasting spring, or any stream or drop of water that issues from it? And he who hath a true touch or taste thereof given him, can his wisdom add to it? Nay, can he so much as retain it?

Consideration of a Position Concerning the Book of Common Prayer (1660)

II.119   ... "But wisdom" in all ages "is justified by her children" [Lk 7:35], and of none else. He that is born of the wisdom, he can discern the womb, and own the fruit and branchings forth thereof under the mean, dark veil, whereby it hides itself from all the fleshly-wise of every age. "The kingdom of God cometh not by observation" [Lk 17:20]; the wisest Scribes and Pharisees could not know it by all the observations which they could gather out of Moses' and the prophets' writings; nor can any now know it by any observations which they can gather out of the apostles' writings; but by being born of that Spirit whereof they were born, and by being formed in that womb wherein they were formed, by this means alone is the thing come to be known which they knew.

Concerning Persecution (1661)

II.195   ... Stubbornness, or such a kind of stiffness and resolvedness, ariseth from the strength and corruption of the natural will and earthly wisdom. The wisdom which is from above is gentle, easy to be entreated; and the will which is created by God is mild and flexible, and easy to be led by the least child, in the line of goodness. And I can truly say this, that I never in my whole course and conversation (who have long been a spectator and uninterested person, both as relating to the civil state and the various professions of religion, till the power of truth and presence of God appearing in this people drew my heart after them), yea, I cannot but say, in the singleness of my heart, I never met with a more mild, gentle, flexible-spirited people. And he that can reach the ground of the thing, cannot but see it to be thus; for he that is daily exercised in denying his will and wisdom; he on whose back the Lord lays the cross, and crucifies him every day, his self-will and self-wisdom, with all the conceitedness and stiffness which arise therefrom, must needs be much broken in him.

To All Such as Complain that They Want Power (1661)

II.287–88 ... Of himself he cannot: but being touched, being quickened by the eternal power, being turned by a secret virtue and stirring of the life in his heart, then he can turn towards that which turneth him. Being drawn by the life, by the power; he can follow after the life, and after the power. Finding the sweetness of the living vine, and his soul made alive by the sap of the vine, his heart can now cleave to, and abide in, the vine, and bring forth the fruit of the living faith and obedience to the husbandman, who daily dresseth the heart, that waiteth in the living principle for further life from the fountain, that it may bring forth the fruits of life more and more.

II.293 ... The fear is the dwelling of the upright heart, and the love is within the fear. He that distrusts himself, feels his own nothingness, finds no power to do any thing God requireth, and yet also fears to stay behind the light of God's Spirit, in any thing it requires, and so finds a putting on forwards in the faith; in him the power delights to appear. He that would feel strength before-hand, and act in the sense of that strength, from him the power withdraws; but he that is weak, and hath no strength, but still as it freely drops into him from moment to moment, this is the vessel the power chooseth to manifest itself to, and to be continually appearing in. This is the new covenant, "I will put my fear in their hearts" [Jer 32:40]. And where the fear of the new covenant is found, so much life, power, and eternal virtue, as is necessary for the present state of that heart, cannot be far off.

Some of the Mysteries of God's Kingdom Glanced At (1663)

II.338, *Quest.* 1. What is faith?
Ans. It is a belief in the appearances of the Lord to the soul, and a cleaving to, and drinking in of, their virtue.

II.340   *Quest.* 1. What is hope?
Ans. The expectation of somewhat from the Lord, in the season of his good-will. The expectation of the crown of life at last; the expectation of deliverance from snares and temptations at present; the expectation of receiving his promises of the divine nature, or of any mercy or blessing which he hath given to pray for.

II.341
Qfp §
26.30

Quest. 1. What is love?
Ans. What shall I say of it, or how shall I in words express its nature! It is the sweetness of life. ... It fulfils the law, it fulfils the gospel; it wraps up all in one, and brings forth all in the oneness. It excludes all evil out of the heart, it perfects all good in the heart. A touch of love doth this in measure; perfect love doth this in fullness.

II.342   O! how sweet is love! how pleasant is its nature! how takingly doth it behave itself in every condition, upon every occasion, to every person, and about every thing! How tenderly, how readily, doth it help and serve the meanest! How patiently, how meekly, doth it bear all things, either from God or man, how unexpectedly soever they come, or how hard soever they seem! How doth it believe, how doth it hope, how doth it excuse, how doth it cover even that which seemeth not to be excusable, and not fit to be covered! How kind is it even in its interpretations and charges concerning miscarriages! It never overchargeth, it never grates upon the spirit of him whom it reprehends; it never hardens, it never provokes; but carrieth a meltingness and power of conviction with it. This is the nature of God.

II.342–43   *Quest.* What is obedience?
Ans. It is the subjection of the soul to the law of the Spirit; which subjection floweth from, and is strengthened by, love. To wait to know the mind of God, and perform his will in every thing, through the virtue of the principle of life revealed within, this is the obedience of faith. This is the obedience of the seed, conveyed into the creature by

the seed, and it is made partaker of the seed. He is the son who naturally doth the will.

II.344 Joy is the gladness of the heart in God, chiefly springing from the refreshings and presence of his life, which carries through and over all, even the greatest trials and tribulations. When the poor, panting, weary soul, which hath longed after God, and long felt the bitterness and misery of its separation, begins to feel his love, and its union with him, in his letting of it forth into the heart, and its assurance of his goodness, righteousness, power, wisdom, and salvation, oh, how is it filled with joy and delight in the earnest of its portion!

II.345 Liberty is the enlargedness of the heart in the Spirit of the Lord, wherein it hath scope in all that is good, and is shut out of all that is evil. The Spirit of the Lord is free, and maketh free. The earthly spirit is in bondage with her children; but they which are begotten of the Lord, and wrapped up in his Spirit, find the power and freedom of the new life therein, and are thereby perfectly out of the reach of that, which (let into the mind) hath power to captivate and enthral. Therefore it is not all manner of scope and latitude, wherein the true liberty consisteth; but in the scope and latitude proper to its nature.

"To Friends of Both the Chalfonts" (1667)
II.498–99 Let us then not look out like the world, or judge or fear according to the appearance of things, after the manner of the world; but let us sanctify the Lord of hosts in our hearts, and let him be our fear and dread; and he shall be an hiding place unto us in the storms, and in the tempests, which are coming thick upon the earth.

To the Jews Natural and to the Jews Spiritual (1677)
III.389 ... Ye desire outward liberty, and the enjoyment of your outward rights; would ye not be free inwardly? Free from the base, earthly, selfish nature and spirit, which man, fallen from God, and the glory wherein he created him, is

degenerated into? O! is not the power of God, and life of Christ, able to restore man to this? He that created man at first so glorious, in his own image, is he not able to create him anew?

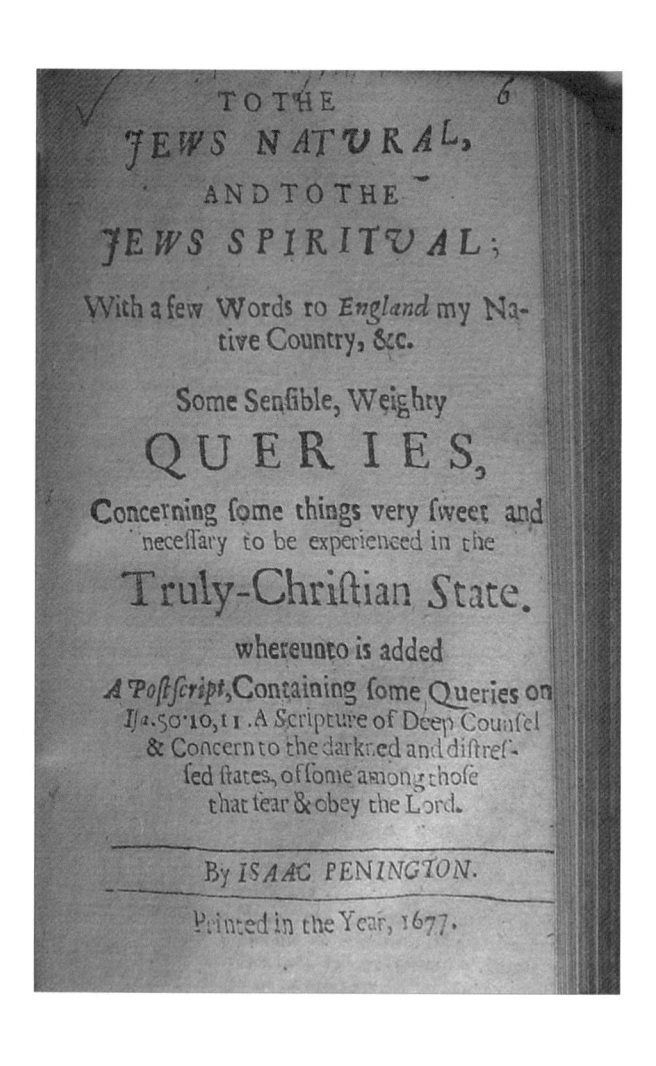

TO THE
JEWS NATURAL,
AND TO THE
JEWS SPIRITUAL;

With a few Words to *England* my Native Country, &c.

Some Sensible, Weighty
QUERIES,
Concerning some things very sweet and necessary to be experienced in the
Truly-Christian State.

whereunto is added

A *Postscript*, Containing some Queries on *Isa.* 50:10,11. A Scripture of Deep Counsel & Concern to the darkned and distressed states, of some among those that fear & obey the Lord.

By ISAAC PENINGTON.

Printed in the Year, 1677.

CHAPTER 8

Prayer and Worship

From the way in which Penington defines prayer we can see how inseparable prayer is from the knowing and doing of the previous two chapters. While prayer is often thought in western traditions to be a certain use of words, for Penington prayer is a way of being, which will from time to time manifest in words. He takes seriously Paul's injunction to pray without ceasing (1 Thes 5:17). This obviously is impossible if prayer is simply speaking. Penington defines prayer not as words but as breathing. Prayer is "the breath of the living child to the Father of life, in that Spirit which quickened it" (*Some of the Mysteries*, II.345). True prayer is God's breath breathing through us. Prayer is unceasing when we have learned a moment by moment attentiveness to the presence of divine breath – spirit – in us (see chapter 3, pp. 147–150).

Addressing prayer to God does not make it authentic. What makes it genuine is if it "is from and in the spirit" (*Babylon the Great*, I.164). The "living child" is the person filled with the Spirit, hence newly birthed in the life: "The birth of the true child is the only true prayer; and he prays only in the moving and in the leading of that Spirit that begat him: and this is a prayer according to the will, in the life, and from the power" (*Axe Laid to the Root*, I.259). What this means is that prayer is an activity of inwardness. Beneath words, prayer is dwelling in the life and being filled with its motions. Prayer is "nothing of man's invention" (*Concerning the Worship*, I.212), but is the teaching of the Spirit "which giveth it the right sense of its wants, and suitable cries proportionable to its state, in the proper season . . ."

(*Some of the Mysteries*, II.345). Prayer is the condition of living with and in the Spirit, unveiling the veiled self to divine presence and leadings. Such a life of indwelling spirit is dynamic, as the Spirit courses through us, stirring each of us in ways fitting to our individual lives and desires – what the Spirit wants through our wants.

What is uttered from these breathings may be words drenched in life, weighted with the depth of Spirit, or may be inarticulate groanings. Taking Paul seriously on prayer, Penington quotes him: "We know not what to pray for as we ought; but the Spirit maketh intercession for us with groanings which cannot be uttered" (Rom 8:26). Hence "the very groanings that come from God's Spirit, from his breathing and work upon the heart, are right prayers in God's sight" (*Naked Truth*, III.293). What is important in prayer is neither the words nor the sounds uttered but that they come from and with divine breathing. Hence "praying in the Name of Christ" is worthless if it comes not from the Spirit's immediate inspiration. It is a mistake to think "that praying in the Name of Christ consists in using some outward words." Rather "the name...is living" ("To My Friends at Horton and Thereabouts", II.469–70). "Living" here means to be "in the motion of the Spirit" (II.470). When moved by the breath of God, prayer is in and from the Spirit and therefore "in the name of Christ" regardless of what words are used. I remember being at a Quaker meeting for marriage where a Protestant member of the wedding party deplored the absence of the couple being married in the name of Christ; yet Christ's presence – though not the word – was palpable.

Prayer is both individual and corporate. In a long extract below Penington describes the nature of silent meeting for worship. Assembling together for worship is very important, for beyond what individual meditation offers, we, like coals from a fire, warm one another when together. Silence is the silencing of the flesh (our normal self-preoccupied understanding and will). As we settle into silence, we turn to the light. The veil covering the self is removed as we are filled with life and drawn into a larger felt whole, which strengthens, invigorates, refreshes. If so led, we are to speak; if not, then we are to remain silent. In such silence we may know the nourishing of the Spirit more immediately than when speaking occurs. We may discover many different degrees of participation in the life. Some may know temptations and get caught up in thoughts from the surface of our lives. When this experience of inner darkness is endured with a desire to grow towards the light, the time spent in worship is not futile. Others may go deep, waiting in silence, until they are led to rise to speak (in a metaphor John Woolman will use again in the eighteenth century) as a trumpet. Whether entirely silent or issuing in speaking, whether individual or communal, prayer is to take us down into the sacred depths of being where in awe (Wisdom's "fear"; Prov 9:10) we feel the breath or streams of divine life coursing through us – stirring, filling, directing us, sometimes devastating us and sometimes evoking joy and a sense of divine glory that binds us together with one another and the whole of being in divine love.

Like Howard Brinton and Thomas Kelly in the twentieth century, Penington depicts a life lived on two levels simultaneously. We engage outward issues even as we pray continuously by being open to the divine breath filling us in every moment. While Penington presumably succeeded at this in his living, there are moments when the breath is blocked. At the end of the last extract below, Penington is caught up in exclusiveness, no doubt weary from persecution. He not merely declares the worship Friends have been called to, but denies the possibility to others of meeting the transforming divine presence in their form of worship. Even as we aspire to be the breath of God, we know many moments in which our breathing seizes up.

Some of the Mysteries of God's Kingdom Glanced At (1663)

II.345   Prayer is the breath of the living child to the Father of life, in that Spirit which quickened it, which giveth it the right sense of its wants, and suitable cries proportionable to its state, in the proper season thereof. So that mark: prayer is wholly out of the will of the creature, wholly out of the time of the creature, wholly out of the power of the creature, in the Spirit of the Father, who is the fountain of life, and giveth forth breathings of life to his child at his pleasure.

"To My Friends at Horton and Thereabouts" (1665)

II.469–70, ... professors grieviously mistake ... about praying in
JP 1.149   the Name of Christ in which he that asketh receiveth, and out of which there is no right asking of the Father. They think that praying in the Name of Christ consists in using

some outward words, as do this for thy Son's sake, or we beg of thee in Christ's name; whereas that in the heart which knoweth not the Father, may use such words; and that which is taught of the Father to pray, and prayeth in the Son, may not be led to use those words. The name, wherein the asking and acceptance is, is living; and he that prayeth in the motion of the Spirit, and in the power and virtue of the son's life, he prayeth in the Name, and his voice is owned of the Father, and not the other, who hath learned to use those words of the sons name (or for his sake) in his own will, time, and spirit.

"To Widow Hemmings" (28 Ninth Month [Nov] 1670)

III.451–52 ...we are to pray continually – nor in praying in a formal way without life, without God's Spirit – who gives us to pray, and who makes intercession – can there be any peace within... But, that it is manifest prayer is not in the time, will or power of the creature that is manifest, for it is a gift of God, and the ability lodges in his Spirit; it is not ours, but as it is given of his Spirit which therefore is to be waited upon, when it will move and breathe in us. ... For there is no true sense of one's condition or one's wants, but from the Spirit of the Lord. ... And O that every one, that hath any true sense of God, might wait on him, to savour this little which ariseth from God, from [amidst] the multitude of his thoughts, words, and desires which are from another root.

"A Further Testimony to Truth Revived out of the Ruins of the Apostasy" (1680 pub.)

IV.47–49 A brief Account concerning Silent Meetings; the nature, use, intent, and benefit of them.

This is a great mystery, hid from the eye of man, who is run from the inward life into outward observations. He cannot see either that this is required by the Lord of his people, or any edification therein, or benefit thereby; but to the mind that is drawn inward the thing is plain; and the building up hereby in the life of God, and fellowship one with another therein, is sweetly felt; and precious refreshment from the presence of the Lord received by them, who singly herein wait upon him according to the leadings and requirings of his Holy Spirit. Now, to open the thing a little to the upright-hearted, if the Lord please.

After the mind is in some measure turned to the Lord, his quickenings felt, his seed beginning to arise and spring up in the heart, then the flesh is to be silent before him, and the soul to wait upon him (and for his further appearings) in that measure of life which is already revealed. Now, this is a great thing to know flesh silenced, to feel the reasoning thoughts and discourses of the fleshly mind stilled, and the wisdom, light, and guidance of God's Spirit waited for. For man is to come into the poverty of self, into the abasedness, into the nothingness, into the silence of his spirit before the Lord; into the putting off of all his knowledge, wisdom, understanding, abilities, all that he is, hath done, or can do, out of this measure of life, into which he is to travel, that he may be clothed and filled with the nature, Spirit, and power of the Lord.

Now, in this measure of life which is of Christ, and in which Christ is, and appears to the soul, there is the power of life and death; power to kill to the flesh, and power to quicken to God; power to cause the soul to cease from its own workings, and power to work in and for the soul what God requires, and what is acceptable in his sight. And in this God is to be waited upon and worshipped continually, both in private and in public, according as his Spirit draws and teaches.

For the Lord requireth of his people not only to worship him apart, but to meet together to worship him, in the seasons, and according to the drawings, of his Spirit: and they that are taught of him, dare not forsake the assembling of themselves together, as the manner of some is; but watch against the temptations and snares, which the enemy lays to deceive them therefrom, and to disturb their sense by, that they might not feel the drawings of the Father thereunto.

And this is the manner of their worship. They are to wait upon the Lord, to meet in the silence of flesh, and to watch for the stirrings of his life, and the breakings forth of his power amongst them. And in the breakings forth of that power they may pray, speak, exhort, rebuke, sing, or mourn, etc. according as the Spirit teaches, requires, and gives utterance. But if the Spirit do not require to speak, and give to utter, then every one is to sit still in his place (in his heavenly place I mean), feeling his own measure, feeding thereupon, receiving therefrom, into his spirit, what the Lord giveth. Now, in this is edifying, pure edifying, precious edifying; his soul who thus waits, is hereby particularly edified by the Spirit of the Lord at every meeting. And then also there is the life of the whole felt in every vessel that is turned to its measure: insomuch as the warmth of life in each vessel doth not only warm the particular, but they are like a heap of fresh and living coals, warming one another, insomuch as a great strength, freshness, and vigor of life flows into all. And if any be burthened, tempted, buffeted by Satan, bowed down, overborne, languishing, afflicted, distressed, etc., the estate of such is felt in Spirit, and secret cries, or open (as the Lord pleaseth), ascend up to the Lord for them, and they many times find ease and relief, in a few words spoken, or without words, if it be the season of their help and relief with the Lord.

For absolutely silent meetings, wherein there is a resolution not to speak, we know not; but we wait on the Lord, either to feel him in words, or in silence of spirit without words, as he pleaseth. And that which we aim at, and are instructed to by the Spirit of the Lord as to silent meetings, is that the flesh in every one be kept silent, and that there be no building up, but in the Spirit and power of the Lord.

Now, there are several states of people: some feel little of the Lord's presence; but feel temptations and thoughts, with many wanderings and rovings of mind. These are not yet acquainted with the power, or at least know not its dominion, but rather feel dominion of the evil over the good in them. And this is a sore travelling and mournful state, and meetings to such as these (many times) may seem to themselves rather for the worse than for the better. Yet even these, turning, as much as may be, from such things, and cleaving, or at least in truth of heart desiring to cleave, to that which disliketh or witnesseth against them, have acceptance with the Lord herein: and continuing to wait in this trouble and distress (keeping close to meetings, in fear and subjection to the Lord who requireth it, though with little appearing benefit), do reap a hidden benefit at present, and shall reap a more clear and manifest benefit afterwards, as the Lord wasteth and weareth out that in them, wherein the darkness hath its strength. Now, to evidence that the Lord doth require these silent meetings, or meetings after this manner silent, it may thus appear.

God is to be worshipped in spirit, in his own power and life, and this is at his own disposal. His church is a gathering in the Spirit. If any man speak there, he must speak as the oracle of God, as the vessel out of which God speaks; as the trumpet out of which he gives the sound. Therefore there is to be a waiting in silence till the Spirit of the Lord move to speak, and also give words to speak. For a man is not to speak his own words, or in his own wisdom or time; but the Spirit's words, in the Spirit's wisdom and time, which is when he moves and gives to speak. And seeing the Spirit inwardly nourisheth, when he giveth not to speak words, the inward sense and nourishment is to be waited for, and received as it was given when there are no words. Yea, the ministry of the Spirit and life is more close and immediate when without words, than when with words, as has been often felt, and is faithfully testified by many witnesses. Eye hath not seen, nor ear heard, neither hath entered into the heart of man how and what things God reveals to his children by his Spirit [1 Cor 2:9–10], when they wait upon him in his pure fear, and worship and converse with him in spirit; for then the fountain of the great deep is unsealed, and the everlasting springs surely give up the pure and living water.

"Life and Immortality" (1671)

IV.161   XXIX *A brief Account of the Ground of our Worship, and how it cometh to pass that we cannot conform to the spirit of this world, or to the wills of men therein, but only to the Spirit and Will of our God.*

We fear God, who made heaven and earth, whose power is over all, who hath caused the light of his Holy Spirit to shine in our hearts, thereby teaching us how to worship him acceptably in Spirit and truth; which worship he hath required of us, and that we meet together so to do in those assemblies, which he hath gathered by his power, and ordereth by his Spirit, either in silence or sound of words, according to his pleasure.

IV.162   Besides, we have found God's presence with us, and blessing upon us, in this way of worship; and our hearts greatly melted and warmed therein, and power given us over our passions and corruptions inwardly, and to order our lives and conversations holily, righteously, and innocently outwardly: which presence of God, and holy power over sin and vanity, affections and lusts, we would not lose for ten thousand worlds. And what an unjust and unthankful thing were it in us to turn from this way of worship which God hath called us to, where we have met with these things, to that way of worship where we did not meet with these things, and where others do not, nor can, meet with them!

CHAPTER 9

Religion, Language, and the Self

The word "religion" may be problematic for modern readers today. Some refuse to call themselves religious because they take it to mean acceptance of certain beliefs, belonging to an institutional group, engaging in particular ritual practices, or ascribing to morality handed down through religious tradition. Often such people will call themselves "spiritual" because they are serious about growth in their inward life. While agreeing with this sentiment, and often using "spiritual" as synonym for "true religion", Penington does not oppose religious to spiritual. Religion for him comprehends both outward and inward forms, whether they are expressions of the life- or of the death-dealing spirit. Religion as such is neither positive nor negative, but a term that encompasses all faith and practice. Like others in his time, Penington uses "religion" to speak not only of Christian groups but of others, such as Jews, Muslims, and Native Americans.

Authentic religion is not, however, identified with any outward or inward forms, but is a way of life that expresses itself through such forms. It is a pattern of living that is grounded in and grows from the Life. In its ordinary meaning people are religious if someone espouses certain beliefs, belongs to a group, participates in rituals, endorses certain morals – all things that can be explicitly identified. For Penington religion is situated in a level of consciousness deeper than what can so easily be named. Beneath understanding and will is the level of feeling. Penington locates religion in feeling, a dimension in the self of experience that is noticeable but also extends beneath the conscious threshold of what can be told or seen. Sometimes we can name our feelings. Sometimes we have difficulty doing so. Sometimes we are not even aware of what we are feeling.

In autobiographical anecdotes about his pre-Quaker years, Penington talks about feeling God stirring life in him but being unable to interpret what was happening. One example:

> The Lord hath been kind to me in breaking of me in my religion, and in visiting me with sweet and precious light from his own spirit; but I knew it not. I felt, and could not but acknowledge, a power upon me, and might have known what it was by its purifying of my heart, and begetting me into the image of God; but I confined it to appear in a way of demonstration to my reason and earthly wisdom. ... (*Way of Life*, 1.17)

Rather than knowing or doing, religion for Penington is to feel the divine life within, so as to be transformed into a pure vessel of life and to manifest outwardly, and to interpret truly, the divine life in all that we say and do.

As the feeling of the Life within, religion has its seat in the conscience. Religion and morality are inseparable, but neither is reducible to the other. Religion is conscience's depth. The divine life illuminates moral consciousness through which we judge right and wrong. The religious and moral aspects of self are functioning harmoniously if judgments of right and wrong are made by and in the Life. They are out of harmony if the veiled self seeks to determine things, ignoring feeling of the divine.

We behave differently depending on whether we act from our veiled self or the Life. To open within our conscience to the religious, to the inward light, is therefore to be changed in all our moral relations to others, world, and our own self. While many religious (or spiritual) people in the west see their morality flowing as a consequence from what they believe, Penington, in locating religion in feeling rather than in understanding or willing, defines religion in its very first stirrings as changing the self morally, as our existence shifts from natural understanding's domination to Spirit indwelling and leading. Hence he says that "true religion" is "a new creation" (*Some Obs ... Scripture*, II.305).

Whereas understanding and willing can be very definite, locating religion in feeling plunges us into mystery. Because it is a mystery,

Penington stresses waiting. Locating true religion in feeling and a changed life confronts us with mystery, in which we must wait for clarity to emerge from this "tacit dimension" (as Michael Polanyi has named it in *The Tacit Dimension*; see ch. 1). Reason and will are not eliminated but operate out of what one is sensing. Later, Quakers emphasised the distinction between human capacity and divinely informed will and understanding to the point that some meetings for worship could go for years with no one speaking in worship. Penington is not this pessimistic but he does stress not only the need for, but the possibility of, religious transparency.

Penington stresses not only mystery but purity. Purity is moral righteousness. But it is so by unimpeded opening and responding to the presence and leadings of the Life within, not by conforming to some objective standard nor by striving for some unrealised goal. Purity is both religious and moral at the same time, rather than being moral behaviour that follows from right belief or good goals, because it is openness to mystery that exceeds our conceptual grasp and moves us in unanticipated ways to do and to be. Rather than pursuing his own will and understanding, Penington wants to wait upon divine creativity and revelation to arise within and become expressed through our outward living.

Penington contrasts two types, or two seeds, of religion: one he names "true" (as described above), and the other "profane" (*Concerning Persecution*, II.188–89); *in* the Life and Spirit or *out* of them; dwelling in mystery or devoted to forms; centred in heart's core or focused on doctrinal belief; creativity or conformity; power that transforms and fulfills or power that dominates and constricts; knowing from experiencing divine presence or knowing from intellectual construction; wisdom that makes us like God or wisdom that makes us like our veiled self. True religion in its sum and substance is the way of love. From dwelling in the life and its light, love flows forth. When we are grounded in the mystery of the life rather than fixated on forms of belief or practice, we are capable of transcending conflicts between religions and the persecuting spirit, for it is the different forms, held too tightly, that divide us: "do but come into the power of that religion which ye yourselves profess, not so much minding the outward form (for it is not of so much value), and ye shall find that we shall agree in religion sooner than ye are aware." Then we can love one another, however different we are, in the "life and power which was before all forms and ways of religion" (*Three Queries*, II.318, 319). To dwell in the life, light, and love of true religion is to become stewards of mystery treasured in earthen vessels.

If religion is centred in feeling and immersed in mystery, it requires a special kind of language. Frustrating as Penington's language is because of slipperiness, vagueness, repetitiveness, and frequent metaphors, I find his insights into how words function profound and very relevant to the contemporary current discussion on the nature of language. We have seen that the self for Penington has levels of awareness ranging from explicit to tacit: understanding and will are explicit, feeling can be explicit but varies from easy to name, through noticeable but difficult to conceive, to an unconscious sense. The words we speak relate to these different levels of awareness from explicit ideas, through feeling and sensing, to being affected unconsciously. Words can present ideas and use them to refer to things. Words can express or evoke feelings. Words can make present to our conscious awareness something of what we are experiencing tacitly. And words can transform our whole way of seeing and relating to things, and thus our way of being in the world, by certain evocations of feeling and drawings from the unconscious.

The realities we relate to through words on these different levels are different. Our explicit ideas name something, setting boundaries around it that distinguish it from other things. These are things, whether mental things, like the idea of freedom or beauty, or physical things, like a tree or tool. Feelings are not things nor ideas but experiences. Even though not tangible, they are real: they have a force that affects us and are a tangle of connections with other people, our own past and future, and other phenomena – cultural and natural – which we may have difficulty discovering. Our unconscious experiences are not objects; they cannot be measured, quantified, or identified directly. Freud, Jung, and others have defined psychological processes and symbolic meanings in the unconscious, but it is fundamentally a place of mystery, of that which is unknown, with aspects knowable only with great effort or inherently unknowable. While mystery is more evident at this level, mystery is also experienced at the level of feeling and idea. Feelings connect us to mystery and are themselves mysterious. While the ideas of freedom, Darwinian evolution, or the light spectrum – as ideas – attempt to define and explain so as to leave no mystery, the phenomena they refer to have a dimension of mystery like that in our psychological depths.

In the way Penington talks about language and uses religious language, he recognises that words are more than their content, more than their explicit ideas. In this he anticipates the difficult philosophical thought of several twentieth-century thinkers, such as Ludwig Wittgenstein (see *Philosophical Investigations*) and Maurice Merleau-Ponty (see *Phenomenology of Perception*). In speaking of religious language he distinguishes content from the divine reality about which he is speaking: "to distinguish the thing itself from the garment wherewith it was clothed" (*Professors*, III.49). The "garment" is the explicit content. The "thing itself" is not a thing, an object. It is, as we have seen Part II, ch. 6), the "life and power which was before all forms" (*Three Queries*, II.319) – the divine mystery. Religious words, for him, aim to take us beneath ideas and objects to which they refer, into that mystery: "the end of words is to bring men to the knowledge of things, beyond what words can utter" ("To___", III.458). If God, the "thing itself", is known beyond words, then this "knowing" is not through ideas; it is experiential, through feeling and a tacit knowing in our unconscious of which we are unaware explicitly: "Indeed there is so much wrapped up in it, as the heart of man cannot conceive, much less the tongue utter; yet somewhat have I felt, and somewhat is upon my heart, to say" ("Seed of God", IV.341). God is "the unlimited One" (*Reply to Queries*, IV.191) who cannot be limited by word and idea, yet this boundless reality can be felt and, despite the inadequacy of words, can in some way be expressed.

How can one speak truly of the unutterable, unlimited One? Religious language for Penington is doing something very different from defining a conceivable thing. It is not trying to identify God as an Object nor to define that Object's nature. Rather it is trying to bring us to experience God's mysterious reality. While God is beyond our conceiving – including beyond "One," an idea he seldom uses – we feel "somewhat" of divine reality and upon reflection realise that God has been stirring the life in our unconscious lives unnoticed by us. Penington says that we are all connected with God; the light is present in all. This feeling of mystery is our connection with divinity rising into awareness. To speak truly of God, then, we need words that evoke this feeling, this experiencing, of divinity – now, as we talk of God. This is why Friends eliminated a set liturgy and prepared sermon: they wanted the words – spoken and heard in their meetings for worship, and in their religious talking and writing – to come from the present experience of this creative mystery as it was felt "somewhat" and laid upon their hearts to say "somewhat".

What kind of words can elicit such feelings? What kind of language is it that Penington speaks of when he says: "mind the words of his lips, which beget sense, and in that sense his life stirs, and in the stirrings of his life the drawings of the Father are felt" (*Of the Church*, III.158)? What kind of words will not "fix or stay upon words concerning the thing, but may sink in spirit into the feeling of the life itself" (*Some of the Mysteries*, II.343)? Words of reason stand over against their subject matter, detached, observing something at a distance, seeing it clearly and coolly. They move ideas around and identify things in our world but they do not awaken us to our connections – beyond being part of a category – and to mystery. Words that evoke feeling, that "sink" us into spirit, that draw out what is stirring in our unconscious life are meditative, poetic, metaphoric. Of such is the language of the Spirit that raises up the life: "to speak the word of life, requires the tongue of the learned in the language of God's Spirit" (*Concerning the Worship*, II.213).

This is why Penington uses so many metaphors (see discussion of metaphor in Introduction to Part II). While in his arguments he uses concepts to isolate and identify something he is talking about, and thus to transmit a clear idea of it, his more powerful writing for us stirs our affections. We know what he is talking about by having an experience of a reality that is hidden from our thinking, yet present in our being. Even his most complex theological writing attempts to clarify precisely in order to touch us in inwardness. Metaphors, I believe, do this most effectively, setting connections vibrating so they become visible. They bring into our awareness several relations simultaneously that enable integrating them into new patterns of living.

What does this mean? It means to experience joy and peace and aliveness rather than just talking about them as fruits of the Spirit: "the Lord so teacheth him things, as words cannot utter; that is, he so knoweth the peace of God, the joy of his Spirit, the life and power of the Lord" (*Question to the Professors*, III.27). The metaphor "to sink in spirit" (*Some of the Mysteries*, II.343) entices us to entrust ourselves to the unknown depths within our selves and to find a comfort and sustenance there. The metaphors of "new creature" (II.305), "leavening the heart with the savour of life," "the light of life spring[s] in the love" (*Weighty Qn... to the King*, II.325), and "a mysterious womb that conceives and brings forth... a mysterious birth" ("Reply [Concerning... New Covenant]", IV.396) – all bespeak and elicit a transformed self and sense of wholeness. Before our pattern was through reason and will to control situations for the good as we perceived it, but now we wait for a creative response to rise in us, not from the surface self but from the unknowable depths, and feel a love and fearlessness at work in us beyond our doing and imagining. The self that rigidly applied a rational plan is now "flexible" (*Concerning Persecution*, II.195) in response as it comes "to know the times and seasons of the spirit" (*Concerning the Worship*, II.213).

When people argue about the true nature of God and the religious life, it matters for Penington whether they speak from this changed self, that is irradiated by its depths, or speak out of the veiled self, for what seems according to its values to be rational. For Penington unless you are in this opened state where you are feeling the divine presence, then your words about God are airy notions referring to ideas but not manifesting the very reality of which they intend to speak. While he argues frequently, I find his metaphorical evocativeness – within and outside his arguments – a more communicative way of talking that does not oppose and defend, but describes one's own experience and elicits a deeper response from others. We can always learn more about what it is we are experiencing, both by hearing others and trying to say what it is for ourselves. The language of the spirit then expresses what our deep feelings of the life are, and the deeper stirrings of which we are only beginning to become aware: "The uttering of the words is but the declaration of what the light in the heart hath done before" (*Scattered Sheep*, I.110).

While Penington nowhere explores the nature of the self in a concerted way, the picture that emerges from his various remarks is of a self that has explicit and tacit levels of awareness, that knows on the experiential basis of feeling and sensing rather than reason or belief cut off from our experience, and that is free to interact with the divine presence within so as to achieve virtue and fullness of being. While the idea of "the self" is problematic today (see Hans Bertens, *Literary Theory: The Basics*, 136–37; Christopher Butler, *Postmodernism: A Very Short Introduction*; Jonathan Culler, *Literary Theory: A Very Short Introduction*, 50–56, 108–120), Penington would agree with its critics who reject the idea of a self as a mental reasoning consciousness or an objective thing. The self is neither a subject nor an object, the two options Descartes inscribed in the beginning of the modern age. Nevertheless, it is still "real" because there is a third option. The self is a mystery – the mystery that we are, in simply being ourselves as we relate, one way or another, to our context and the mystery of God.

The Scattered Sheep Sought After (1659)

I.133 Let thy religion be to feel the pure principle of life in the pure vessel of life; for the eye must be pure that sees the life, and the heart that receives it. And faith is a pure mystery, and it is only held in a pure conscience. Know that in thee that purifies thee, and then thou knowest Christ, and the Father, and the Spirit and as that lives and grows up in thee, so shalt thou know their dwelling-place, and partake of their life and fullness.

Babylon the Great Described (1659)

I.147 ... ye must look at home, and read within; and there having found the thing, and seen it in the true light, ye will be able to see it certainly abroad also. Now do not go about to distinguish these things in the notion of the understanding; but come to feel the life, to unite with the life, and the eye will open which can see into the nature of things, and will behold all in its season; for that eye which is so eager to see, shall never see these things; but that eye alone which waits in stillness and quietness on the pleasure and good-will of the opener.

The Jew Outward Being a Glass for the Professors of this Age (1659)

I.217 ... we can only pray in the Spirit; sing in the Spirit; wait in the Spirit; speak in the Spirit (as that gives utterance [Acts 2:4]), and not of ourselves, or when we will; but as we see life, strength, and power from on high, leading and assisting us. And our religion consists neither in willing nor running, but in waiting on the Spirit and power of the Lord, to work all in us and for us.

9. Religion, Language, and the Self

The Axe Laid to the Root of the Old Corrupt Tree (1659)

1.227–228   . . . when they [Christians not "in the life" from Corinthians to the present] had overcome them that had the living testimony of Jesus, and the true power and presence of the Spirit among them, then they set up their own dead form, making a cry all over the nations of the earth: "Revelation is ceased! there is no looking now for such an infallible Spirit, and such immediate teachings as the Christians had in the apostles' days, who had the anointing to teach them all things;" but they pointed men to traditions, to the church, as they called it (which title the whore hath engrossed since the days of the apostles), or to searchings of the scripture, and reading expositions upon it, and bodies of divinity, formed by the understanding-part in man to instruct the understanding-part. Thus the whole course of religion, and of the knowledge of God, came to be out of that Spirit and life wherein it first came forth (and wherein it first stood), and consisted in doctrines of men, and a form of worship and knowledge which the wisdom of man had framed, in an imitation of that which formerly stood in the life.

1.232–33   . . . The ground wherein men's religion grows (even the most zealous) is bad; even the same ground wherein the Pharisees' religion stood and grew; and it hath brought forth such a kind of fruit; namely, such a kind of conformity to the letter as theirs was; which stands in the understanding and will of man, rearing up a pleasant building there, but keeps from the life, and from building in it. But the true religion stands in receiving a principle of life; which, by its growth, forms a vessel for itself; and all the former part, wherein sin on the one hand, or self-righteousness on the other hand, stood and grew, passeth away.

An Examination of the Grounds or Causes which are said to Induce the Court of Boston . . . (1660)

1.378–79   . . . For it is not so much speaking true things that doth good, as speaking them from the pure, and conveying them to the pure: for the life runs along from the vessel

221

Part II The Spirituality and Thought of Isaac Penington

of life in one, into the vessel of life in another; and the words, though ever so true, cannot convey life to another, but as the living vessel opens in the one, and is opened in the other.

1.383–384 …the main thing in religion is to keep the conscience pure to the Lord, to know the guide, to follow the guide, to receive from him the light whereby I am to walk; and not to take things for truths because others see them to be truths; but to wait till the Spirit make them manifest to me; nor to run into worships, duties, performances, or practices, because others are led thither; but to wait till the Spirit lead me thither.

The Consideration of a Position Concerning the Book of Common Prayer (1660)

II.128 …religion is not such an outward form of doctrine, or worship of any sort,…but it consists in Spirit, in power, in virtue, in life: not in the oldness of any form that passeth away; but in the newness of the Spirit, which abideth for ever; in being born of the Spirit, in abiding in the Spirit, in living, walking, and worshipping in the Spirit; yea, in becoming and growing into Spirit, and into eternal life:…that they might become like God, be formed into, and live in his image!

Some Directions to the Panting Soul (1661)

II.207 Indeed this is the true religion, to feel God beginning the work, and to wait on him for his carrying it on. The feeling of God's Spirit beginning somewhat in the heart, the heart's waiting on him for more of his Spirit, and walking on with him in his Spirit, as he pleaseth to quicken, lead, draw, and strengthen; this is the spiritual and true religion.…

Some Observations upon that Portion of Scripture, Romans 14:20 (1662)

II.305 …Religion, true religion, is not a matter of opinion (as men, who have not tasted of the power, are apt to imagine), but a new creation and work of God in the heart of the creature, sowing the light and life of his Spirit there, and by it working man out of the darkness and death of sin (which is the destruction and misery of the soul), into his life and blessedness.

A Weighty Question Propounded to the King and Parliament (1663)

II.325 ... What is the sum and substance of the true religion? Is it not love from a principle of life? Is it not a travel out of the enmity of the creature into the love of God? Doth not the light of life spring in the love, and gather into the love? Doth not Christ, revealed in the heart, and leavening the heart with the savour of life, teach love to enemies, to bear with them in love, to seek them in love, to forgive them in love, to pray for them in love, to wish good to them, and wrestle with God for mercy towards them, even while they are hating and persecuting?

Concerning the Sum or Substance of Our Religion (n.d.; ca. 1666)

II.441 This is the sum or substance of our religion; to wit, to feel and discern the two seeds: the seed of enmity, the seed of love; the seed of the flesh, the seed of the Spirit; the seed of Hagar, the seed of Sarah; the seed of the Egyptian womb, the holy seed of Israel; and to feel the judgments of God administered to the one of these, till it be brought into bondage and death; and the other raised up in the love and mercy of the Lord to live in us, and our souls gathered into it, to live to God in it.

II.443 So that this is our religion, to witness the two seeds, with the power of the Lord bringing down the one, and bringing up the other; and then to witness and experience daily the same power, keeping the one in death, and the other in life, by the holy ministration of God's pure living covenant. And so to know God in this covenant, (in this covenant which lives, gives life, and keeps in life) and to walk with God, and worship and serve him therein, even in his Son, in the light of his Son, in the life of his Son, in the virtue and ability which flows from his Son, into our spirits. ...

Part II The Spirituality and Thought of Isaac Penington

Some Things of Great Weight and Concernment to all (1667)

III.2   That it is a great and hard matter to come into a capacity of knowing and receiving the truth. It is no hard matter to take up any religion that a man finds in the world. To read scriptures, to believe what a man finds related there, according to his understanding of them; yea, to believe that he hath the light and help of the Spirit in his reading and understanding; to apply himself also to practise and observe what he finds therein required; and to aim at holiness, etc.; this is no hard matter; every man that is serious, and seeks religion of any kind but in the weight of a man's spirit, may go thus far. But all this administers not the true capacity, but he that meets with it, must go further than thus. ...

III.4–5, 13   ... this is the main thing in religion, even to know Christ revealed in the soul ..., to be gathered under his banner, which is the cross, or that living principle in the heart which resisteth the corrupt principle; ... to mind the seed of the kingdom [Mk 4:2–20], the leaven of the kingdom [Mt 13:33], its growth in the mind, soul, and spirit, and the mind's, soul's, and spirit's gathering into, and growth in it.

III.15   ... For religion, the true religion, is a mystery; life is a mystery; Christ is a mystery; the Spirit is a mystery; faith is a mystery; obedience (the pure obedience) is a mystery; worship (the spiritual worship in and according to the new covenant) is a mystery; hid from the eyes of all the wise searchers of the world, but revealed to the least babe that is of God, and abideth in the quickened life of his Son.

A Question to the Professors of Christianity (1667)

III.27   ... the Lord so teacheth him things, as words cannot utter [Rom 8:26]; that is, he so knoweth the peace of God, the joy of his Spirit, the life and power of the Lord Jesus Christ, his wisdom, righteousness, and pure, precious ways of sanctifying the heart, the tender mercy, faithfulness, and rich love of the Father, etc. as he cannot utter to any man; nay, so as he never learned (nor could

learn) from words about the things; but by the sense
and experience of the thing itself, the Lord (in whom
are the depths of life, and who giveth the sense and
understanding of the deep things of the Spirit) opening
them in him, and manifesting them to him. And indeed
this is the right and excellent way of knowledge, to come
into the union, to come into the thing itself; to learn in the
union, to see and know in the thing. This is the way that
the Lord teacheth all his children in the new covenant, by
the inward life, by the pure light within.

Some Things Relating to Religion Proposed to the Consideration of the Royal Society (1668)

III.111 Our religion stands wholly out of that which all
their religion stands in. Their religion stands in the
comprehension, in a belief of a literal relation or
description. Our religion stands in a principle which
changeth the mind, wherein the Spirit of life appeareth to,
and witnesseth in the conscience to and concerning the
things of the kingdom; where we hear the voice, and see
the express image of the Invisible One, and know things,
not from an outward relation, but from their inward
nature, virtue, and power. Yea, here (we must profess) we
so know things, that we are fully satisfied about them, and
could not doubt concerning them, though there never
had been word or letter written of them; though indeed
it is also a great comfort, and sweet refreshment to us, to
read that testified of outwardly, which (through the tender
mercy of our God) we feel and enjoy inwardly. And in
this our whole religion consists; to wit, in the silence and
death of the flesh, and in the quickening and flowing life
of the Spirit. For he who is of the new birth, of the new
creation, of the second Adam (the Lord from heaven),
is as really alive to God, and as really lives to him in his
Spirit, as ever he was really dead in trespasses and sins in
the time of his alienation and estrangement from God.

"To the Friend of Frances Fines" (n.d.; ca. 1668–1670)

III.459, JP 1.100, Qfp § 19.30

I am satisfied in God's Spirit, that that which I have written in the last I sent to thee, is the sum and substance of true Religion;... whereof doth not stand in getting a Notion of Christ's righteousness, but in feeling the power of the endless life, receiving the power and being changed by the power. And where Christ is, there is his righteousness.

"To Nathaniel Stonar" (1671)

III.475, JP 1.128

There was no true religion in the Apostles' days, without turning to the inward light (and that the true ministry was sent to turn men to) nor is there any true religion now without being inwardly turned to and walking in the same light: nor canst thou try any truth or understand any Scripture aright, but in the Light of God's Spirit. No man can understand the things of God but the Spirit of God.

"Reply [Concerning...New Covenant]" (1667/8)

IV.191

... call the light, which is spiritual and eternal, (and gives the true and certain knowledge of Christ) natural? What! of God, of Christ, (having received the Spirit, the living well) and yet not know the mystery of life within, nor its pure voice in this present day! but limit the unlimited One to a form of words formerly spoken by him!... Surely they are deeply in the mist. ... Now, we are one with any of you (though ye know it not) so far as ye know and are of the truth, and feel true union with whatever is of God in you.

"Reply to an Answer of Some Queries Concerning the Gospel-Baptism" (1679)

IV.396

He that would know God and Christ to salvation, must know them in that mystery of light and life, wherein and whereby they save and deliver from the mystery of sin and death; for there is the mystery of God, the mystery of the Father, the mystery of Christ, the mystery of the gospel, the revelation of the mystery, the preaching of the mystery, the mystery of the kingdom of God, the speaking the wisdom of God in a mystery, the riches of the glory of the mystery, the acknowledgment of the mystery, the fellowship of the mystery, and the mystery of the faith held in a pure conscience. The true ministers of Christ are stewards of the mysteries of God. They have the treasure of life in their earthen vessels, and are to give forth from that treasure to those they minister to, and bring them to the discerning and partaking of the same treasure in themselves.

O, consider, consider all ye professors of Christ, and of the Christian religion! There is a mysterious power that begets, a mysterious womb that conceives and brings forth, a mysterious birth that is begotten and brought forth, which hungers after the mystery, and is fed with the knowledge, life, and virtue of the mystery.

"Some Experiences" (1679)

IV.430 O that Protestants, Papists, Jews, Turks, [American] Indians, did all know and own this light, that there might be an end of the darkness and misery, wherewith mankind hath been so long overwhelmed; and happiness both in particular nations, and in the whole world, might be experienced in the stead thereof. For men's erring from the light and spirit of God, hath been the cause of all their misery; and their returning to the light and Spirit of God (from which all have erred) will take away the cause of their misery, and in it (as they faithfully subject to the Lord and travel therein) they shall find his power, love, and mercy revealed, towards their restoring unto happiness.

CHAPTER 10

Interpreting the Bible

The Bible for many Quakers is, as we have seen (in Part II Introduction), a centre of contention. Some disregard the Bible because they find it oppressive in its doctrinal and judgmental language, its support of various forms of social oppression, and its picture of God as dominating power. Others love to live within its words of salvation, reassurance, and guidance. Each group is critical of, if not repelled by, the other group. And ranging between are many Friends perplexed about what to make of it all, interested yet not knowing how the Bible relates to their spiritual growth and ethical action. Some Friends in each group are discovering the explosive creativity of current biblical studies and are being challenged and nourished by those who in their view of Jesus and the religious life are similar to a Quaker perspective as they stress experience of divinity and concern for justice. Consider works by Marcus Borg, John Dominic Crossan, Elisabeth Schussler Fiorenza, Robert W. Funk, John P. Keenan, Jean-Yves LeLoup, Ched Myers, Elaine Pagels, and Walter Wink (see Bibliography). Amidst this exciting conversation Penington can show us a Quaker starting point and approach to the Bible (cf. Joanne and Larry Spears, *Friendly Bible Study*).

Penington reads scripture as language of the Spirit. To share his method, we have to be open at the deeper level of feeling and tacit stirrings, allowing the words of scripture to touch us in inwardness. Their meaning is not simply their content, the ideas we can think, but making the divine present through this deeper level. Reading the Bible should evoke experience of God rather than merely clarify ideas about God. We need to get beneath the form of ideas to feel the life and power that grasps us. As we saw in *The Way of Life and Death*, the rule for living is "the measure of life which they receive", which is to be a "new creature" (*Way of Life*, 1.26–27). This new creature – the self opened to its depths – living by the received measure of life is the same rule for reading scripture:

> This will open the scriptures aright; yea, this is the true key, which will truly open words, things, and spirits. ... The prophets and apostles, who wrote the scriptures, first had the life in them: and he who understands their words, must first have the life in him. He that understands the words of life, must first have life in himself. And the life, from which the words came, is the measurer of the words, and not the words of the life. (*Scattered Sheep*, 1.115–16)

The life within includes "the unity, the love, the peace" (1.116). If we dwell within these we can begin to understand the Bible whose true spirit is this life. If we approach it from our veiled self, we will pick up words in the Bible of domination and exclusion, and then use these, because they are scriptural, to measure – constrict, twist – the freely creative and compassionate life in the Life. If the life is the measure of words, and not words of the life (which differentiates Quakers fundamentally from mainstream Protestantism), then we understand scripture from our experience of the life, and not from our knowledge of the right words (doctrine). When we interpret scripture to others, then, we speak with authority out of our own experience. However much our "days" are encounters with "small things" (*Way of Life*, 1.89), we speak with integrity, simplicity, and power. Being well informed by reading other interpreters can enrich our understanding but the insights must be measured by the life we know within ourselves (see Rosemary Moore, *The Light in Their Consciences*, ch. 4).

Interpreting scriptural words as they bear in upon the meaning of our lives in their particularity is best exemplified in Penington's weave of biblical allusions into accounts of his personal experience, because his words carry the immediacy of experiencing the divine life within. Look again at the first extract in Part II ch. 2 ON P. 138 (*Scattered Sheep*, 1.106); within the very first paragraph of his account of his religious experience before convincement, he alludes to specific biblical passages or expresses more general biblical resonances (in RSV): "witness" (Rom 8:16), "light" and "darkness" (Jn 1:4–5, 8:12), "measure" (Rom 12:3), "sold myself" (1 Kings 21:20), "appearance of life" (2 Tim 1:10), "Lord blew" (Gen 1:2, 2:7), "comeliness" (Isa 53:2), "inward beauty" (Psal 29:2), "freshness" (Job 29:20, 2 Cor 2:14–16), "hardest heart" (Ex 7:13–14), "forming of me to himself" (Jer 1:5), "taste" (Psal 34:8, Heb 6:4–5). His language is made powerful by using biblical words, whether by quotation or allusion, to illumine his experience and to pour his experience into those words showing what they mean in his life in the Life. While Penington's contemporaries would have recognised that their power came from biblical origins, we who are unwitting or intolerant of biblical words need to wait with his words, to sense the life in them. They may become powerful for us too.

This personal weave of biblical allusions into the texture of his life both to illumine and express the Life in his experience is, I believe, Penington's most powerful way of handling scripture. He takes two other approaches: symbolic interpretation, that shows how a passage is revealing of our own condition, and argument, that explains how a passage or passages exhibit Quaker themes. In his symbolic handling of the two trees in the midst of the Garden of Eden (Gen 2:9), he takes the tree of life as symbolic of our life in the Spirit and the tree of knowledge as symbolic of a life of knowledge without the Life. In his prophetic mode he speaks of Babylon symbolically: they who "come from the spirit of deceit... shall never come out of Babylon; but only be translated into some of the more refined chambers of it, and fed with some more fresh likenesses of truth" (*Babylon the Great*, 1.146). This is clearly symbolic talk about an inward condition of captivity and alienation from God, not literal reference to a city in present-day Iraq known among sixth-century BCE Jews for its sensual degradation and conquest of Jerusalem. Much of local history in the Bible Penington reads symbolically, so that it reveals his spiritual condition rather than merely referring to ancient history. Penington and early Quakers read the Old Testament primarily not as pointing to salvation history but as illumining their own lives – beginning with Fox's earliest "opening" that things in the Hebrew Bible were interpreting him (*Journal*, 19).

Penington's third use of scripture, in argument, either quotes from various places in the Bible or interprets one biblical passage in order to present a Quaker view of some religious point. For instance, in the first extract in Part II ch. 1 (see pp. 130–31), Penington quotes Ephesians, Hebrews, Romans, and Galatians to show that the scripture defines the rule for a Christian as the same rule for Christ: the measure of life in the new creature, and in its fullness in Christ. Occasionally, Penington will analyse one passage. He does not pause, however, for an extended commentary on a passage, and never for one on an entire book of the Bible. Again, this distinguishes Quakers from mainstream Protestants, like Luther and Calvin, and their followers, who wrote long commentaries interpreting many biblical books. This difference is understandable given that they locate authority in the Bible, while early Friends locate it in the Spirit known in inward experience, and manifest in and corroborated by the Bible. This is not to say that no early Friends were interested in biblical studies. Samuel Fisher did pioneering canonical research (i.e. examining the formation of the contents of the Bible, what was included and excluded in different Bibles) in *Rusticus ad Academicos*; see Barbour and Roberts, eds., *Early Quaker Writings*, 304–14.

We have already seen excerpts from Penington's commentary on Mt 20:25-28 in which he argues that Jesus' power was not dominating but that of a servant (*Examination... Boston*, I.377–80, in Part II chapter 4 pp. 161–62). Elsewhere he offers readings of Rom 2:14-15 that Gentiles who respond can be saved by the inward light without explicit knowledge of Christ, and learn to do by nature what is contained in the Jewish law – over against the usual Protestant reading that denies salvation to any who do not know Christ through scripture ("Life and Immortality", IV.135-38; cf. "Reply [Concerning... New Covenant]", IV.182); of Rom 7 (*New Covenant*, II.40–42) that the law condemns us, not that we cannot live up to it, since Paul says he succeeded, but because we seek to live in conformity with an outward form rather than being transformed into a new inward way of being; and of Rom 9:18 that God's mercy is not selective but universal in intent (see chapter 11 section 2, ALVATION, PP. 246–47 AND 255–61). Penington has found illumination of his own pre-Quaker condition through the biblical text, rather than taking the usual Protestant view that the text is presenting the doctrinal truth that the law condemns us as sinners, but that we are forgiven through knowing Christ in the Bible.

Below, I extract one such short commentary on Genesis 2:4bff, the second creation story, of Adam and Eve, (on two creation stories of Genesis 1:1–2:4a and 2:4b–3:24 see Bernhard W. Anderson, *Understanding the Old Testament*). This is presented in the form of a catechism – yes, some early Quakers wrote catechisms (a pedagogical device for learning the beliefs of a faith community). As with the allusive life-texturing and symbolic approaches, Penington looks from the life within his own experience for the life in the story. He finds it in the Tree of Life. The fall into sin was not principally humans' disobeying God, but their choosing the Tree of Knowledge – which he takes to be a knowing not rooted "in the life" – in preference to the Tree of Life. Eden then illumines his own discovery that he had been operating, prior to convincement, in his understanding rather than in the life.

All three of Penington's biblical approaches – life-textured insight, symbolic, and argumentative – seek to interpret the Bible by living in the feel of the life, and to express it in the language of the Spirit. Most biblical commentators would say such approaches do not offer an objective grasp of the biblical meaning. Penington would agree but say that was not the proper aim of interpreting the Bible anyway. Rather "the true end of men's reading the Scriptures, is to turn them to the light" (*Scattered Sheep*, I.131) in their own experience.

This means that the Spirit is still active, empowering people with the life as they read, but also as they speak and write. The canon (the writings chosen for inclusion in the Bible) is not closed. Writings made since Christians decided on the Bible's contents can have as much authority as those included in it, insofar as the Spirit speaks through them and is received in that same divine life (see "Reply [Concerning...New Covenant]", IV.172). Revelation continues.

Not only do we need to be in the life so we can have the life speak to us through different texts, we need the Spirit's guidance in how we apply texts to our lives, for all biblical truths are not relevant to all situations. We must come "to know the times and seasons of the spirit" (*Concerning the Worship*, II.213). Learning the language of the spirit we become sensitive to how biblical texts are fitting to our own concrete circumstances.

The gospel, the apostles' message, as Penington reads it illumined by the Light within, is that "God is light" (IV.232), but we need to learn how that meaning plays out in our own lives given whatever measure of light we have. Living in and from that light we live in the life which *is* the kingdom of God. What we know in the scripture and in our own life, both in our words and our silence, is the mystery of life in inwardness which engenders language of the spirit with the feel of the kingdom: "the life is the kingdom, and words from the life yield the savour of the kingdom" (*Jew Outward*, 1.210). Identifying the kingdom of God with living in the life avoids conceiving the kingdom as triumphal domination, and returns us to reading scripture within the life's stirrings in our "day of small things" (*Way of Life*, 1.89).

"Short Catechism", in *The Scattered Sheep Sought After* (1659)

1.120–21 *Quest.* What brought Adam to this estate?...
Ans. Feeding on the tree of knowledge, from which man is not excluded to this day, though he is from the tree of life [Gen 3].
Quest. How came Adam at first, and how come men still, to feed on the tree of knowledge?
Ans. From a lustful appetite and desire after the forbidden wisdom....
Quest. What is the forbidden fruit?
A. It is knowledge without life; knowledge in the earthly part; knowledge acquired from below, not given from above. This promiseth to make men as God, and to give them the ability of discerning and distinguishing between good and evil, which is God's peculiar property. Eating of this fruit undid Adam, undid the Gentiles, undid the Jews, undid the Christians; they all feeding on the tree of knowledge, and departing from the life in their several dispensations.
Quest. How doth this fruit undo man?
Ans. The wisdom and knowledge, which they thus gather and feed upon, perverts them; makes them wise in the wrong part; exalts them against the life; dulls the true appetite, and increases the wrong appetite; insomuch as there is not so much as a desire in them after God in truth; but only to get knowledge and wisdom from what they can comprehend. By this means, whatsoever was afterwards ordained to life, became death to man....
Quest. What is the food which man should feed on?
Ans The tree of life; the word which liveth and abideth for ever, which is in the midst of the garden of God

Part II The Spirituality and Thought of Isaac Penington

[Gen 2:9]; which word was made flesh for man's weakness' sake, on which flesh the living soul feeds, and whose blood the living spirit drinks, and so is nourished up to eternal life.
Quest. But had Adam this food to feed on?...
A. God breathed into man the breath of life, and man became a living soul: and nothing less than life itself could satisfy his soul at first, nor can to this day. Every word of God that cometh fresh out of his mouth, is man's food and life. And God speaketh often to man, showing him what is good: but he cannot relish nor feed on this, but desireth somewhat else, through the error and alienation of his mind. ...

I.122   *Quest.* This is too mysterious for me; give me the plain, literal knowledge of the Scriptures.
Ans. Is not the substance a mystery? Is not the life there? The letter of any dispensation killeth: it is the spirit alone that giveth life [2 Cor 3:6]. ... when it [soul] awakes, it will feel.

I.131   ... The true end of men's reading the Scriptures, is to turn them to the light. The Scriptures contain messages concerning God, concerning Christ, concerning the spirit; the end whereof is to turn men to the power and life, which can do the thing for them; which God, which Christ, which spirit, fill all things, and are within in the heart, as well as without. The Word is nigh thee in thy heart, and in thy mouth, saith Moses to the Jews [Deut 30:14], saith Paul to the Christians [Rom 10:8].

I.132   *Quest.* Then by this a man may be saved, though he should not know the literal name Jesus, or the literal name Christ, etc.
Ans. The names are but the signification of the thing spoken of; for it is the life, the power (the being transformed by that) that saves, not the knowledge of a name. And Christians mightily deceive themselves herein: for they think to be saved by believing a relation

concerning Christ, as he appeared in a fleshly body, and suffered death at Jerusalem. Whereas Christ is the same yesterday, today, and for ever; and the saving knowledge reveals him, not only as he was then, but as he was the day before, and will be for ever. And this knowledge is also revealed in the Scripture; but they are so drowned in the letter, wherewith the carnal part is so filled, that the spiritual eye cannot open in them to see: so that which was ordained for life, becomes death to them.

The Jew Outward Being a Glass for the Professors of this Age (1659)

I.221 ... the disciples who were illiterate, and not so knowing of the scriptures that were written of Christ, yet they knew Christ: but the Scribes and Pharisees, who were very skilful in the letter, could not know him. What was the reason? The reason lay in the difference of the eye, or light, wherewith they looked: the one looked with an outward eye, the other with an inward eye. And a little inward light will do that, which a great deal of outward light will not do. And this I can certainly affirm, that all the light that men can gather from the Scriptures, cannot give them the knowledge of Christ as he hath appeared in this age; nay, nor as he hath appeared in any age, since the days of the apostles: but a little true inward light will give the knowledge of this thing. ...

The Axe Laid to the Root of the Old Corrupt Tree (1659)

I.243 ... Man's faith ... receiveth a literal knowledge of him from what it heareth from men, or from what it readeth related in the Scripture concerning him; but refuseth the nature of the thing. And it cannot be otherwise; for man's faith, not being of the nature of it, cannot but refuse it. But this faith, which is given of God, which is from above, being of the same life and nature with Christ, cannot refuse the spring of its own life; but receiveth him immediately. There is no distance of time; but so soon as faith is received, Christ is received, and the soul united to him in the faith. As unbelief immediately shuts him out, so faith lets him in immediately, and centres the soul in him: and the immortal soul feels the immortal virtue, and rejoices in the proper spring of its own immortal nature.

1.246 He that hath Christ, or the seed of eternal life, which is Christ, formed in him (which seed the Spirit always dwells in, and never is absent from, which is the same Spirit which gave forth the Scriptures), he is in a capacity of understanding those scriptures which that Spirit gave forth, as that Spirit leads him into the understanding of them. But he that hath not received that which is like the grain of mustard-seed [Mk 4:31–32], and so hath not Christ nor his spirit (whatever he may pretend to), he, by all his studies, arts, languages, reading of expositors, conferences, nay, experiences, can never come to the true knowledge of the Scriptures; for he wants the true key, which alone can open.

1.248 ...To them under the gospel, to them who are come to the substance, to them who are begotten and born in the life, there can be no rule proportionable to their state, but Christ the substance, Christ the life. Here he alone is the light, the way, the truth, the rule [cf. *Way of Life*, 1.26–27]; the Spirit is here the rule, the new creature is the rule, the new covenant the rule; all which are in unity together, and he that hath one of them hath them all, and he that hath not them all hath none of them. So that directions taken out of the scripture cannot be the rule to him who is the true Christian; but the measure of grace, the measure of the light, the measure of the Spirit, the measure of the gift received into the living soul from the spring of life, this is the alone rule of life. But Christians in the degeneration have lost this, and so have taken up words for a rule (which were not given to that end); and so with deductions by the earthly part, they feed the earthly part.

1.249–50 ...The Spirit of the Lord is the true expositor of scriptures; he never addeth nor diminisheth: but man, being without that Spirit, doth but guess, doth but imagine, doth but study and invent a meaning, and so he is ever adding or diminishing. This is the sense, saith one; this is the sense, saith another; this is the sense, saith a third; this, saith a fourth: another that is witty, and large in his comprehension, he says they will all stand; another, perhaps more witty than he, says none of them will stand, and he invents a meaning different from them all. And then, when they are thus expounding them, they will say, take the sense thus, it will yield this observation; or take it thus, and it will afford this observation. Doth not this plainly show, that he who thus saith, hath not the Spirit of the Lord to open the scripture to him, and manifest which is the true sense, but is working in the mystery of darkness? And yet this very person, who is thus working with his own dark spirit in the dark, will in words confess, that there is no true understanding or opening of scripture, but by the Spirit of God. ...

Now he that is the adder, he that is the diminisher, he crieth out against the Spirit of the Lord, and chargeth him with adding and diminishing: for man being judge, he will judge his own way to be true, and God's to be false. That which is the adding and diminishing, he calls the true expounding of the place; but if the Spirit of the Lord immediately open any thing to any son or daughter, he cries, "This is an adding to the word: the scripture is written; there are no more revelations to be expected now; the curse," saith he, "is to them that add." Thus he removes the curse from his own spirit, and way of study and invention, to which it appertains; and casts it upon the Spirit of the Lord. And man cannot possibly avoid this in the way that he is in; for having first judged his own darkness to be light, then, in the next place, he must needs judge the true light to be darkness [1 Jn 1:5–7]. He that hath aforehand set up his own invented meaning of any scripture to be the true meaning, he must needs oppose the true meaning, and call it false, and so apply himself to form all the arguments he can out of other scriptures, to make it appear false.

1.254–55 ... Wait for the key of knowledge, which is God's free gift. Do not go with a false key to the Scriptures of Truth; for it will not open them. Man is too hasty to know the meaning of the Scriptures, and to enter into the things of God, and so he climbs up over the door with his own understanding; but he has not patience to wait to know the door, and to receive the key which opens and shuts the door; and by this means he gathers death out of words which came from life. And this I dare positively affirm, that all that have gone this way to work have but a dead knowledge; and it is death in them that feeds upon this knowledge, and the life is not raised. Consider now the weight of this counsel in the true balance: there is no opening of the Scriptures but by the true key, nor is there any coming at the key till the Lord please to give it. What then is to be done, but only to wait (in the silence of that part which would be forward, and running before-hand) till the key be given, and to know how to receive it, as it is offered in the light; and not to wait in the will, or expect to receive it according to observations in the fleshly wisdom from the letter.

An Examination of the Grounds or Causes which are said to Induce the Court of Boston... (1660)

1.315 Now is not this sound according to the Scriptures? And is it not a good way to know this by unity with it, by feeling a measure of the same life made manifest in our mortal flesh? 2 Cor 4:11. This we confess is our way of understanding things; and likewise of understanding the Scriptures, which speak of these things. And we have found it a far surer kind of knowledge; namely, to understand the Scriptures by experience of that whereof the scripture speaks, than to guess at the things the scripture speaks of, by considering and scanning in the earthly part what the Scriptures speak of them. Such a kind of knowledge as this, a wise man may attain to a great measure of; but the other is peculiar to him who is begotten of God, whose knowledge is true and certain, though it seem ever so different from his who

10. Interpreting the Bible

hath attained what he hath by the search of his wisdom.

I.387 ...Not to know Paul, or Apollos, or Cephas, but the Spirit ministering in them [1 Cor 1:12]. Paul may err, Apollos may err, Peter may err (and did err, when he compelled the Gentiles to live as the Jews, Gal. 2:14, for which Paul withstood him to the face, ver. 11), and Barnabas also did err. ver. 13. But the Spirit cannot err; and he that keeps to the measure of the Spirit in himself, cannot let in any of their errors, if they should err, but is preserved.

A Question to the Professors of Christianity (1667)

III.48–49 ...such as have received the spiritual understanding know it to be distinct from the natural; and we experimentally find a very clear distinction, between scriptures searched out by the reasonings of the mind (and so practices drawn therefrom), and scriptures opened by the Spirit, and felt in the life.

Now that professors generally have not received their knowledge of Christ from the Spirit, or from scriptures opened in the Spirit (and so know not the thing, but only such a relation of the thing as man's reasoning part may drink in from the letter of the Scriptures), is manifest by this, in that they are not able in spirit and understanding to distinguish the thing itself from the garment wherewith it was clothed, though the Scriptures be very express therein. Speak of Christ according to a relation of the letter, there they can say somewhat; but come to the substance, come to the spirit of the thing, come to the thing itself, there they stutter and stammer, and show plainly that they know not what it is.

"Reply to Queries and Animadversions [Concerning the Rule of the New Covenant]" (1667)

IV.172 ...Whether the writings of any now be of equal weight with the Scriptures; I have this to say:

The weight of the words which are from God's Spirit is according to the strength of life which he pleaseth to clothe them with. He sent forth Moses, the prophets, the Son in that body of flesh, the apostles in his name and authority; and the angel that he sends with the everlasting gospel [Rev 14:6], after the apostasy, to preach to every nation, kindred, tongue, and people, he sends not without his authority; yea, the message that he thus sends in any age hath a peculiar reference to the state of the world, and the state of the people of God in that age; and none can slight it (whether it be signified by word or writing) without dashing against God's authority, and despising him that speaketh in these latter days. Yea, the immediate word of the Lord, spoken and declared at this day, by any man to whom it pleaseth the Lord to commit the same, is of no less authority, nor more to be slighted now, than it was in his servants in the days past, by whom the Scriptures were given forth.

IV.176 That a man's doctrinals are right according to scripture in all the main substantials, is no infallible rule to try what power it is that works in him, or what his spirit is; because deceit works in a mystery; and the spirit of error may come in sheep's clothing [Mt 7:15], and may get good words and fair speeches to deceive the hearts of the simple.

"A Treatise Concerning God's Teachings, and Christ's Law" (1671)

IV.232 ... they [the apostles] were to preach the light to them (even this message, that God is light, and in him is no darkness at all, [1 Jn 1:] ver. 5), and to turn them to the light (Acts 26:18) in which alone men can see and receive the life which is eternal. Men may know or comprehend many things concerning the Messiah from the letter; but they can only know the Messiah himself in the light which shines into their hearts, and which he sent his apostles to direct and turn their minds to. For they directed them to the Word within, light within, life within, Spirit within; to feel after the manifestation of God within, which was communicated to the very Gentiles. Rom. 1:17.

"A Question Answered Concerning Reading the Scriptures Aright" (n.d.; ca. 1671–75)

IV.269 And here the truth, sweetness, and fullness of words is known, felt, and witnessed, even in that which comprehends them, and gives them their due weight and measure.

IV.270 ... All truths are not proper to every state, nor all remedies to every disease. Christ had many things to teach and say to his disciples, which they were not able to bear; and a man in reading the Scriptures, though he should understand the truth of what he reads, yet he is apt to misapply things, as to himself or others, unless the Lord guide and help him. He is apt to apply that to him which belongs not to him, and thrust that from him which belongs to him.

CHAPTER II

Answering Theological Controversy

Mid-seventeenth-century England was a time of great theological controversy. Penington's essays not only present his view of the spiritual life individually, communally, and in the nation; his philosophical insights into the nature of the self in its knowing, freedom, and use of language; his religious thinking about prayer and worship, the nature of religion, and how to interpret the Bible; and autobiographical accounts of his own spiritual development; they also give his answers to the theological issues of the day. Much of his writing uses a question and answer or objection and reply format. He varies targets of his answering. He writes to the "simple-" or "tenderhearted" (who are serious about their spiritual growth and who might respond sympathetically to what he has to say); "professors" (who profess theological ideas but do not live them); Protestants, Papists, and Jews; specific theologians; and political leaders in England and America. His effort is to persuade, clarify, and defend the Quaker way. Much of this shows his Quaker response to doctrine, for his audience is thinking and arguing in doctrinal concepts.

Doctrine is a hard nut for Friends to crack. We do not have a creed and many Friends reject all doctrine as well. What is doctrine and why do many of us oppose it? If we think about religious experience, as Penington presents it, it begins with the presence and stirrings of the Spirit beneath the threshold of consciousness. Emerging from the unconscious, awareness of divine presence and action first becomes conscious through feeling and sensing, whether in silent worship or going about our daily existence. When Penington writes about this, he has lifted experience into thought, using ideas to describe and explain its meaning.

Lifting experience into thought is what doctrine did for early Christians, providing them with ideas of their experience of Jesus and of God through Jesus. Whenever we talk to our children about our religious endeavours, to other Christians inquiring about the meaning of "Quaker", or to other religious or so-called secular people about what it means to be religious, we use such ideas. They are called "beliefs". When we speak of our beliefs, however, we know that such ideas are abstractions from rich experience, the whole and centre of which cannot be expressed. Beliefs, then, are the conceptual aspect of religious experience. Doctrine is the organised pattern of beliefs of a religious community.

The early church sought through doctrine to name what was central to their religious experience. They did this to clarify their identity within and later outside of Judaism, and amidst several Roman religions. Very quickly, however, doctrine became not merely a way to identify one's own religious group but a standard of right belief (which is what "ortho-doxy" means) to exclude heretics, who were seen as a danger in time of persecution. Once the church became imperial, when the Roman Empire became Christian in the fourth century, doctrine also came to be used to ensure obedience to the state.

Seventeenth-century Friends opposed doctrine insofar as it was an instrument of domination, forcing conformity of belief. Through suffering and advocacy, they succeeded eventually with other dissenters in persuading the royal government to grant religious toleration to British subjects. They also opposed doctrine because it so often had become an empty form, separated from the life of the Spirit, making people feel powerful through assurances that they were right, and obscuring the shockingly transformative potential of the "weak stirrings of the Spirit". Quakerism began as a return to experience of divine reality and of our human condition. Nevertheless, the fact that Friends rejected lifeless forms abstracted from experience, and their use for domination, does not mean that they did not use ideas to express their religious experience, nor that they did not disagree with those whose ideas they did not approve.

Quakerism arose amidst a lively discussion of theological and ethical ideas during "the world turned upside down" (Acts 17:6; *Way of Life*, 1.80) of the English Civil War. To come to consciousness of oneself as a spiritual being in that context was to learn to speak in theological and therefore doctrinal terms. Theology was the language of common discourse in which not only religious but political, economic, psychological, and social matters were discussed. In order to gain the ears of contemporaries, to explain oneself and to persuade others, it was necessary to locate Quaker identity through these concepts. Doctrinal talk, which is pervasive among early Friends, was a container that held their experience of the life. As they used such terms, they tried to show how those forms could be filled with the life, even while criticising others, using many of the same concepts, for the absence of life in their ideas. Where the content of others' ideas denied the rising of the life in one's own experience here and now, Quakers rejected them, and sought to show scripture's support for their own perspective.

Such doctrinal talk is alien to many Friends today, and if we want to understand it, we need when we encounter it to find a way of reaching through its theological form to the life within. Why should we want to do that? While early Friends' metaphors and life stories can move us, we will understand our Quaker origins better if we explore the whole expression of their experience of the life, and not just the forms with which we feel comfortable. Moreover, there is a power, I have found, in the life as it is contained in theological language that can nourish our own spiritual growth – if we will confront, rather than avoid, this strangeness, and find a way through its forms into its life. Not simply discerning the life there but thinking about its relevance to the life in our lives can enhance the quality of our spiritual existence. We need such religious thinking not only to clarify for ourselves who we are, but to nurture the next generation and to share with others our deepest life-orientation. Understanding how Penington used his ideas to make sense of and to express experience of the life can enrich a thoughtful life. His way of putting things may not be ours, but it can clarify the relation of life and idea, and draw from us discovery of how we want to speak, and how we want to remain silent. He will confirm our search for something much deeper which ideas cannot comprehend nor words express.

How then can we discern the life in the doctrines Penington articulates – of sin, salvation, perfection, creation, last things, and Christ and trinity? We should look for the idea of life but more importantly feel the life in how he is using doctrine, and catch his efforts at engendering a sense of the life through these common concepts, now alien to so many of us.

1. Sin

The doctrine of sin, naming the damaged condition of our humanity, is defined by Penington as not living in the life, not being transformed, filled, and led by the divine life, but living in "any form, out of the life", which "kills the life" (*Axe Laid to the Root*, 1.229). While other Christians define it as the will's disobedience to God's command or the understanding's loss of the vision of God (see H.R. Niebuhr's *The Responsible Self*, ch. 5), Penington locates it in the refusal to live by feeling or sensing the life of God within our own life.

The story Christians focus on to picture how our lives got damaged is the Fall of Adam and Eve, the second, but older, creation story in Genesis 2:4b ff (see Anderson and pp. 231–32 above). While taken as a historical event by early Friends as well as other Christians, what is significant about this story for Penington is that it is a symbol of our own desire, like Adam's "enlarging his blessedness" (*Some Qs . . . Jews Natural*, II.234) by pursuit of knowledge and wisdom that is "out of the life" (*Axe Laid to the Root*, 1.229). In the story there are two trees in the Garden of Eden, one of Knowledge and one of Life (Gen 2:9). The usual Protestant interpretation is to see the Fall as the result of disobedience to God's command not to eat of the Tree of Knowledge of Good and Evil (Gen 2:17). What Penington focuses on, however, is not rules and their violation but that humans' choice was and is of Knowledge rather than Life, out of a desire to enhance their religious state but mistakenly, by seeking a life in themselves "out of the fountain" (*Some Qs . . . Jews Natural*, II.234; cf. *Scattered Sheep*, 1.120–22 in Part II ch. 10 pp. 233–34).

Thinking of this condition in story form as an historical event, Christians speak of life in Eden as "original righteousness" and the Fall as "original sin". Stressing symbolism, as Penington does, "original" does not mean first in a sequence but what is underlying. He says we were created originally as "a vessel of light [and]...life" but our vessels have been "emptied of their proper liquor," even though the "vessels still remain the same in being" (*Some Qs . . . Jews Natural*, II.234 & 235). This means for Penington that residing in our depths now in our present lives is this vessel of light, but the way we live is not light-filled. Rather all our senses without the light's irradiation are "benumbed". We have lost the flow of the divine life within, what he calls (following Genesis 1:26–27) "the image of God". Switching the metaphor from vessel and image, he says each person has, however, "a little seed" (*Warning of Love*, I.405) in their original inward depths that can fructify into dwelling fully in the life of God. What stands in our way is our insistence on living by our own understanding and will rather than opening to the life within.

2. Salvation

Correlative to sin being defined as not living in the life, salvation is defined as dwelling in the life of the divine Spirit, being opened to, transformed by, and feeling, God's presence in the present: "The gospel state is a state of substance, a state of enjoying the life, a state of feeling the presence and power of the Lord in his pure, holy Spirit. ... Now art thou here, in the living power, in the divine life, joined to the spring of life, drawing water of life out of the well of life with joy?" (*Some Dirs to the Panting Soul*, II.203). The Spirit stirs the life within every person. If we will own it and open to it, grace will transform our life – the seed will grow – so as to be filled and guided by the Life. The traditional sequence of being saved by being accepted by God ("justification") and then after salvation being cleansed ("sanctification") is reversed for Penington. Salvation is not acceptance by God because of Christ's crucifixion but is the beginning of transformation of us by Christ's Spirit in us: "faith, which purifies the heart, and through which sanctification is, must needs be in order of nature before the justification which is by it" (*Holy Truth*, III.207; cf. "Further Testimony to Truth", IV.4). God loves us damaged or not, because "His nature is love; love to all his creatures" (*Ancient Principle of Truth*, III.273). God's "good pleasure" (*Ancient Principle of Truth*, III.276) is for us to become open to the divine seed within (*To All Such...Power*, II.289-290) and to "flourish" (*Warning of Love*, I.410; cf. *Somewhat...Weighty Qn*, II.153) in its growing within us into maturity.

Salvation, then, is the germinating of the divine seed, which is within everyone. It is not an event in the historical past – Jesus sacrificing himself for us, thereby providing "satisfaction" to God's justice (*Consid...the Book*, II.120) – but is an event in the present within the individual, letting go of control by the veiled self and allowing God to guide and grow in us. Penington seldom uses sacrificial language, but when he does the stress falls, not on Jesus' death, but on our inward dying to our own will and understanding ("To the Fd of F Fines", III.461–63; "Life and Immortality", IV.86–87; *Ep to all Serious Profs*, IV.360–61). A "true Christian" is then not someone who professes the name of Christ but someone who is a "new creation" ("Some Misreps...Church Gov.", IV.334) by the divine Spirit, who is most fully revealed in Jesus (*Holy Truth*, III.209–10; "Reply [Concerning...New Covenant]", IV.172–73). This can be anyone from the beginning of the human race who turns by grace to the seed or light within, regardless of whether they know anything about Jesus and the Bible (*Great Question...Swearing*, II.143–44; *Some Qs...Man His Duty*, II.267–68; "Reply [Concerning...New Covenant]", IV.182).

3. Perfection

Our life can become what God intended in our origin, the present possibility in our depths – a vessel filled again with light and life. Penington rejects the idea that the body prevents recovery of original righteousness: "The sinful body, the...flesh is within. The outward body, that is not hell; that is the temple of God, where...the pure Word of life sanctifies throughout, even in soul, in body...(*Holy Truth*, III.229). Being filled and led, moment by moment, by the Spirit is what Penington calls "perfection". Perfection for him is not a fixed ideal state beyond reach in this life, but is a dynamic, humble, daily dwelling in God (*Examination...Boston*, I.318–21). Each person has a certain measure of the light within. Perfection is being faithful with this degree of light. Like Jesus, but in our own degree, we "partake of the divine life" (*Naked Truth*, III.303) and it becomes "natural" to love and manifest the "fruits of life" ("To ____" (1670), III.449; cf. "fruit of the Spirit" in Gal 5:22).

4. Creation

Christian theologians have looked at the history of the world as having a narrative pattern that goes from the creation of the world through the time of Jesus to its final end. This is known as "salvation-history". With Jesus as the centre the stress usually falls on his life as a past event which made salvation possible. Penington, however, stresses the present as the time in which we open to and experience God's presence, which is salvation: "by his inward and spiritual presence...Immanuel, the gospel state, God with us,...living in us" (*Naked Truth*, III.301). God was present in the creation, and subsequently, and will be at the end of the world. Divine power is "the same" at the beginning and throughout cosmic history. Penington does not logically separate God's creating from his preserving power, although he acknowledges that the creating act involves more "immediate force" whereas God's preservation of creation involves more personal attention and even artifice – "a way of care, industry, art, and skill" (*Some Qs...Jews Natural*, II.256). We know God's creating and preserving power are the same because we experience that same power in our own lives.

The result of focusing on the Presence in the present is that Penington has little to say about the doctrines of creation and the last things. He thinks metaphorically rather than chronologically or logically. God is not the Cause at the beginning but the originating "pure fountain, and wellspring of life" (*Warning of Love*, I.402) underlying every moment of history from beginning to end: "God...Christ... spirit, fill all things and are within in the heart, as well as without" (*Scattered Sheep*, I.131). When he writes approvingly to the Royal Society, who in Britain are inventing modern science, he affirms "the excellency of nature" and that "God is not an enemy to nature", but his interest is not in figuring out the doctrine of creation in the light of scientific thinking. Rather, he is concerned about scientists' spiritual lives, that they "partake of that wisdom from which nature came" (*Some Things...Royal Society*, III.107).

5. Last Things
While Penington makes remarks about the end of the world, he draws no picture of it. He does believe in a final judgment in which God holds people accountable "for sinning against God" – adding his angle on inwardness – "and for oppressing that in your consciences which discovers to you, and checks you for, your sins" (*Salutation of Love*, II.321). Writing from prison of an "everlasting punishment in the fire of his wrath" (referring to Mt 25:31–46), he does not dwell on it but seeks rather to make his imprisoners aware of God's "temporal judgments" on the suffering they are now inflicting on Christ in his followers, referring to Jesus identifying with the suffering of the least significant, including prisoners (Mt 25:34–46; *Concerning the Church*, II.437–40; cf. *Warning of Love*, I.410, *Salutation of Love*, II.321–22). And

he makes it very clear, replying to accusations, that he does not believe that only Quakers are saved (*Jew Outward*, 1.210). He speaks of a tempter or Satan who draws us away from the life to live in empty forms (see *Scattered Sheep*, 1.107–08), but never portrays him, though he knows experientially a power in his own life which pulled him away from the life to live in his veiled self. For myself, I see this talk of Hell and Satan as a mortgage to Penington's Puritan past, hard to reconcile with his experience of God's indwelling presence as life-enhancing love. His experience of divine presence contradicts belief in an eternal separation from God, and his use of symbolism contradicts the impression he leaves of Satan as an external metaphysical entity, rather than an inward power. In the last days on earth he looks, not for an apocalyptic destruction of evil, but for the establishment of a peaceable kingdom through the "pouring out of the Spirit, even upon all flesh" resulting in "no more war" nor "oppressing of the creation" (*Some Qs...Jews Natural*, II.230).

6. Christ and Trinity

There is no question of the centrality of Christ for Penington – "every spiritual thing, refers to Christ, and centres in him" (*Some of the Mysteries*, II.343); the question is how is he central. Christ, for Penington, is God, "the infinite eternal Being" which was most fully present in the man Jesus but "cannot be confined to be nowhere else but there" (*Question to the Professors*, III.49–50). Penington's approach is experiential. He knows Christ is God and was fully manifest in Jesus because he knows in some measure that "Being" in his being: God "did all in him [Jesus], as it is a measure of the same life which doth all in us" ("To the Fd of F Fines", III.462). He rejects, therefore, the frequent accusation thrown at Quakers that they spoke of "two Christs, one manifested without, and another revealed within", for the "mystery of life, and hope of glory" was manifest in the earthly Jesus that is "revealed and made known within unto us, by the same eternal Spirit" ("Life and Immortality", IV.166).

As scripture sheds light on what Penington discovers growing within, it is the biblical metaphors that he draws upon. The people he is answering approach the Bible through logic rather than metaphor, with the intention of getting it conceptually "right". He approaches the Bible metaphorically in order to express and grow in experience, and evoke it in others. He writes: "my spirit hasteneth from words" to "sink in spirit into the feeling of the life itself, ... and cease striving to ... comprehend concerning it" (*Some of the Mysteries*, II.343).

He uses such metaphors for Christ as seed ("Spiritual Travels", I.10), breath, light, life, image, substance, son, mystery (*Scattered Sheep*, I.117–18), wisdom and power (*Some Qs ... Jews Natural*, II.238), spring of life, quickening Spirit, discoverer, reprover, condemner, justifier, strengthener, comforter, fountain of perfect love, sweetness (*Some of the Mysteries*, II.334, 338). He does play with the traditional threeness – Father, Son, and Spirit – but he refuses to embrace the doctrine of the trinity because "they find it not in Scripture". It is a result of men's "own invention to express their apprehensions" but we, he says, "are content with feeling the thing which scripture speaks of" (*Examination ... Boston*, I.312–14).

Traditional trinitarian thought distinguishes three "persons" in the Godhead. Penington refuses to speak of "persons" since this word does not occur in scripture in connection with God. Nor does he make sharp distinctions in functions between these three, as logic will do. Rather he speaks metaphorically of Father, Son, and Spirit (which already are metaphors) all as light or all as breath. From his experiential approach he says they each "draw" to each other, because he has experienced them drawing himself out of darkness into their unity of light and life (*Scattered Sheep*, 117–18).

The significance of Jesus is that the divine life – of Father, Son, and Spirit – dwells within him in its fullest manifestation. His reality is incarnation; his power is revelation. Penington rejects the idea that Christ's death was a transaction through sacrifice that released God's mercy by satisfying God's justice (an idea going back to Anselm in the eleventh century, now used by evangelical Christians). While the transaction is supposed to change God's attitude towards humanity, allowing him to be merciful at least to some, Penington sees no change in God's loving attention to all, stirring the life in all people throughout salvation history. Jesus reveals this indwelling life most fully. His difference from us is, therefore, one of degree. Like Jesus, we can partake of the divine nature and "become light" (*Ancient Principle of Truth*, III.256; cf. *Naked Truth*, III.303). The power of Jesus' revelation is to make us aware of the indwelling presence of life in its potentiality within each of us, and to draw it forth so as to pervade our lives.

As his contemporaries focus more on doctrine, they show less interest in the quality of life exhibited by Jesus. For Penington, on the other hand, he sees certain particulars in the biblical portraits of Jesus' life that illumine his experience of moving beneath the veiled self to wait on the Spirit in inwardness. We have already seen Penington underscore Jesus' servanthood, that he did not seek to dominate and require conformity of belief from his disciples but nurtured the life in them (Part II ch. 4 "Life in the Church"). Jesus, Penington recognises, taught not in doctrine but in parables (now stressed by recent New Testament scholarship). Because parables are an indirect form of teaching that leave you wondering if not upset, Jesus used them, Penington says, to be "offensive...to man's wisdom" (*Jew Outward*, 1.206). Similarly, Jesus said various contradictory things: he judges no one, yet he is frequently condemning the Pharisees; he is one with the Father, yet the Father is greater than he; he preaches the gospel of peace yet says he came not to send peace but a sword. As in his use of parables, Jesus speaks paradoxically as "contradictions to the fleshly understanding" (*Jew Outward*, 1.202). Similarly, Jesus and his disciples did work miracles but not for the satisfaction of man's will and wisdom. They were performed by the power of the Spirit. In his day, Penington sees the "same power" performing "inward miracles in Spirit." The important thing is not to interpret visible miracles but "to feel and live in the moving of the power." Even "if we did work outward miracles," Penington goes on, "if thou hadst not an inward eye to see them with, thou wouldst not be able to distinguish by what power they were wrought" (*Jew Outward*, 1.217). Jesus' life – his parabolic and paradoxical teaching, miracle working, even silence when refusing to give an answer (*Jew Outward*, 1.206) – all served, as Penington views it through his own experience, to drive the hearer off the self's surface to wait in the inward life.

Penington is a Christian universalist whose commitment to Christ opens up the entire history of the world as the arena of God's salvific activity as the Spirit, or eternal Christ, stirring the life in everyone regardless of their belief in the external Jesus. In his passionate pursuit of inwardness, while he nowhere speaks of the superiority of Christianity and does affirm diversity of Christian and non-Christian ways, he always advocates the religious life in Christian terms. Moses, and many other Hebraic leaders, he recognises, to be filled in inwardness with the life of the Spirit, which he identifies as the eternal Christ. But the outward covenant of Moses is superseded by the inward covenant of the Messiah. All must, and can, turn inward, and there they discover reality, not as Jews understand it – even though he calls it becoming an "inward Jew" – but as Christians do (see *Jew Outward*, I.195–225; *Some Qs...Jews Natural*, II.218–33). He has, therefore, like many Christians throughout the history of the church contributed to the belief that the Christian perspective has superseded the Jewish way, the tradition of anti-Judaism which shaped the context of the Holocaust.

While Penington lends support to Christians' anti-Judaism, he is primarily concerned with transcending all outward forms not filled with the life (among Christians and Jews, and all others) and opening to the divine presence within. The inward will issue in outward forms. The challenge is to keep those forms vital by their ongoing reemergence from the life within. So also with theological forms: the challenge is to use them as they arise from the "presence...in the midst" ("Some Misreps...Church Gov", IV.330), and to know that all words are manifestations of the mystery of life.

1. Sin

The Scattered Sheep Sought After (1659)

I.102 ...the Lord God of life lived not in them; but they lived upon such things as once came from the life; but, being separated from the spring, were dead, and nourished but the dead part in them, the estranged from God. And thus, though their professions were great, and they multiplied prayers, sacrifices, and fasts, and drew nigh to God with their lips, yet their hearts were far from him. They had forsaken the fountain; they drank not of the waters of the spring, of the rock that followed them [this phrase would appear to be a conflation of the cloud and fire that followed Moses day and night (Num 9:15–16), and the rock he struck to bring forth water (Num 20:10–13)]; but they drank of the waters of their own cisterns. They set up that knowledge of the law for their light which they had hewed out with the tools of their own understanding, without the spirit that wrote it. This was Israel's error of old: they drank very zealously of the waters of the law; but they drank it not from the spring, but out of the cisterns which themselves had hewed.

The Axe Laid to the Root of the Old Corrupt Tree (1659)

I.229 ... any form, out of the life, kills the life; and its reward is death to itself. The form kills the life, which stirred underneath, and made it appear with some freshness; and when the life, from which it had its seeming beauty and lustre, dies, then it soon withers and dies also: so that the living principle being once slain, there remains nothing but the dead spirit, feeding on the dead form.

A Warning of Love from the Bowels of Life (1660)

I.404–05 The fall of man from God is such, that it hath benumbed all his senses; yea, so bereft him of them, that he cannot feel his own estate. He is dead, spiritually dead; and can no more feel his death, his spiritual death, than a man naturally dead can his natural death. He is bewitched into a fool's paradise, where he hath a new life, a new virtue, a new wisdom, a new kingdom, a new dominion (which is indeed but death). ... Nay, nay; the spiritual image, the divine image, the eternal life, the pure power and virtue is wholly lost; and there is nothing left, but what is captivated and destroyed through the degenerating power. There is nothing at all of the eternal kingdom, of the spiritual image, of the divine life, to be found in fallen man, but a little seed. ... And now, who can read this riddle? The kingdom is within every man, and yet not so much as sown in any man, till the springing up of the eternal virtue, according to the eternal pleasure: nay, the earth is not so much as prepared to receive the seed, until the Lord send his plough into the heart. So that it is impossible for fallen man to attain to so much as one true breathing or desire after God again; this must arise from the grace. ...

Some Questions and Answers for the opening of the Eyes of the Jews Natural (1661)

II.234–35 ... Man was made a vessel of light, a vessel of life, a vessel of pure freedom. He was formed in the eternal image and had a pure being in that image. He was light in the Lord, living in the Lord, free unto all good, and from all evil in the Lord. This was the state of his being at first, and thus was he made in the image a pure resemblance of the eternal purity and blessedness: but, besides this, he had the eternal life, the eternal substance, the eternal purity itself dwelling in the vessel, shining in it, and manifesting itself from it according to its pleasure.

Quest. How came man to fall from this estate?

Ans. Not willingly, not of an inclination of his own; but he was deceived, through the subtlety of temptation, to entertain a desire of enlarging his blessedness, out of the limits of the will of his Creator.

Quest. How could such a temptation enter man, he being pure and holy, inclined to good, and against evil, after the image of his Creator?

Ans. Man was not made to enjoy a perfection in himself separate from his Creator, or to live of himself, but by dependence. Now though he had no inclination in him not to depend, or to seek a life in himself out of the fountain, yet there was a capacity of so doing: before which capacity the tempter laid his bait of advancing him to a greater wisdom, glory, and excellency than his Creator had placed him in; with which he consulting out of the dependence upon his Creator fell from that which alone was able to uphold him in the pure state wherein he was made. ...

Quest. What was the state of man in and since the fall?

Ans. A state of darkness, a state of death, a state of deep captivity. ... Man is not dead as to his being either in soul or body, but as to the right, pure, and sanctified state of each. The vessels still remain the same in being; but they are emptied of their proper liquor, and filled with other wine. The understanding is the same, the reason the same, the will the same, the memory the same, the bodily members the same, as to their being or matter; but they are all otherwise leavened, and another king now dwells in them, and reigns over them.

Some of the Mysteries of God's Kingdom Glanced At (1663)

II.347 ... Man is indeed fallen, and hath no strength or will of himself to serve or obey the Lord; but there is a visitation of life and love (for Christ's sake) issuing forth towards mankind in general, wherein there goeth forth a quickening life, and a secret, hidden virtue, which giveth ability to the hearts which the Lord maketh willing to follow his drawings. And this dispensation is so managed by the Lord, that no man perisheth for want of power, but only from the stubbornness and choice of his own will.

2. Salvation

"Short Catechism", in *The Scattered Sheep Sought After* (1659)

1.126–27 *Quest.* How will this [believing in the light] save me?
Ans. By this means; that in thee which destroys thee, and separates thee from the living God, is daily wrought out, and the heart daily changed into the image of him who is light, and brought into unity and fellowship with the light, possessing of it, and being possessed by it; and this is salvation.

Quest. We thought salvation had been a thing to be bestowed hereafter, after the death of the body; but if it be thus, then salvation is wrought out here.

Ans. So it is, even in all that are saved; for there is no working of it out hereafter, but here it is wrought out with fear and trembling; and the believer, who is truly in unity with the life, daily changed from glory to glory, as by the spirit of the Lord.

Quest. But show more particularly how faith, or believing in the light, worketh out the salvation.

Ans. First, it causeth a fear and trembling to seize upon the sinner. The Lord God Almighty, by the rising of his light in the heart, causeth the powers of darkness to shake, the earth to tremble, the hills and mountains to melt, and the goodly fruit-trees to cast their fruit; and then the plant of the Lord springs up out of the dry and barren ground, which by the dews and showers from above, thrives, grows, and spreads till it fills God's earth.

2. In this fear and trembling the work of true repentance and conversion is begun and carried on. There is a turning of the soul from the darkness to the light; ... from all

false appearance and imaginations about holiness, to that which the eternal light manifesteth to be truly so. ...
3. In the belief of the light, and in the fear placed in the heart, there springs up a hope, a living hope, in the living principle, which hath manifested itself, and begun to work. ...
4. Faith, through the hope, works righteousness, and teaches the true wisdom. ... Faith in the light works out the unrighteousness, and works in the righteousness of God, in Christ. And it makes truly wise, wise in the living power; even wise against the evil, and to the good, which no man can learn elsewhere.

Some Questions and Answers for the opening of the Eyes of the Jews Natural (1661)

II.238–39   *Quest.* What is the work of redemption?
Ans. To purge the old leaven out of the vessel, to purify the vessel from all the false appearances of light, to batter down all the strongholds of the enemy in the mind, all the reasonings, thoughts, imaginations, and consultations, which are not of the pure, nor in the pure; and so to new-create and new-form the vessel in the image of the wisdom and purity wherein it was at first formed.
Quest. Who doeth this work, or who is man's redeemer out of the fall?
Ans. The Eternal Word or Son of the Father, even the wisdom and power which went forth from the fountain in the creation, the same goeth forth from the bosom of the Father to purify the creature, and so bringeth the creature back (being purified and cleansed) into his bosom again.
Quest. With what doth this Word, or Redeemer, redeem?
Ans. With his own life, with his own blood, with his own eternal virtue and purity. He descendeth into the lower parts of the earth, becomes flesh there, sows his own seed in his prepared earth, begets of his flesh and of his bone, in his own likeness, and nourisheth up his birth with his flesh and blood unto life everlasting.
Quest. What is this life? Or how doth it first manifest itself in the darkness?

Ans. It is the light of men. It is that which gave light to
Adam at first, again to him after the fall, and to all men
since the fall. It enlightens in nature; it enlightened under
the law; it did enlighten under the gospel before the
apostasy, and again since the apostasy.
Quest. How doth the light enlighten?
Ans. By its shining. The eternal Word moves, the life
opens, the light shines: this, in the least degree, is a
beginning of redemption; in its fullness it is redemption
perfected.
Quest. How doth the light work redemption in its shining?
Ans. Two ways: first, By turning the heart from the
darkness towards itself; secondly, By exercising the heart,
being turned.
Quest. How doth it turn the heart from the darkness?
Ans. The light, by its shining and enlightening, findeth out
its own, openeth it, and toucheth it with a secret virtue,
which persuades out of, and draws the heart from, the
principle and power of death and darkness, towards its
own native spring.

To All Such As Complain that They Want Power (1661)

II.289–90 The seed of the kingdom is sown man knows not how,
even by a sound of the eternal Spirit, which he is not
a fit judge of; and it grows up he knows not how; and
the power appears and works in it, in a way that he is
not aware of. He looks for the kingdom, the power,
and the life, in a way of his observation, answerable to
the thoughts and expectations of his heart. But thus it
never comes; but in the way of its own eternal motion,
it springs in the hearts of many, and they overlook the
thing, and turn from it daily, not knowing its proper way
of appearance, but expecting it some other way. And thus
the enemy holds them in the bands of death, and they are
captives in the strange land. ... I myself was long withheld
from obedience to the light eternal, in its low appearance
of discovering and convincing of sin, through this very
deceit, believing that my condition required the manifest
appearance of a very great power to help me; and so

when sin overcame me, I did only mourn over it, crying after and waiting for power, but was kept from joining with, and cleaving to that, wherein the power springs up and manifests itself according to its own pleasure, quite contrary to the way of man's expectation.

Concerning the Sum or Substance of Our Religion (n.d.; ca. 1666)

II.451–52 It is objected against us, who are called Quakers, that we deny Christ (and look not to be saved by him) as he was manifested without us, but look only to be saved by a Christ in us. To which this is in my heart to answer such as singly desire satisfaction therein.

We do indeed expect to be saved (yea, and not only so, but do already, in our several measures, witness salvation) by the revelation and operation of the life of Christ within us; yet not without relation to what he did without us. For all that he did in that body of flesh was of the Father, and had its place and service in the will, and according to the counsel, of the Father. But the knowledge and belief of that, since the days of the apostles, have been very much held in the unrighteousness, and in the separation from the inward work of the power and life of Christ in the heart; which, as so held, cannot save any. But whoever feels the light and life of Christ revealed in him, and comes into union with God there-through, he feels the work of regeneration, of sanctification, of justification, of life, and redemption; and so comes to reap benefit inwardly, and to partake of the blessed fruits of all that Christ did outwardly. ... This indeed is the main thing, to witness salvation wrought out in the heart.

Of the Church (1668)

III.152–53 ... The grace, in itself, is of its own nature everywhere. This is true. And that it hath power in it everywhere, and that this power is over and above sin; this is true also. But yet there is a greater or lesser proportion of it given, according to the pleasure and goodwill of the giver: and according to the measure of it (which is freely given), and the soul's growth therein, so is the power of it manifested in the heart.

Now, the difference in every man is by the grace: not of himself; for he can do nothing that is good, as of himself; but only by the grace, which is alone able to work that which is good in him, and to cause him to work in it. Yet thus it is: as the grace reacheth to him, draweth him, quickening and causing him, in the virtue, life, and obedience of the grace, to answer the grace; so doth the work thereof go on in him.

The Ancient Principle of Truth (1672)

III.273–74 Rom. 9:18. "Therefore hath he mercy on whom he will have mercy, and whom he will he hardeneth."

Now many apprehend from this scripture, as I also formerly did, that God hath chosen out a certain number of persons on whom he will have mercy, and save by Jesus Christ the Lord; and that he hath passed over the rest, so that they were never intended to have any benefit by Christ's death as to their eternal salvation. This the wisdom of man, from the letter of the scripture and many other places, may easily apprehend and strongly reason for. But as the Lord openeth the mind, and men come to a sense of his nature and Spirit, and his intent in sending his Son, and receive the key which openeth the truth as it is in Jesus, they will easily see that this is contrary to God's nature, and his intent in sending his Son, and the universal covenant of light and life, and the manifest testimony of the Scriptures.

First, As touching the nature of God. His nature is love; love to all his creatures. He would not have it go ill with any of them. He needeth not their misery to make himself happy. His nature is to love, to bless, to save; not to destroy or cut off, nor to afflict or grieve the children of men; not to hurt either the body or soul of any: he preserveth man and beast. Ps 36:6.

Secondly, As touching his sending his Son. He sent him in his love to mankind, to save mankind. His love was not to a few only; but he loved all his creatures, he loved all lost souls, and he sent his Son to save them all. He gave him light to enlighten them all, and he gave him life to quicken them all; only he dispenseth this in different ways, according to the infinite wisdom and good pleasure of his Father.

So that, Thirdly, The covenant of light and life is universal, and nigh all mankind, by which the darkest parts and corners of the earth are at some times enlightened, and feel somewhat of the quickening life. For the life is the light of men, and the light comes from the life, and is a quick, piercing, quickening light, conveying warmth and life, yea, living virtue into the darkest hearts, as it moves and finds entertainment in them.

Lastly, As for the testimony of the Scriptures, it is very clear that God would have none to perish. "All souls are mine," saith the Lord. Ezek. 18:4. "I have no pleasure in the death of him that dieth," ver. 32. And again, "As I live, saith the Lord God, I have no pleasure in the death of the wicked," chap. 33:11. I have sent my light to enlighten all men, and turn all men, and I would have all men receive it, and be turned by it. I have showed every man what is good, and what I the Lord require of him; and I would have every man answer the manifestation of my light and Spirit in him.

"Reply to Queries and Animadversions [Concerning the Rule of the New Covenant]" (1667/8)

IV.182   ... For though they had never heard the outward sound or name Christ; yet feeling the thing, and being gathered to God by the thing, the value and virtue of it could not but redound to them; for it is not the outward name, but the inward life and power, which is the Saviour.

"Some Misrepresentations of Me Concerning Church Government" (n.d.; ca. 1675–1679)

IV.334   ... Ever since the fall of man, man hath been secretly, or more manifestly, directed by a light, or the principle within to direct or guide his ways. To Adam the holy seed was promised, which was not only to appear outwardly in a body of flesh, but also within in man's heart, to bruise the serpent's head there [Gen 3:15]. And the holy patriarchs had not the letter outwardly, but God's Spirit inwardly, to be their guide and teacher, which did also strive with the wicked old world before the flood. The Jews also were directed to the Word nigh in the mouth and heart [Rom 10:8]: and by this Word God showed also to the Gentiles what was good, and what the Lord required of them; and by this Word such of the Gentiles as hearkened to it felt somewhat of the new creation, and of the new nature, by which nature they did in measure answer the holy law of God, and do the things contained in the law, which by the old, corrupt nature no man can do. Also Christ preached the kingdom, or seed of the kingdom within. And the apostles preached the same Word of faith within, which Moses had testified of.

3. Perfection

The Scattered Sheep Sought After (1659)

1.127–28   In the righteousness, and in the true wisdom which is received in the light, there springs up a love, and a unity, and fellowship with God, the Father of lights, and with all who are children of the light. Being begotten by Christ, the light, into the nature of the light, and brought forth in the image, there is a unity soon felt with God, the Father, and with those who are born of the same womb, and partake of the same nature. And here are a willingness and power felt in this love, to lay down the life, even for the least truth of Christ's or for the brethren. ... Yea, in them that turn towards it, give up to it, and abide in it. In them it cleanseth out the thickness and darkness, and daily transformeth them into the image, purity, and perfection of the light. And this nothing can do but the light alone.

An Examination of the Grounds or Causes which are said to Induce the Court of Boston ... (1660)

1.318–19   ... The ... last instance which they [Boston Puritans] give of the destructiveness of their [Quakers'] doctrine to the fundamental truths of religion, is, That opinion of theirs of being perfectly pure and without sin, which (say they) tends to overthrow the whole gospel, and the very vitals of Christianity: for they that have no sin, have no need of Christ, or of his satisfaction, or blood to cleanse them, nor of faith, repentance, etc.

Ans. That the Lord God is able perfectly to redeem from sin in this life; that he can cast out the strong man, cleanse the house, and make it fit for himself to dwell in; that he can finish transgression and sin in the heart, and bring in everlasting righteousness; that he can tread down Satan under the feet of his saints, and make them more than conquerors over him; this they confess they steadily believe. But that every one that is turned to the light of the spirit of Christ in his heart, is presently advanced to this state, they never held forth. ... Yet for all this, saith Christ to his disciples, "Be ye perfect" [Mt 5:48]; directing them to aim at such a thing; and the apostle saith, "Let us go on unto perfection" [Heb 6:1]; and Christ gave a ministry "for the perfecting of the saints" [Eph 4:12]: and they do not doubt but that he that begins the work, can perfect it even in this life, and so deliver them out of the hands of sin, Satan, and all their spiritual enemies, as that they may serve God without fear of them any more, in holiness and righteousness before him all the days of their lives.

1.320–21 ... as for purifying themselves daily, and putting off the old man, and putting on the new [Eph 4:22-24]; it is that which their hearts delight to be continually exercised about; and all this with a hope that it may be effected, that the vessel may be made holy to the Lord, a fit spiritual temple for him to dwell in, that he may display his life, glory, power, and pure presence in them. ...

... in the state of perfection, the blood is not laid aside as useless, but remains to keep pure for ever. It is the blood of the everlasting covenant, Heb. 13:20, both the covenant and the blood last for ever, and are useful even to them that are perfect. ... That which unites and ties the

soul to Christ, the life, abides in the soul for ever, even as
the union itself abides. And there is a growing in the life,
even where the heart is purified from sin, even as Christ
did grow and was strong in spirit; for a state of perfection
doth not exclude degrees. And so there is also a need of
watching against temptations in a perfect state; for Adam
was perfect, and yet he needed a watch: and Christ was
perfectly pure and without sin, and yet he did both watch
and pray. So that if any were brought to the perfect state
of a man, even unto the measure of the stature of the
fullness of Christ, which the ministry was given to bring
all the saints unto, Eph 4:11–13, if any were taught and
enabled so to walk in the light, as to be cleansed by the
blood from all sin, and to have such fellowship with the
Father and the Son, as might make their joy full, 1 John
1:3–4,7, if any were brought to that state of glory, as to
be chaste virgins, 2 Cor 11:2, without spot or wrinkle of
the flesh, but holy and without blemish, Eph. 5:27, if any
should be made perfect in every good work to do his will,
which was a thing the apostle prayed for, Heb. 13:21, if
any should have so put off the old man, and have put on
the wedding garment, as to be made ready and fit to be
married to the Lamb, Rev 19:7, yet this would not exclude
faith in the blood, or prayer, or watchfulness, to keep the
garment pure, etc., nor growth in the life. And this we
are not ashamed to profess, that we are pressing after,
and some have already attained very far, even to be made
perfect as pertaining to the conscience; being so ingrafted
into Christ the power of God, so planted into the likeness
of his death and resurrection, so encompassed with
the walls and bulwarks of salvation, as that they feel no
condemnation for sin, but a continual justification of the
life; being taught, led, and enabled to walk, not after the
flesh, but after the spirit. Rom 8:1.

Some of the Mysteries of God's Kingdom Glanced At (1663)

II.341–42 … The great healing, the great conquest, the great
salvation is reserved for the full manifestation of the love
of God. His judgments, his cuttings, his hewings by the

word of his mouth, are but to prepare for, but not to do, the great work of raising up the sweet building of his life, which is to be done in love, and in peace, and by the power thereof. And this my soul waits and cries after, even the full springing up of eternal love in my heart, and in the swallowing of me wholly into it, and the bringing of my soul wholly forth in it, that the life of God in its own perfect sweetness may fully run forth through this vessel, and not be at all tinctured by the vessel, but perfectly tincture and change the vessel into its own nature; and then shall no fault be found in my soul before the Lord, but the spotless life be fully enjoyed by me, and become a perfectly pleasant sacrifice to my God.

II.351–52 ... By his blood; by his life; by his power; by his nature sown in the vessel, and transforming the vessel into its own likeness. Yea, this is indeed redemption, when the creature is changed into, and brought forth in, the image, power, nature, virtue, and divine life of him that redeemeth; and the old contrary image perfectly blotted out, by the presence and indwelling of the new. This is perfect redemption, the least measure whereof is redemption in a degree.

"To ___" (1670)

III.449, ... he receives life in abundance in and through the Lord
JP II.255 Jesus Christ; then the fruits of life become easy and natural to him, and the fruits and ways of sin, unbelief, and disobedience unnatural; and here the yoke is easy and the burden light, and none of the commandments of our Lord Jesus Christ grievous.

4. Creation

A Warning of Love from the Bowels of Life (1660)

I.402 There is an everlasting, infinite, pure fountain, and wellspring of life, from whence all creatures came; from whence their life, being, motion, virtue, and rest flow; in which they all have a place and standing according to their nature, estate, temperature, and course of operation in his eternal counsel, who made all, disposeth of all, ruleth in and over all eternally. ...

Some Questions and Answers for the Opening of the Eyes of the Jews Natural (1661)

II.256 ... The creating power and preserving power is the same; but the work is somewhat different, both in the outward, visible creation, and inward, new creation. The preservation of that which is created and planted (unto its growth and perfection) is by the same power which created and planted; but rather in a way of care, industry, art, and skill, than of such immediate force and power, though by the exercise and putting forth of the same virtue and power.

5. Last Things

Some Questions and Answers for the Opening of the Eyes of the Jews Natural (1661)

II.230 The Spirit was once poured down from on high on the disciples of the Messiah, upon his ascending into his glory, and the wilderness then became a fruitful field, and the fruitful field was accounted for a forest; but over that glory the defence was not so stretched forth, but that a night overtook that day, and the wild beasts made a prey of that vineyard and fruitful field also, as well as of the former. But there is to be a more general pouring out of the Spirit, even upon all flesh, and the wilderness is more generally to be visited, and become a fruitful field, and the fruitful field is more generally to be blasted and made a forest; insomuch as all flesh everywhere shall appear grass, and the glory thereof as the flower of the field, which shall fade and wither before the breath of God's Spirit. Then judgment shall dwell in the wilderness which is then visited, and righteousness shall remain in the field which is then made fruitful; and righteousness shall be powerfully operative, working out the lasting peace; and the effect of it shall be "quietness and assurance for ever." No more war, no more fighting with creatures, no more burdening and oppressing of the creation, no more sinning and offending against the Creator, no more being dispossessed of his life and glory; but the dwellings which God reareth up in the last days for Israel, his people, shall be peaceable habitations, sure dwellings, and quiet resting-places for evermore.

A Salutation of Love (n.d.; ca. 1662–1663)

II.321–22 Certain I am, there is a day of giving account for sinning against God, and for oppressing that in your consciences which discovers to you, and checks you for, your sins. And this will as certainly come, as the day of sinning now is; and then every man must receive from God according to his works, and reap the fruit of the deeds done in the body; then every soul must inherit according to its nature, and every vessel be filled with what it is fitted to receive: that which is fitted for mercy, with mercy; that which is fitted for wrath and misery, with wrath and misery. . . .

6. Christ and Trinity

The Scattered Sheep Sought After (1659)

I.117–18 The work of the Son is to reveal the Father, and to draw to the Father. He reveals him as light, as the spring of light, as the fountain of light, and he draws to him as light. When he gave to his apostles the standing message, whereby they were to make him known to the world, and whereby men were to come into fellowship and acquaintance with him; this is it, "that God is light, and in him is no darkness at all" [Jn 1:5].

Christ Jesus, the Son of God, he is the image of his substance, the exact image of this light, the light of the world, who is to light the world into this substance. So that as God the Father is to be known as light, so Christ the Son also is to be known as light. He is the only begotten of the Father of lights, the only image wherein the eternal substance is revealed and made known. And he that receives this image, receives the substance;

and he that receives not this image, receives not the substance.

Now there is a breath or spirit from this substance, in this image, which draws to the image; thus the Father draws to the Son; and the image again draws to the substance; thus the Son draws to the Father. And so hearkening to this breath, the mind and soul is led out of the darkness, into the image of light (which is the Son), and by the image into the substance: and here is the fellowship which the gospel invites to. Joining to this breath, being transformed by this breath, living in this breath, walking in this holy inspiration, there is a unity with the Father and the Son, who themselves dwell in this breath, from whom this breath comes, in whom this breath is, and in whom all are, who are one with this breath.

This breath purgeth out the dark breath, the dark air, the dark power, the mystery of death and darkness; and fills with the breath of light, with the breath of life, with the living power, with the holy, pure mystery.

Now, as the Father is light, and the Son light; so this breath, this spirit which proceeds from them both, is light also. And as the Father, who is light, can alone be revealed by the Son, who is light; so the Son, who is light, can alone be revealed by the spirit, who is light.

He then who hears this message, that God is light; and feeleth himself darkness, and in darkness, and is willing to be drawn out of the darkness into fellowship with God, who is light; this is requisite for him to know; namely, how he may be drawn out, who is it that draws, and which are the drawings; that he may not resist or neglect them (waiting for another thing) and so miss of the true and only passage unto life. Wherefore, observe this heedfully.

None can draw to the Father, but the Son; none can draw to the Son, but the Father: and both these alone draw by the spirit. The Father, by his spirit, draws to the Son; the Son, by the same spirit, draws to the Father: and they both draw by the spirit as he is light, as he is their light lighted to that end. For as the Father is light, and the

Son is light; so that spirit which draws them must be light also. He is, indeed, the breath of light, eternally lighted, to draw to the eternal image of light, and then to the eternal substance, which eternally dwells in that eternal image.

The Jew Outward Being a Glass for the Professors of this Age (1659)

1.202–03 … in his doctrine there seemed many contradictions to the fleshly understanding; for one while he said, "I judge no man" [Jn 8:15]; for I came not to condemn the world: and yet was not he continually judging and condemning the Scribes, the Pharisees, the Priests, the Lawyers, and that whole generation of professors? So again, he came to seek and save that which was lost; to preach the gospel of peace; and yet another while he saith, he came not to send peace, but a sword, and to kindle a fire, and to set men at variance, etc. Again, one while he said, "I and my Father are one" [Jn 10:30]; another time, "My Father is greater than I" [Jn 14:28]. One while he bid men do as the Scribes and Pharisees taught [Mk 12:28–34]; another while he bid men beware of the leaven or doctrine of the Pharisees and Sadducees. Mt 16:12.

But to what purpose should I heap up any more instances? O thou that readest this, wait to know in thy self the ear that cannot hear Christ's doctrine; while thou condemnest the Jews, do not run into the same error of unbelief and gainsaying; but wait to know the voice of Christ in this day, and to receive the ear that can hear it; for though thou shouldst be willing to hear, yet thou canst not till thy ear be opened. Nicodemus, who could acknowledge Christ "a teacher come from God," yet could not receive the doctrine of the new birth from him. John 3:4. And there were many things the disciples themselves were not able to bear: for when, at a certain time, he spake of "giving his flesh to eat," not only the Jews, John 6:52, but they also, stumbled, ver. 61. And who is there among professors that can now bear it, or receive Christ's own interpretation of it? who saith, that "the flesh" (which they understood) "profiteth nothing;" but the flesh which he meant was "spirit and life," ver. 63.

I.206–07 There were many other things which they could not but except against [Jesus]; as at his answers to their questions, to which sometimes he was silent, and gave no answer at all; at other times, he answered not directly, but in parables. And how offensive is this to man's wisdom, who requires a positive and direct answer! . . .

. . . He showed not respect to Herod the king; . . . the reverend and grave doctors of the law; . . . the high priest; . . . his own disciples; . . . his own mother (as man's spirit, by its rule of respect, would judge and condemn him); but said, "Woman, what have I to do with thee?" John 2:4. And in a manner denied all his relations. Mat. 12:48.

Some of the Mysteries of God's Kingdom Glanced At (1663)

II.343 Mark how every thing in the kingdom, every spiritual thing, refers to Christ, and centres in him. His nature, his virtue, his presence, his power, makes up all. Indeed he is all in all to a believer, only variously manifested and opened in the heart by the Spirit. He is the volume of the whole book, every leaf and line whereof speaks of him, and writes out him in some or other of his sweet and beautiful lineaments. So that if I should yet speak further of other things, as of meekness, tenderness, humility, mercy, gentleness, patience, long-suffering, contentedness, etc. (all which I had much rather should be read in his book, even in the living book of the eternal Word, than in my writings), I should but speak further of his nature brought up, manifested, and displaying itself in and through the creatures, by his turning the wheel of his life in their hearts. But my spirit hasteneth from words, therefore can I not but cut short and pass over these openings in me, that neither my own soul nor others may fix or stay upon words concerning the thing, but may sink in spirit into the feeling of the life itself, and may learn what it is to enjoy it there, and to be comprehended of it, and cease striving to know or comprehend concerning it. And then I am sure he that hath a taste of this cannot but be willing to sell all the knowledge that can be held in the creaturely vessel, for that knowledge which is living.

A Question to the Professors of Christianity (1667)

III.49–50 Now the Scriptures do expressly distinguish between Christ and the garment which he wore; between him that came, and the body in which he came; between the substance which was veiled, and the veil which veiled it. "Lo! I come; a body hast thou prepared me" [Heb 10:5–7]. There is plainly he, and the body in which he came. There was the outward vessel, and the inward life. This we certainly know, and can never call the bodily garment Christ, but that which appeared and dwelt in the body. Now if ye indeed know the Christ of God, tell us plainly what that is which appeared in the body – whether that was not the Christ before it took up the body, after it took up the body, and for ever.

And then their confining of Christ to that body, plainly manifesteth that they want the knowledge of him in Spirit. For Christ is the Son of the Father; he is the infinite eternal Being, one with the Father, and with the Spirit, and cannot be divided from either; cannot be anywhere where they are not, nor can be excluded from any place where they are. He may take up a body, and appear in it; but cannot be confined to be nowhere else but there; no not at the very time while he is there. Christ, while he was here on earth, yet was not excluded from being in heaven with the Father at the very same time; as he himself said concerning himself, "The Son of man which is in heaven." John 3:13. Nor was the Father excluded from being with him in the body; but the Father was in him, and he in the Father: whereupon he said to Philip, "He that hath seen me hath seen the Father" [Jn 14:9]. What! did every one that saw that body, see the Father also? Nay, not so; but he that saw Christ, the Son of the living God, whom flesh and blood revealed not, but the Father only (Mat. 16:16–17), he saw the Father also.

O friends! look to your knowledge of Christ, and to your faith and knowledge of the Scriptures, and to your prayers also; for it is easy missing of the living substance in all these, and meeting with a shadow; which may please, and make a great show in the earthly part, in the natural understanding and affections, but satisfieth not the soul, or that which is born after the Spirit, but still the cry goes out (where the soul is awakened) after truth, substance, life, virtue from God's Spirit in the spirit which it alone can feed upon.

These four things following I am certain of; which he that cometh into the true light, shall infallibly experience them there.

First, That nothing can save but the knowledge of Christ, even of that very Christ, and no other, who took upon him the prepared body, and offered it up at Jerusalem.

Secondly, That no knowledge of Christ can save but the living knowledge. Not a knowledge of him after the letter (which the carnal part may get much of, and value itself much by), but a knowledge of him in the Spirit; which is only given to that which is begotten and born of the Spirit, and only retained by that which abides and remains in the Spirit, and runs not out into the fleshly reasonings, imaginings, and conceivings, about the things mentioned in the Scriptures.

Thirdly, That that man who knoweth not Christ in Spirit, nor keepeth close to him in spirit; but (through darkness and misguidance of the spirit of deceit) calleth the shinings of his light (his reproofs, his checks for that which is evil, and his secret motions to that which is good) natural; this man, though he seem to own Christ ever so much according to the letter, yet in truth denies him.

Fourthly, He that denies Christ, in his knockings and visitations of him in his own heart, and before men in the truths which he holds forth by his servants and ministers of his Spirit, him will he deny before his Father in heaven.

"To the Friend of Frances Fines" (1670)

III.461–62   Now consider I pray thee, if this be not contrary to the
JP 1.100   Scriptures. Was the work laid by the Father upon the Manhood or upon the Son, who in the Life and by the Life was mighty to save? Who took up the Manhood? Was it not the Son? Lo I come, saith he, a body, hast thou

prepared me [Heb 10:5–7]. And was it not he that laid down his glory, that made himself of no reputation, but came in the form of a servant [Phil 2:7] (took upon him man's Nature?) did not he do the work in man's Nature? Did not the eternal Spirit sanctify the body in the womb? Did not the eternal power act in him all along? Yea, did not the eternal Spirit offer the body to God as a sacrifice? For the manhood would fain have avoided the cup (Father if it be possible let this cup pass from me [Lk 22:42]) but the Spirit taught him to subject to the will of the Father herein. So that his giving up to Death was rather to be attributed to his eternal Spirit, than to his manhood: for that was the chief in the work, and not only assistant to him. And doth not Christ confess as much to his Father, when he saith, I have glorified thee on the earth, I have finished the work which thou gavest me to do: and now, O Father, glorify thou me with thy own self; with the glory which I had with thee before the world was [Jn 17:5]. Though we are willing to honour the manhood of Christ (the Father having honoured it) with the honour wherewith the Father hath honoured it: yet we cannot honour it in the first place, and attribute Redemption to it in the first place, making the Spirit and life of God but supporting, assisting, and carrying on therein. For God was in Christ [2 Cor 5:19]; and it was his power, life, and virtue did all in him, as it is a measure of the same life doth all in us: in which measure we partake of his Death, and not only so, but also of his Life and resurrection.

CHAPTER 12
God

What can we learn today about God and the spiritual life from Penington's way of talking about "the mystery of the life within" ("Reply [Concerning...New Covenant]", IV.191)? Can we benefit from how he uses "God" in the language of the spirit?

The word "God" has become problematic for many people in the modern world. "God" is used in politics to justify war and oppression. Psychologically, it is used to twist the meaning of greed, domination of others, and self-destructiveness into reassuring ideals, and to focus attention outwards, away from the self. In economic relations "God" endorses charity without concern to change the roots of injustice, and redirects passion for fairness and reform to a future life. In science God as cause and controller of everything is undercut by explanations of cosmic and organic evolution in terms of natural principles and causes. Human suffering inflicted by humans, not to mention natural suffering, undercut "God" as the world's administrator. In morality "God" is used to support order, to oppose energy and change, and enforce conformity to the rules of an external authority. And in theology "God" as unchanging distances God from the dynamism and particularity of our lives.

For Penington the way many Protestants and Catholics speak of "God" is also problematic. He starts from his own experience. The word "God" comes to mean something that he becomes aware of in his own life. While there is no doubt that he is steeped in traditional Christian language, his convincement, like that of others to Quakerism, was not to become Christian, since he already was a serious

Christian, but was to discover the divine presence in his present life. On the basis of this personal discovery he could then make sense of various ideas he knew in scripture and tradition. He could also look backwards from this point to his past and see the divine presence stirring the life in him beneath, and often contrary to, his former Protestant beliefs.

Penington's theological thinking starts from experience – and stays with it, not by telling anecdotes but through remaining open to the level of depth from which to speak. He knows "there is so much wrapped up in" God which "the heart...cannot conceive", that he speaks of the "somewhat" of the divine mystery he has "felt" and can "say" ("Seed of God", IV.341). He knows God through sensing, feeling, tasting rather than rational "striving to know" (*Some of the Mysteries*, II.343). He thus urges a profound simplicity of thought – to avoid the abstract complexities of the theological tradition and to speak only what one experiences within: "not making likenesses of him in our minds, but...worshipping him in his own appearances" (*Obs... Muggleton*, III.83).

Penington is speaking of what we today call "continuing revelation": God is revealed or appears in our own lives. Thinking of God as the incomprehensible whole—implied in Paul's phrase "In him we live and move and have our being" (Acts 17:28) – I would say for Penington that aspects of that Whole appear to us at different moments in our experience. Theology, then, should gather up these moments and be based in them, using words and ideas to grasp conceptually and to convey what these appearings are. Penington's words and ideas about God come from scripture and the Christian tradition, and are articulated in his difficult seventeenth-century language. The measure of their truth is not however their conformity to scripture or tradition, nor their logical coherence and systematic connectedness, but their bearing life as it issues forth from having sunk down into the Life.

Whatever "God" means for Penington, it is known through experience in its depths. Through the use of metaphor and symbol he reaches this experiential level where the Life is stirring, and speaks of what he knows of this mysterious presence. If we are responsive, the use of symbol can make us aware of something hidden. The use of metaphor can evoke connections in our lives, transform us, and engender an authentic humility, teaching us to be "flexible" and "pliable" in our thinking, for we can only say what God is "like" since we grasp only the "somewhat" of an incomprehensible Whole which we sense in our lives.

It should be evident that for Penington what we know of God and how we know God are inseparable. God is not the same object that can be known through a variety of modes of knowing. The known is different if approached rationally or experientially. Approached rationally within scripture and tradition, without a present sense of divine reality, the "God" spoken of is not the same reality as what is spoken of as we are experiencing it. Speaking the language of Spirit conjoins, therefore, the how of "experience", "sensing", "feeling", "tasting" with the what of "presence", "mystery", "Pure Being" (*Some Qs...Jews Natural*, II.252), "Whole", in Penington's variety of metaphors. We know God thus as we are feeling our relatedness, being changed, and becoming open to the divine "More".

Throughout my commentary on Penington's thought, I have focused on the metaphor that I see as paramount for him – the Life. In the early chapters of Part II, I have shown how Penington, from the period of his convincement, conceives the divine life as a seed within each of us which can grow into fullness. "Seed" we have seen is a fitting metaphor to bear the life Penington experienced in its transformative power. "God" when used by Penington in the language of the Spirit means a reality which changes us to live creatively from the Spirit indwelling us; to live harmoniously with diversity in community; to work for justice and an end to oppression in the nation; and to participate in the wisdom of the Spirit that originates, orders, and fills nature. This reality Penington knows "somewhat" in the changes in his life is love. God loves all creatures; it is God's "holy pleasure" (*Naked Truth*, III.283) for each person to open to the seed and to flourish. God is primarily life and the engenderer of life, drawing us into the divine nature of Life. Involved intimately in our lives, God works in and through the afflictions of body and soul, not to destroy out of judgment, but to transform us deeper into the life, out of love. In this Penington locates himself in the Christian tradition of those who liken God's love to a mother's (*Holy Truth*, III.205; *To Fds in England etc.*, III.418). From the "hidden womb of wisdom", or of the "Spirit" (*Babylon the Great*, I.148; *Consid...the Book*, II.119), we are born into new life, again and again, and nourished into maturity.

God in Penington's experience is, as well, liberator from self-deception and social oppression. God works in history by working in people's hearts, using them whether opened or closed, to achieve divine intentions in the world to overturn oppression, to beget a tender conscience, and to awaken people from "benumbed sense" (*Question...England*, 1.293) in the way of death to live here and now in the land of life, the kingdom of God – the way of freedom, justice, peace, and fullness of life. In this God is cause, but not an external cause of the world or of historical events. Rather God is the "wellspring of life" (*Warning of Love*, 1.402.) underlying all being and doing in inwardness, out of which creation has come, and guiding those who are open to dwelling in the Life. God "fill[s] all things" (*Scattered Sheep*, 1.131). As "the inward substance of all that appears" (*Some Qs...Man His Duty*, II.270), "God" is not an object to be known but a mystery to feel and to dwell within.

Some Questions and Answers for the Opening of the Eyes of the Jews Natural (1661)

II.252   It [God's exercise for us] prepares for a clearer entrance into, and safer enjoyment of, the fullness; As the soul is more emptied of the strength and riches it received from God; so it is more prepared to enter into, and live in, the Pure Being itself. For nothing can live there which veils. In the life God was, and is, and is to be all in all for ever.

Some Questions and Answers Showing Man His Duty (1662)

II.270–71 *Quest.* What is God?
Ans. The fountain of beings and natures, the inward substance of all that appears; who createth, upholdeth, consumeth, and bringeth to nothing, as he pleaseth. ...
Quest. How may a man come by a principle of life from God?
Ans. God is near to every man with the breath of his life, breathing upon him at times according to his pleasure; which, man's spirit opening unto, and drinking in, it becometh a seed or principle of life in him, overspreading and leavening him up to eternal life.

To All Such as Complain that They Want Power (1661)

II.293–94   ... It is necessary that his [God's] power and life should spring up in the creature in its own way, according to the counsel of his own wisdom, suitable to his own nature, and not in the way which the creature chalks out, and expects it in. God must be like himself, and walk in his own path in every thing he does. He is a God that hideth himself in the mystery of his working, throughout the whole track of man's redemption; and man must be wrought out of himself, out of his own thoughts, expectations, gathered apprehensions concerning the kingdom and way to life, and led in a path he doth not know (nor ever can know any longer than he is in it); and in ways he hath not been acquainted with.

Some of the Mysteries of God's Kingdom Glanced At (1663)

II.341 ...[Love] is the sweet, tender, melting nature of God, flowing up through his seed of life into the creature, and of all things making the creature most like unto himself, both in nature and operation.

Observations on Some Passages of Lodowick Muggleton (1668)

III.95–96 "...I [Lodowick Muggleton] marvel what satisfaction any man can have in his mind in believing in a Quakers' God, to tell a man that God abides in himself, and is what he is."

...Doth not God say to Moses concerning himself, *I am that I am*. When Moses desired to know how he should answer the Israelites, when they should enquire who sent him to them, God bid him tell them that I am had sent him, Exod 3:14. How could the Israelites understand what God was by this? what satisfaction could they find in this answer of Moses, would this spirit say? But God is not to be known by the description of words of the earthly wisdom, but in his own feeling Spirit and life.

The Ancient Principle of Truth (1672)

III.261 ...Consider the great love of God to mankind, and the great care he hath of them. First, as touching their bodies; how doth he provide for the bodies of all mankind! He would have none hurt, none destroyed; but feedeth all, nourisheth all, making plentiful provision, and giving fruitful seasons; causing his sun to shine, and his rain to descend on all. Then as to their souls, he knoweth the preciousness thereof. ...

"Life and Immortality" (1671)

IV.62 ... Did they [the apostles] not preach this message of the gospel (which they had from Christ to carry to men), that "God is light, and in him is no darkness at all" [1 Jn 1:5]? And did they not preach it to this very end, to turn men, and bring men from the darkness within to the light within, that in it they might have union and fellowship with God, who is light? Can any have fellowship with God, who is light, but as his spirit is brought out of the inward darkness into the inward light?

"Somewhat Relating to Church Government" (1675)

IV.294 ... God is the fullness, the seed is a measure and manifestation of him, the infinite fullness. And as he is light and Spirit, so the seed that comes from him, or that the good husbandman sows, is light and Spirit also.

"Seed of God" (n.d.; ca. 1675–1679)

IV.343 ... As God is love, so the seed that is of him partakes of his love. There is no enmity in it, and no enmity or ill-will springs from it. This is it that makes it so natural to the children of God to love; because they are born of that seed which came from the God of love, whose nature is love.

APPENDIX A

Short titles used for extracts from Works, and notes on texts

Items not published in IP's lifetime are in quotes, without italics. Notes are by Rosemary Moore. All items are referenced to their location in the *Works: The Works of Isaac Penington A Minister of the Gospel in the Society of Friends, Including His Collected Letters* 4 v. Glenside, Pennsylvania: Quaker Heritage Press, 1995–1997. Available online at www.qhpress.org/texts/penington/index.html See pp. x–xi for earlier collected editions, and Bibliography p. 294.

Ancient Principle of Truth
  The Ancient Principle of Truth or the Light Within Asserted [1672]. *Works* III.244–278. Probable date from position in first edition of *Works*, this is a solid book and a date soon after Penington's release from Reading, when he could work at leisure, is likely.

Axe Laid to the Root
  The Axe Laid to the Root of the Old Corrupt Tree (Lodowick Lloyd, 1659). *Works* I.226–275. A collection of short theological papers, probably published early in this year, before political matters outweighed all other interests.

Babylon the Great Described
  (Lodowick Lloyd, 1659). *Works* I.134–194. The notoriously wicked city of Babylon was frequently used at this time as a metaphor of evil. George Thomason, who made a large collection of

pamphlets now in the British Library, purchased this book on 8 August, when it was probably newly written. At this date the nation was sliding into anarchy, and people were beginning to despair of a political solution to the nation's troubles: "This nation hath long been wounded and sick... many are spending their judgment upon her, some thinking a King would help, some a Parliament, some hoping for good from the Army, but every eye sees her case to be desperate" (1.194).

Concerning the Church
Concerning the Church or of the Church State under the Gospel Whereby It May Appear (1666). Works II.422–440.

Concerning God's... Israel
Concerning God's Seeking out His Israel (Wilson, 1663). Works II.388–408. An epistle to Friends in Godmanchester, near Huntingdon. Penington had been visiting them with John Crook, and "had a word unto you from the Lord", while Crook was speaking. But when Crook had finished "those words which had often sprung in me before, sprung not again". Later, the Lord gave him "a pointing to write them down", with additions.

Concerning Persecution
(Wilson, 1661). Works II. 170–199. Written at a time when the persecution of Quakers and others was gathering strength, a plea for freedom of conscience.

"Concerning the Rule of the New Covenant"
See "Reply [Concerning... New Covenant]"

Concerning the Sum or Substance of Our Religion
[1666]. Quaker faith in relation to traditional Christianity. II.454–455

Concerning the Worship
Concerning the Worship of the Living God (n.d.; ca. 1661). Works II.210–217.

Appendix A: Short Titles and Notes on Works

Consid...the Book
The Consideration of a Position Concerning the Book of Common Prayer (Wilson, 1660). *Works* II.101–130. This was probably written during the autumn of 1660, when the new church settlement was being debated.

Ep to All Serious Profs
An Epistle to All Serious Professors of the Christian Religion (n.d.; ca. 1675–1679). *Works* IV.358–366.

Examination...Boston
An Examination of the Grounds or Causes which are said to Induce the Court of Boston in New England to make that order of Banishment upon Pain of Death against the Quakers (1660). *Works* I.301–390. *Qfp* §27.13; cf. §23.74 and §19.18. The persecution of Quakers in New England is a frequent theme of Quaker pamphlets at this time. Four were hanged before the newly restored Charles II ordered the death sentences to cease.

Flesh and Blood
The Flesh and Blood of Christ in the Mystery, and in the Outward (1675). *Works* III.341–369. An account of Quaker faith, with particular reference to the human nature of Christ, written in connection with a debate with Baptists that took place in 1672. See page 94.

"Further Testimony to Truth"
"A Further Testimony to Truth Revived out of the Ruins of the Apostasy". *Works* IV.1–49. A miscellaneous collection of short papers only published in posthumous collected works.

Great Question...Swearing
The Great Question Concerning the Lawfulness or Unlawfulness of Swearing Under the Gospel (1661). *Works* II.140–150.

Holy Truth
The Holy Truth and People Defended (1672). *Works* III.202–243.

Jew Outward
: *The Jew Outward Being a Glass for the Professors of this Age* (1659). *Works* 1.195–225.

"Life and Immortality"
: "Life and Immortality Brought to Light through the Gospel". *Works* IV.50169. Written in Reading Gaol, part dated 26 May 1671. Only published in posthumous collected works.

Many Deep Considerations have been upon my heart concerning the State of Israel (n.d.)
: See *Some Deep . . . Israel*

Naked Truth
: *Naked Truth or Truth Nakedly Manifesting Itself* (1674). *Works* III.279–340. The mature Penington is now at peace with himself, but there is a reference to earlier controversy.

New Covenant
: *The New Covenant of the Gospel distinguished from the Old Covenant of the Law* (Wilson, 1660). *Works* II.29–83. On the nature of the Sabbath, in answer to some queries of a Seventh-Day Baptist, W. Salter. This group observed Saturday instead of Sunday as their Sabbath.

Obs . . . Muggleton
: *Observations on Some Passages of Lodowick Muggleton* (1668). *Works* III.78–105. Lodowick Muggleton founded the only other 1650s sect that survived into the twentieth century. Like the Quakers, Muggletonians taught that the final age, the age of the Spirit, had now arrived. Muggletonians had no regular worship, and when religious controls were reimposed after the restoration of Charles II, they were prepared to compromise with the laws requiring attendance at parish services. See Christopher Hill, William Lamont and Barry Reay, *The World of the Muggletonians*, esp. pp.23–42, 111–153 for the character and personality of Lodowick Muggleton. The Quakers had several written disputes with Muggleton, and George Fox, Richard Farnworth and other Quakers were formally cursed by him.

Appendix A: Short Titles and Notes on Works

Of the Church
Of the Church in Its First and Pure State, in Its Declining State, in Its Declined State, and in Its Recovery (1668). *Works* III.125–195.

"A Question Answered Concerning Reading the Scriptures Aright"
Works IV.263–272. Only published posthumously, with no evidence as to when it was written.

Question...England
A Question Propounded to the Rulers, Teachers, and People of the Nation of England (1659). *Works* I.293–300.

Question to the Professors
A Question to the Professors of Christianity Whether They Have the True, Living, Powerful, Saving Knowledge of Christ, or No (1667). *Works* III.18–67. From Aylesbury gaol, part dated to August 1666.

"Reply [Concerning...New Covenant]"
"Reply to Queries and Animadversions". *Works* IV. 170–206. This overall title is given in the 1861 *Works* to two essays, "Concerning the Rule of the New Covenant", and "A Reply to thy Animadversions" (addressed to an unidentified person): in the 1681 folio collected works these are separate items with no overall title, and each are given their own dates at the end, 25 of 11 month 1667 [Jan 1668] and 19 of 12 month 1667 [Feb 1668], respectively. Extracts and references in the present book all come from "Concerning the Rule of the New Covenant".

"Reply to...Gospel-Baptism"
"A Reply to an Answer of Some Queries concerning the Gospel-Baptism". *Works* IV.367–396. Dated 18th July 1679, so one of Penington's last works. Only published in posthumous collected works, this gives answers to a paper signed N.B.

"Reply to Queries and Animadversions"
See "Reply [Concerning...New Covenant]"

Salutation of Love
A Salutation of Love and Tender Goodwill to the Commissioners of

the Peace for the County of Bucks [1670]. Works §321–323. Broadside addressed to the civic authorities, warning of the coming wrath of God. Probable date from relation to the passing of the Second Conventicle Act (pages 88–89).

Scattered Sheep
The Scattered Sheep Sought After (Lodowick Lloyd, 1659). *Works* I.101–133. See Part I pp.29–30 for the national events of this year. This book was probably written early in the year, before political considerations became paramount, and it deals with the Quaker understanding of salvation.

"Seed of God"
"The Seed of God and of His Kingdom". *Works* IV.336–357. Undated paper, only published in posthumous collected works.

Some Consids...London
Some Considerations Proposed to the City of London, and the Nation of England, to calm their spirits. Works I.285–287. Broadside, that is, a single sheet printed on one side only, suitable for display. Undated, but presumably published 1659. The current rulers of the country should not have replaced the old nobility with a new one of their own. This angers God. See also Penington's letters to the Council of State, pages 26–28.

Some Deep...Israel
Some Deep Considerations Concerning the State of Israel Past, Present, and To Come with Some Questions and Answers Concerning Unity (n.d.; ca. 1663). *Works* II.374–387. Date 1663 from content relating to Perrot. Originally published as *Many Deep Considerations have been upon my Heart Concerning the State of Israel*; not included in the first collected works; published in later editions under this title. See page 43.

Some Directions to the Panting Soul
(Wilson, 1661). *Works* II.205–206. *Qfp* §26.70. Perhaps Penington's finest brief account of personal mystical religion.

Appendix A: Short Titles and Notes on Works

"Some Experiences"
"Some Experiences which It Hath Pleased the Lord To Give Me Concerning His Way, His Truth, His Church and People, against Whom the Gates of Hell Cannot Prevail" (1679), *Works* IV.425–430. Only published in posthumous collected works. Dated 31st July 1679, a few weeks before his death, the elderly Penington reflects on his spiritual life.

Some Few Qrs ... Cavaliers
Some Few Queries and Considerations Proposed to the Cavaliers, being of Weighty Importance to them (1660). *Works* II.84–91. No printer's date, but George Thomason bought it on 2 May 1660, on the verge of the Restoration. King Charles II was proclaimed on 8 May. Penington is considering the position, under God's plan, of the coming monarchical government.

"Some Misreps ... Church Gov."
"Some Misrepresentations of Me Concerning Church Government" (n.d.). *Works* IV.303–335. Only published in posthumous collected works. A reply to John Pennyman's 1675 criticism of Penington's exposition of church government in *An Examination of the Grounds and Causes...* (1660). For Pennyman see pages 40, 95.

Some Obs ... Scripture
Some Observations upon that Portion of Scripture, Romans 14:20 (1662). *Works* II.305–311.

Some of the Mysteries
Some of the Mysteries of God's Kingdom Glanced At (1663). *Works* II.332–360. *Qfp* §26.30. Questions and answers on the Christian faith.

"Some Queries Concerning Compulsion in Religion"
Works IV.415–418. Written in 1670, at the time of the passing of the Second Conventicle Act (see pages 88–89), but published only in posthumous collected works.

Some Queries Concerning the Order and Government of the Church of Christ
(n.d.). Works II.361–373. Undated, but written from Aylesbury prison, indicating a date 1665–1667.

Some Qrs . . . Work of God
Some Queries Concerning the Work of God in the World (Wilson, 1660). Works II.92–100. This pamphlet suggests a political situation that is still uncertain, and was probably written February–April 1660.

Some Questions and Answers for the Opening of the Eyes of the Jews Natural (1661). Works II.218–265. Originally published in a small format suitable for the pocket. There was a good deal of interest in the Jews at this time. They had been expelled from England in 1290, and later from some other European countries, but by the early seventeenth century there was a Jewish population settled in Holland, refugees from the Spanish Inquisition. The diarist John Evelyn visited their synagogue, and so did Queen Henrietta Maria. Samuel Fisher was invited to address the synagogue when Quakers first visited Holland in 1654. Jews applied for permission to return to England in 1655, and while no formal leave was given, they were in fact already settled in the City of London and soon afterwards built a synagogue not five minutes walk from William Penington's house. (The present synagogue in Bevis Marks is a replacement building from later in the seventeenth century.) Londoners seem to have accepted the Jews with a mild friendly curiosity, and Samuel Pepys mentions a visit to the synagogue. Christians at this time generally believed that the conversion of the Jews to Christianity must precede the end-times of the world, and Cromwell included the Jews in his prayer for the unity of "all godly people". Quakers wrote a number of tracts inviting them to accept Quaker ways, and John Pennyman (pages 40, 95) invited "all the synagogue of the Jews" to attend his wedding. Penington would certainly have known about these developments, and may have visited the synagogue. His criticisms should be taken as on a par with his criticisms of any non-Quaker worship, and by no means anti-Semitic in the modern sense. The early Quaker relationship to the Jews is described in Kathleen Thomas,

"An Evaluation of the Inward Light as a Basis for Mission – as exemplified by Quaker approaches to Jews and Muslims in the seventeenth century" (*Quaker Studies* 1/1, Winter 1996, 54–72).

Some Qs ... Man His Duty
Some Questions and Answers Showing Man His Duty and Pointing Him to the Principle of God in His Heart (Wilson, 1662). *Works* II.266–286. A brief introduction to Quaker faith, similar to others written around this time of the inception of the Restoration church settlement. It includes several sets of queries on Christian duty and the nature of the true church.

Some Things of Gt Weight
Some Things of Great Weight and Concernment to All (1667). *Works* III.1–17. Notes and questions on Quakerism written in Aylesbury Gaol. III.2

Some Things ... Royal Soc
Some Things Relating to Religion Proposed to the Consideration of the Royal Society, So Termed (1668). *Works* III.106–124. The Royal Society was incorporated in 1660. Scientific enquiry was then in its infancy, but burgeoning, and Penington distrusted the tendency to rely too heavily on human reason.

"Somewhat Relating to Church Government"
Works IV.273–302. Probably written about 1675, but not published till 1681, after Penington's death. A reply to an attack on the Quaker doctrine of the Light.

Somewhat ... Weighty Qn
Somewhat Spoken to a Weighty Question concerning the Magistrate's Protection of the Innocent (Simmons, 1661). *Works* II.151–169. *Qfp* §24.21. Thomas Simmons (husband of Martha, the friend of James Nayler) was a regular publisher of Quaker books during the 1650s, and it is thought that Robert Wilson may have taken over his press early in the 1660s. Written in the aftermath of the publication of the Quaker "Peace Testimony" in 1661, this is a development of the theme of Quaker refusal to take part in war.

"Spiritual Travels"
"A True and Faithful Relation, in brief, Concerning Myself, in reference to My Spiritual Travails [sic in *Works*], and the Lord's Dealings with Me" (1667). *Works* I.7–11. This appears as part of Ellwood's "Testimony".

Three Queries
Three Queries Propounded to the King and Parliament (n.d.). *Works* II.312–320. The new monarchical government had come to power because the previous government had disobeyed the Lord. But the new government is also in danger if it disobeys the Lord. This message suggest a date before the permanence of the change of government was fully accepted by everyone. Probably written 1661 or 1662.

"To ___" (27 Nov 1670)
JP II.255. *Works* III.449. To an unknown correspondent, 27 Ninth Month [Nov] 1670. For a different letter, undated: JP II.278.2. *Works* III.458, see pp. 91–2.

To All Such . . . Power
To All Such as Complain that They Want Power Not Applying Themselves To Yield Subjection to What of God is Made Manifest in Them, upon a Pretence of Waiting for Power So To Do (Wilson, 1661). *Works* II.287–300. Spiritual power may come unexpectedly, as it did for Penington. The book includes a letter from John Crook written at the time of Penington's convincement, see page xx16.

To Fds in England, etc
To Friends in England, Ireland, Scotland, Holland, New England, Barbadoes, or Anywhere Else, Where the Lord God Shall Order This To Come (1666). *Works* II.409–418.

"To Friends in Truth, in and about the Two Chalfonts"
(20 June 1666). JP I.87. *Works* II.471. Chalfont St Peter and Chalfont St Giles, two adjoining villages. Penington wrote several epistles to his own meeting at Chalfont (now Jordans), mostly during times when he was unable to meet with them, being in prison.

Appendix A: Short Titles and Notes on Works

"To Friends of Both the Chalfonts"
(2 and 3 August 1667). JP 1.27.3. *Works* II.494.

"To My Friends at Horton and Thereabouts"
(22 October 1665) Part of JP 1.149. *Works* II.469–470. See pages 50–52 and 81–85 for the difficult Horton meeting.

"To My... Fds in Scotland"
To My Dear Suffering Friends in Scotland (5 July 1676). JP III.374. *Works* III.512–514.

"To Nathaniel Stonar"
(7 June 1671) JP 1.128. See notes on "To Widow Hemmings": he was her son–in–law. III.475

"To the Fd of F Fines"
"To the Friend of Frances Fines". JP 1.100. *Works* III.459–463. *Qfp* §19.30. This letter was written to an unknown friend of Penington's friend Frances Fines. This name is properly Fiennes, the family name of Lord Saye and Sele. The peer of that day was a noted supporter of the Parliamentary cause. His wife was a Frances, and maybe the person named in the correspondence, as she is elsewhere referred to in the Penington manuscripts as "Lady Fines". The widow of Nathaniel Fiennes, a younger brother of Lord Saye and Sele and a member of Cromwell's Council of State, was also a Frances, but less likely to be referred to as "Lady". The family had connections with Buckinghamshire. This letter contains references to Penington's "Cousin Brise", and a letter to this (female) cousin follows in the manuscript. It is undated, but was probably written 1668–1670, in the period of time when Penington wrote several dated letters to Frances Fines and Cousin Brise. In the original there are seven closely-packed pages of theological discussion, and only part is included in *Works*.

To the Jews Natl & Spiritual
To the Jews Natural and to the Jews Spiritual (1677). *Works* III.370–411. See notes on *Some Questions and Answers for the Opening of the Eyes of the Jews Natural*. III.390–391.

"To the Lady Conway" (undated, probably 1679)
JP II.183.3. Anne Conway, wife of the Viscount Conway, was learned in metaphysics and theology, and in her later years (she died in 1679) she accepted Quakerism. Penn, Barclay and Fox visited her house. Penington corresponded with both her and her husband. III.463–465

To the Parliament
To the Parliament, the Army, and all the Well–affected in the Nation, Who Have Been Faithful to the Good Old Cause (1659). *Works* I.276–281.

"To Widow Hemmings (26/8)"
("26 Eighth Month" [=Oct] 1670). JP 1.77. *Works* III.441–446. See notes on Widow Hemmings and family, pages 89–91.

"To Widow Hemmings (28/9)"
("28 ⅓INTH ⅞ONTH" [=Nov] 1670), JP 1.79. *Works* III.450–453.

"Treatise"
"A Treatise Concerning God's Teachings, and Christ's Law". *Works* IV.229–262. *Qfp* §26.69. Written 1671 but published only in posthumous collected works. A collection of papers on Quaker faith written in Reading Gaol.

"A True and Faithful Relation"
See "Spiritual Travels"

Warning of Love
A Warning of Love from the Bowels of Life (Wilson,1660). *Works* I.402–410. Robert Wilson published a number of Quaker books in the early 1660s. This is addressed to 'professors', that is, other Christians, on the nature of salvation.

Way of Life
The Way of Life and Death Made Manifest and Set Before Men (Lodowick Lloyd, 1658). *Works* I.14–100. Lloyd was not a regular Quaker printer, and it may be that Penington made his own arrangements for publication. This is Penington's first work

Appendix A: Short Titles and Notes on Works

written as a Quaker, and the original edition contained brief papers by George Fox and Edward Burrough, thus emphasising Penington's position as a Quaker apologist.

Weighty Qn ... to the King
A Weighty Question Propounded to the King and Parliament (1663). Works II.324–331. "Proposed" in 1663 ed.; "propounded" in 1681 collected works.

Where is the Wise?
Where Is the Wise? Where is the Scribe? (Wilson, 1660). Works I.411–420. Human wisdom is made foolish by God. Probably written during the summer of this confusing year, after the restoration of the King in May.

> A
> **Weighty Question,**
> Propoſed to the
> **KING,**
> And both HOUSES of
> **PARLIAMENT:**
> Together, with some
> **QUERIES**
> ABOUT
> **RELIGION,**
> For the good of mens Souls, that they may seek after, and be established in that which gives Life.
>
> By ISAAC PENINGTON.
>
> LONDON, Printed for R. Wilson, 1663.

APPENDIX B

Quotations from Isaac and Mary Penington's writings

in *Quaker faith and practice: the book of Christian discipline of the Yearly Meeting of the Religious Society of Friends (Quakers) in Great Britain* (1995).

Qfp ref.	Pages	
§2.48	83, 84	A combination of two short passages from a long letter to Bridget Atley [1669]. A long section of the original letter has been omitted from the middle of the *Qfp* passage. This omission was made by John Barclay, the nineteenth century editor of a selection of Penington's letters.
§10.01	59	Beginning of a letter to Amersham Friends, 1667.
§10.27	59	Part of the postscript to a letter to Chalfont Friends, 1667. Note the omission made by the nineteenth century editor.
§19.14	17, 24	From the paper on his convincement, "A True and Faithful Relation...concerning...the Lord's Dealings with me", 1667. Not complete in our text.
§19.30	226	From a letter to a friend of Frances Fines.
§19.43	51, 52	From a letter to Bridget Atley, 1665. The omissions were made by the nineteenth century editor.
§24.21	175, 174	From *Somewhat Spoken to a Weighty Question*, 1661. Two passages written as one, separated in the original and in the reverse order.
§26.30	202	From *Some of the Mysteries of Gods Kingdom*, 1663.

Appendix B: Quotations

		Part omitted in our text.
§26.70	141	From *Some Directions to the Panting-Soul*, 1661.
§27.13	163	From *An Examination of the Grounds and Causes, which are said to induce the Court of Boston in New England to make that Order or Law of Banishment upon Pain of Death against the Quakers*, 1660.
§27.22	11	From *The Life of a Christian*, 1653.
§27.27	92	From an undated letter to an unknown recipient.

Quotations from Penington used in *Quaker faith and practice* by other authors

§23.74	164	From *Examination...Boston*, slightly misquoted.
§26.69	194	From 'Concerning God's gathering us home to himself', in 'A Treatise concerning God's Teachings, and Christ's Law'

By Mary Penington

§19.13	17	From *Some Experiences of Mary Penington*, pages 44–45. Brief reference only in our text.

Bibliography

1. Editions of Isaac Penington's works

The Works of the Long Mournful and Sorely Distressed Isaac Penington. Folio, 2 vols., London: Benjamin Clark, 1681. Contains most of Penington's previously printed works and some unpublished papers. Several further editions, all in four volumes, followed during the eighteenth and nineteenth centuries, of which the last, 1861–63, included a number of Penington's letters that had recently been published. The modern edition, cited as *Works*, is: *The Works of Isaac Penington: A Minister of the Gospel in the Society of Friends, including his collected Letters*. 4 vols and supplement. Glenside, Pa: Quaker Heritage Press, 1995–97, also available freely on line at www.qhpress.org/texts/penington/index.html. This contains all previously printed Quaker books, letters and papers of Isaac Penington, and also the pre-Quaker book *A Touchstone or Tryall of Faith*. The text in general follows the 1861–63 edition

2. Manuscripts

Letters and papers of Isaac and Mary Penington, and other mss cited. These are all in the Library of the Religious Society of Friends, Friends House, London.

(a) Cash Collection, Temp. MS 747 3A and B. Holograph letter from Isaac to Mary, 1st Sept 65.

(b) Caton MSS, vols 1 & 2: MS Vols 320–321; vol 3: MS Vol S 81. Miscellaneous early Quaker letters.

(c) Crosse Collection MS Vol. 292. "Edmund Crosse his book" is a personal collection of pro-Perrot Quaker letters and papers from the 1660s and 1670s.

(i) 4, "To such who are little and low". See T. Edmund Harvey collection.

(ii) 6. Paper on Perrot. "Some things have been very observable and wonderful unto me concerning John Perrot. 1st the great sufferings which he underwent in Rome for truth's sake."

(iii) 37. Two short epistles (a) "There is a pure birth of life to be brought forth, and all other births are to die and pass away before it." (b) "The true liberty lies hid in the life, and appears as the power of life appears."

(d) Gibson MSS, MS Vols 334–336, six volumes of manuscripts collected during the first half of the nineteenth century.

(i) 2.45. Part of an account of Penington's life, including an autobiographical account of his arrest in 1670, and imprisonment in Reading gaol. Also a letter to Mary from Aylesbury gaol, 19th March 1667, beginning "My dear love who my heart is still with".

(ii) 3.5. A testimony against bone-lace making, 31st March 1669, signed by Penington and others.

(e) Harvey, T. Edmund, collection, MS vol. 214. Undated booklet c. 1663.

(i) Concerning Justification (JP 1.20).

(ii) Undated epistle to Friends, about a "further dispensation of the Lord". "To such who are little and low and broken-hearted in Israel, and cannot lean(?) upon anything they have known or formerly received (See Crosse 4).

(iii) Some queries...to such as...have been convinced.

(iv) Letter to Friends at Hertford "If every one.."

(v) Some things concerning John Perrot (See Crosse 6)

(vi) 1663 To ye Parliament "The Lord pittied..."

(f) John Penington MSS, MS Vols 341–44, cited as JP. Four volumes of letters and papers by or relating to Penington, copied by his son John.

(g) Portfolio MSS, 42 vols, MS Port 1–42. Portfolios of Quaker letters and papers.

(h) Swarthmore MSS, 8 vols. MS Vols 351–60. Large collection of early Quaker letters.

3. Selections from Penington's writings

The first two are commonly available in libraries, and provided the source material for most later selections, of which the first two listed are currently in print.

Barclay, John, ed. *The Letters of Isaac Penington*. London: Harvey and Dalton, 1828, and later editions. Contains most of the letters reproduced in the complete *Works*. There are a number of unmarked omissions from the original texts.

Bevan, Joseph. *Memoirs of the Life of Isaac Penington*. London: Harvey and Doulton, 1830, often reprinted. Extracts from his published writings and some previously unpublished letters.

Leach, Robert J. ed. *The Inward Journey of Isaac Penington*. Philadelphia: Pendle Hill History Studies, 1943. Extracts from the devotional writings.

Penington, Isaac. *The Light Within*. Philadelphia: Tract Association of Friends, 1983, reprinted 1998. Selections mainly from devotional writings.

Saxon Snell, Beatrice, ed. *A Month with Isaac Peningto*n. London: Friends Home Service, 1966. Extracts from devotional writings.

4. General historical background

Coffey, John. *Persecution and Toleration in England 1558–1689*. Harlow: Longman, 2000.

Coward, Barry. *The Stuart Age*. London: Longman, 1994.

Gwyn, Douglas. *Seekers Found*. Wallingford, PA: Pendle Hill Publications, 2000. Good on the Seeker background, and includes a useful chapter on the Peningtons.

Hill, Christopher. *The World Turned Upside Down: Radical Ideas during the English Revolution*. London: Temple Smith, and New York: Viking Press, 1972. Classic work on the ambience from which the Quaker movement sprang.

Kishlansky, Mark. *A Monarchy Transformed: Britain 1603–1714*. London: Penguin, 1996.

Watts, Michael. *The Dissenters from the Reformation to the French Revolution*. Oxford University Press, 1978. Predates recent developments in Quaker history, but shows how Quakers fitted into the general dissenting scene.

5. Quaker history

Barbour, Hugh, and Arthur Roberts, eds. *Early Quaker Writings*. Eerdmans: Grand Rapids, MI, 1973, and Wallingford, PA: Pendle Hill, 2004. Selections from many early Quaker authors.

Braithwaite, William C. *The Beginnings of Quakerism*. 1st edn London: Macmillan 1912; 2nd edn Henry J. Cadbury, ed., Cambridge University Press, 1955.

Braithwaite, W. C. *The Second Period of Quakerism*. Cambridge University Press, 1925; 2nd edn Henry J. Cadbury, ed., 1955, re-issued by William Sessions of York, 1979.

Braithwaite, W. C. "The Penal Laws affecting early Friends in England." Appendix to Norman Penney, ed. *The First Publishers of Truth*. London: Headley, 1907.

Moore, Rosemary. *The Light in Their Consciences: Early Quakers in Britain 1646–1666*. University Park: Pennsylvania State University Press, 2000.

Punshon, John. *Portrait in Grey*. London: Quaker Home Service, 1984. A summary of the whole of Quaker history.

6. Penington background

Ellwood, Thomas. *History of the Life of Thomas Ellwood*. London: Sowle, 1714; Rosemary Moore, ed., Walnut Creek, CA: AltaMira Press/International Sacred Literature Trust, 2004.

Keiser, R. Melvin. "From Dark Christian to Fullness of Life: Isaac Penington's Journey from Puritanism to Quakerism," *Guilford Review* 23 (Spring 1986): 42–63.

Penington, John. *John Penington's Complaint against William Rogers*. London: Benjamin Clark 1681.

Penington, Mary. *Experiences in the Life of Mary Penington*, ed. Norman Penney. London: Headley, 1911, reprinted Gil Skidmore, ed., Friends Historical Society, 1992.

Punshon, John. "The Early Writings of Isaac Penington", in D. Neil Snarr and Daniel L. Smith-Christopher, eds, *Practiced in the Presence: Essays in honour of T. Canby Jones*. Richmond, IN: Friends United Press, 1994.

Saxon Snell, Beatrice, ed. *The Minute Book for the Upperside of Bucks 1669–1690*. Buckinghamshire Archaeological Society, 1937. This was the Peningtons' monthly meeting. Thomas Ellwood was clerk for most of this period.

Summers, W.H. *Memories of Jordan and the Chalfonts*. London: Headley, 1895. Some useful background information from a local historian.

7. Other Works Cited or Referenced

Anderson, Bernhard W. *Understanding the Old Testament*. Englewood Cliffs, NJ: Prentice-Hall, 1975.

Barnard, T. C. *Cromwellian Ireland*. Oxford University Press, 1975.

Bernard of Clairvaux, *On Loving God*. Kalamazoo, MI: Cistercian Publications, 1995.

Bertens, Hans. *Literary Theory: the basics*. London & New York: Routledge, 2001.

Bible: *The New English Bible* (NEB). Cambridge University Press, 1961. *The Revised Standard Version* (RSV). New York: Nelson, 1952; *New Revised Standard Version* (Anglicized edition). Oxford University Press, 1995.

Borg, Marcus. *On Meeting Jesus Again for the First Time: The Historical Jesus & the Heart of Contemporary Faith*. New York: Harper Collins, 1995.

Butler, Christopher. *Postmodernism: a very short introduction*. Oxford University Press, 2002.

Capp, B. S. *The Fifth Monarchy Men*. London: Faber and Faber, 1972.

Carroll, Kenneth L, "Early Quakers and 'Going Naked as a Sign'". *Quaker History* 67.2 (Autumn 1978).

―――. *John Perrot, Early Quaker Schismatic*. London: Friends Historical Society, 1970.

Crossan, John Dominic. *Jesus: A Revolutionary Biography*. San Francisco: Harper San Francisco, 1994.

Culler, Jonathan. *Literary Theory: a very short introduction*. Oxford University Press, 1997.

"Dictionary of Quaker Biography", multi-volumed typescript work in progress. Library of the Religious Society of Friends, London, and Haverford College, Pennsylvania.

Edwards, Thomas. *Gangraena*. London: Ralph Smith, 1646.

Elwell, C. J. L., *Bottrells Close: Some Notes for a History*. Chalfont St Giles: Privately published, 1973.

Fell, Margaret. *Undaunted Zeal: the Letters of Margaret Fell*. Elsa F. Glines, ed. Richmond, IN: Friends United Press, 2003.

Fiorenza, Elisabeth Schussler. *In Memory of Her: A Feminist Theological Reconstruction of Christian Origins*. New York: Crossroad, 1983.

———. *Jesus: Miriam's Child, Sophia's Prophet: Critical Issues in Feminist Christology*. New York: Continuum, 1994.

Fisher, Samuel. *Rusticus ad Academicos*. London: Robert Wilson, 1660.

Fox, George. *The Journal of George Fox*. John L. Nickalls, ed. London: Religious Society of Friends, 1975.

———. *The Short Journal and Itinerary Journals of George Fox*. Norman Penney, ed., Cambridge University Press, 1925.

———. *Friends, the Matter concerning not putting off the Hat at Prayer*. London: Ellis Hookes [1663].

———. *The Epistles of George Fox*, vols. 7 & 8 in *The Works of George Fox*. T. H. S. Wallace, ed., Pennsylvania: New Foundation Publications, George Fox Fund, 1990.

Funk, Robert W. *Honest To Jesus: Jesus for a New Millenium*. San Francisco: Harper San Francisco, 1996.

Hick, John. *Evil and the God of Love*. New York: Harper & Row, 1966.

Hill, Christopher, William Lamont and Barry Reay. *The World of the Muggletonians*. London: Temple Smith, 1973.

Huxter, Robert. *Jordans Meeting*. Jordans: Jordans Preparative Meeting, 1989.

Keenan, John P. *The Gospel of Mark: A Mahayana Reading*. Maryknoll, NY: Orbis Books, 1995.

LeLoup, Jean-Yves. *The Gospel of Mary Magdalene*. Rochester, VT: Inner Traditions, 2002.

Martin, Clare J. L. "Tradition versus Innovation: the Hat, Wilkinson-Story and Keithian Controversies". *Quaker Studies* 8.1 (September 2003) 5–22.

Merleau-Ponty, Maurice. *Phenomenology of Perception*. Trans. Colin Smith. London: Routledge & Kegan Paul; New York: The Humanities Press, 1962; pb 2003.

Mucklow, William. *Tyranny and Hypocrisy Detected*. London: Francis Smith, 1673.

Myers, Ched. *Binding the Strong Man: A Political Reading of Mark's Story of Jesus*. Maryknoll, NY: Orbis Books, 1988.

Niebuhr, H. Richard. *The Responsible Self: An Essay in Christian Moral*

Philosophy. New York, Evanston, London: Harper & Row, 1963; Louisville, KY: Westminster John Knox Press, 1999.

Nuttall, Geoffrey. "Early Quaker Letters". Typescript, 1952. Copies in various locations including the Library of the Religious Society of Friends, London, and in the USA the college libraries of Earlham (Richmond, IN), Guilford (Greensboro, NC), Haverford, and Swarthmore (PA).

Pagels, Elaine. *Beyond Belief: The Secret Gospel of Thomas*. New York: Random House, 2003.

———. *The Gnostic Gospels*. New York: Random House, 1979.

Pepys, Samuel. *Diary of Samuel Pepys*. 11 vols., Robert Latham and William Matthews, eds. Berkeley and Los Angeles: University of California Press, 1970–1983.

Polanyi, Michael. *The Tacit Dimension*. Garden City, NY: Doubleday & Company, Inc., 1966.

Ricoeur, Paul. *Freud and Philosophy: An Essay on Interpretation*. New Haven and London: Yale University Press, 1970.

Smith, Nigel. "Exporting Enthusiasm: John Perrot and the Quaker Epic", in Thomas Healy and Jonathan Sawday, eds, *Literature and the English Civil War*. Cambridge University Press, 1990.

Spears, Joanne, and Larry Spears. *Friendly Bible Study*. Philadelphia: Friends General Conference, 1990.

Stevens, Wallace. *The Collected Poems of Wallace Stevens*. New York: Alfred A. Knopf, 1954; 1961.

Wink, Walter. *Engaging the Powers: Discernment and Resistance in a World of Domination*. Minneapolis, MN: Fortress Press, 1992.

———. *The Human Being: Jesus and the Enigma of the Son of the Man*. Minneapolis, MN: Fortress Press, 2002.

Wittgenstein, Ludwig. *Philosophical Investigations*. Trans. G. E. M. Anscombe. New York: The Macmillan Company, 1953.

Index of Bible References

Old Testament

Genesis		Deuteronomy		4:18	88	Ezekiel	
1:2	148	30:14	234	9:10	87	2:9	57
	230				198	16:8	53
1:1–2:4a	232	1 Kings			207	18:4 32	260
1:26	61	21:20	230	12:1	61	33:11	260
1:26–27	246			13:18	61		
2:4b–3:24	231–2	2 Kings		15:5	61	Daniel	
	245	2:9	117			2:44	4n
2:7	230			Ecclesiastes		4:25 35	172
2:9	230	Job		3:16	173		
	233–4	28:28	87	4:1	173	Amos	
	245	29:20	230			5:8–9 18	138
2:17	245			Isaiah			
3:15	23	Psalms		2:4	174	Zechariah	
	97	8:6	88	5:1–7	22	4:10	52
	261	23:2	144	5:18	56		130
4:8	62	29:2	230	7:14–16	87		131
21:2–12	23	34:8	80	24	57		152
21: 9–21	28		180	25:6	87		155
49:7	138		230	25:7	87		
		36:6	259	27:4	173		
Exodus		52:5	140	30:15	175		
3:7–9	23	75:5	172	45:9	14		
3:14	277	91:3	85	51:1	27		
7:13–14	230		114	53:2	230		
16:4	199	106:17	68	53:3	44		
20:12	20	124:7	68	53:8	66		
			69	55:3	87		
Leviticus		125:3	173				
19:19	77	133:1	165	Jeremiah			
				1:5	230		
Numbers		Proverbs		11:19	66		
9:15–16	252	1:7	87	18:1–6	14		
20:10–13	252	1:23	86	32:40	201		

New Testament

Matthew		12:29	97	20:25–28	158	4:31–32	236
5:6	67	12:46	21		161	9:50	168
5:33–37	33	12:48	269		231	10:15	23
5:48	262	13:33	141	25:36–46	248		82
6:22	135		224	27:51	152	12:28–34	268
7:13	106	16:12	268			14:38	114
7:15	240	16:16–17	270	Mark		14:66–72	159
11:19	87	16:18	100	4:2–20	224		
11:29–30	152	18:15–20	74	4:30–32	154		

301

Luke		2:14–15	231	3:14	87	**Titus**	
2:52	30	2:28	114	4:6	88	1:7	32
7:35	200	2:28–29	133	4:7	137		
8:20–21	21	2:29	91	4:11	238	**Hebrews**	
9:23	152	3:23	11	5:16	193	2:11	130
13:21	141	5:5	78	5:19	272	6:1	262
17:10	185	7	231	6:16	133	6:4–5	230
17:20	200	8:1	263	11:2	263	10:5–7	270
22:16	87	8:1–2	130	12:9	142		272
22:42	272	8:16	91			10:19	91
			230	**Galatians**		12:23	99
John		8:20	88	2:9	57	13:20	262
1:1	80	8:26	206		58	13:21	263
1:4–5	230		224	2:14	239		
1:5	266	8:29	90	4:26	99	**1 Peter**	
2:4	269	8:35	146	5:22	247	2:4	100
3:4	268	9:18	231	6:10	13	2:25	86
3:5	6		259	6:15–16	131	3:6	84
3.8	125	10:8	234				
3:13	270		261	**Ephesians**		**1 John**	
6:52 61 63	268	12:3	230	3:18	144	1:1	80
8:12	230	14:4	164	4:11	59		117
8:15	268	14:5–15	163	4:11–13	263		139
10:3–4	86	14:10	90	4:12	67	1:3–7	263
10:10	133	14:20	222		262	1:5	88
10:30	268		285n	4:13	165		240
13:20	57			4:22–24	262		278
14:6	133	**1 Corinthians**		5:8	88	1:5–7	237
14:9	270	1:12	239	5:27	263	1:7	88
14:28	268	1:20	199	5:30	130	2:1	84
15:1–8	154	1:20–25	23			3:9	131
15:5	185	1:24	86	**Philippians**		4:16	78
15:15	158	2:9–10	211	2:7	272	5:20	199
17:5	272	2:14	141	4:11	149		
		3:16–17	133			**Revelation**	
Acts		3:18	19	**Colossians**		3:18	100
2:4	220		80	3:9–10	98	3:20	130
17:6	129		83	4:17	113	3:20–22	87
	243	3:18–19	36			4:11	118
17:28	274	7:29–31	159	**1 Thessalonians**		12	98
24:26	159	12:28	67	5:17	205	12:5	82
26:18	88	12:31	57			14:6	240
	240			**2 Timothy**		17:14	87
		2 Corinthians		1:10	230	19:7	263
Romans		2:14–16	230	3:5	134	21:5	87
1:17	240	3:6	133			21:9	81
2:9	57		234			22:1–2	81

General Index

Abingdon assizes 89
Adam
    and Eve 231
    perfection of 263
    temptation 233, 234
affections (*see also* desire) 62, 98, 110, 112, 183, 185–6, 188, 218, 271
    God's power over 212
alienation *see* God
Allen, John (maternal grandfather) 3
American Indians 227
Amersham
    arrest of IP at 47
    Berrie House, move to 49
    "To Friends in . . ." 59–60, 292n
    Woodside, move to 94
Anabaptists (*see also* Baptists) 32
Ancient Principle of Truth 246, 250, 279
    extracts 259–60, 277–8
Ancram, Charles Kerr, 2nd Earl of 53, 54
Anderson, Bernhard W. 232, 245
Anselm 250
apostasy of church 97, 98, 158–9, 164
    revival from 208, 240, 257, 281n
apostles
    age of 4, 98, 221, 226, 235, 258
    erring of 239
    gospel as message of 153, 200, 229, 232
    of Jesus 221, 266, 278
    Paul 206, 231, 239
    preaching of 240, 261, 278
    and prophets sent by God 59, 67
appearances/appearings of God *see* presence
appearances (false, misleading; *see also* forms) 183, 188, 274, 256
    IP weary and sick of 13
    not to judge by 203
    Satan's (tempter, etc) 57, 58, 135, 138–9, 189, 190
    shadow 270
appetite *see* desire
argument *see also* controversy
    IP and 167, 218–9, 230, 237

    IP with Ranters 10
    IP's father with Quakers 30
    written queries in 90
Arminian theology 4, 6
Armscote women's meeting 31n, 107–13
assizes 89 (*see also* legal system)
Astrop Wells 107
Atley, Bridget 50–2, 82–5, 292
atonement *see* salvation
authority (*see also* domination; power)
    of church 159
    of G. Fox 102, 104, 159
    of government/law, from God 27, 32, 56, 93
    inward 159, 231
    of man: corrupt nature 161; in hat controversy 40
    of God 56, 58, 59, 61–5, 80, 173, 240, 273; wait for 176
    of Jesus as mentorship 158–9
    of life 49
    of meetings in God's power/life 107–8, 161
    of men (Mary) 111
    of non-canonical writings 232
    of Quakers 15
    of self-will passing for righteousness 173
    of Spirit in experience 229, 231
awakening 22, 49, 137–8, 234, 271, 276
    of nation 171, 176
awareness
    consciousness, levels of 136–7, 213–4; in metaphor 216, 218–9
    experiential/pre-conceptual 178, 180–2, 194, 214–5, 217, 242, 273–4
    through breath 148
    through senses 136, 179
awe 170, 198, 207
Axe Laid to the Root 181, 184, 205, 245, 279
    extracts 140, 151, 185–8, 221, 235–8, 255
Aylesbury Gaol 46–71, 81
    writings from 15, 34, 36, 283n, 286n, 287n, 295n

Babylon the Great 181, 198, 205, 230, 275, 279–80
    extracts 139, 171–2, 199, 220
baptism 6, 11, 90, 134
Baptists 4, 32, 33, 94, 281n
Barclay, John x, 20, 292
Barclay, Robert 5n, 125, 128, 290
Bathurst, Elizabeth 127–8
Beaconsfield 86
beauty
    experience of 147
    inward 138, 230
    seeming 253
being (reality/substance) 179
    fullness of vii, 137, 219
    God/infinite eternal/pure 143, 145–6, 217, 239, 249, 253, 270, 275–6
    levels of (*see also* awareness, unconscious) 11, 136–7, 213–4
    new (way of) 170, 231
    our being in God 274; rooted in mystery 136
    and prayer 205, 207
    sacred 180, 207
    and ultimate meaning/mystery 147, 180, 184, 197
    whole of 207, 210, 274
belief/s 178–95, 243
    biblical forms of 135
    diversity, and unity of Spirit 160, 166
    and experience 162–3, 219, 225
    faith and 139, 149, 185–7, 201
    inward 136
    Jesus did not require 162, 251
    and outward/literal knowledge 153–4, 166, 182–3
    and life of the Spirit 160
    in light 255
    power of, from above 185
    Protestant, IP's former 274
    Quakers and 123–4, 127
    Quaker beliefs 78, 97, 115
    religion, true/profane 213, 215
    and salvation 256, 258
    vain 106
believers 163
    in Christ 182, 183
Berkshire Justices, letter to 93

Bernard of Clairvaux 180
Berrie House, Amersham 49, 94
Bertens, Hans 219
Bible (or Scripture; *see also* gospel; Index of Bible References)
    in argument 230–2, 244
    canon not closed 232, 239–40
    discerning life/light in 24, 91–2, 128, 135–6, 159, 182–3, 229, 232–3, 238
    G. Fox "interpreted by" 230
    interpreting/understanding 158, 222, 228–41
    Jews and 234
    language and metaphor 122, 149, 180, 229–30, 249, 274
    literal knowledge, or in spirit 185–7, 226, 234–6
    philosophy and theology from 149, 185, 224
    present-day scepticism 122, 137, 228
    wisdom in 198
birth (spiritual) 79, 97, 106, 139, 256, 295
    baptism, spiritual 6
    mysterious 219, 227
    new 225
    of true child 87, 205
    two births 23–5, 185, 187
    vessel for 153
    from womb of wisdom 87, 157, 200; wisdom from womb of spirit 198
blood (*see also Flesh and Blood*)
    of Christ/the Redeemer 88, 187, 256, 262–3, 264
    of the living Spirit 234
Board, Edward 81–2
body (*see also* flesh; incarnation) 27, 133, 166, 168, 247
    and senses 181
Bond, Nicholas, letter to 49–50
bond (surety) 37
Book of Common Prayer *see Consideration…*
Borg, Marcus 228
Boston, execution of Quakers (*see also Examination…Boston*) 158–60
Bottrels, Chalfont St Giles 49, 75
bowels (*see also Warning of Love…*) xiii
Brailes 113

General Index

Braithwaite, William C. 14
Bray, Thomas, letter to 113
breath
   creator Spirit (*ruach*) 148, 234
   of God 142, 145, 146, 151, 207, 276; as light 267
   and prayer 205, 207
Bridgwater, Earl of 47, 48, 54
   IP letter to 55–7
Britain Yearly Meeting vii
brotherly love 74
brothers, IP's letters to 23–4, 66–9, 97–9
Burrough, Edward 16–17, 29–30, 33, 43, 47
business meetings 104, 111
Butler, Christopher 219

Calvinism 4, 30
Cambridge University 6
canon (Bible) not closed 232, 239–40
captivity to self 197
catechism (*see also Scattered Sheep*) 232, 233–5, 255–6
Catholicism 3, 5, 93, 227
   IP's brother Arthur 96, 98, 100
Catsgrove 89n
Cavaliers (*see also Some Few Queries*)
   Cavalier Parliament 46
Caversham 13
Chalfont St Giles / St Peter 3, 49, 117
   disputes 57–8, 73–4, 143–6
   "To Friends in Truth, in and about the Two Chalfonts" (20 June 1666) 288; extract 143;
   "To Friends in the Chalfonts" (25 Jan 1667) extract 57–9
   "To Friends of Both the Chalfonts" (2/3 Aug 1667) 125, 150, 181, 198, 289; extracts 143–5, 203
Charles I, *King* 3
   beheading 7, 32
   parliament of 11
Charles II, *King*
   Declaration of Breda 31
   Declaration of Indulgence 89
   Mary's letter to 31–2
children
   behaviour of 61–5
   deaths of 85, 89, 115, 116

Christ (*for NT see* Jesus) 20
   authority as mentor 158–9
   as centre 249, 269
   and the church 98, 164
   covenant of light and life 153, 223, 259–60
   discipleship / "school of" 162, 163
   flesh and blood / incarnation (*see also Flesh and Blood*) 187, 250, 256, 270–2
   fullness of 263
   and honour to parents 20–21
   inward / outward knowledge of 139, 192–3, 224, 231, 234–6, 249, 260, 271–2
   as the Light 266–8
   as Life 149
   and love 12, 223, 250, 255, 259
   metaphors for 250
   ministry and teaching of 14, 241, 251, 261, 262, 268–9
   praying in the name of 206–8
   Quakers and 14, 137, 249, 258
   and Spirit 78, 247
   righteousness of 225–6
   sacrifice / suffering 246, 248
   and salvation 234, 258–60, 271
   seed of eternal life 236
   as servant 161, 247
   and the Trinity 249–52, 266–72
   voice of 268
   as wisdom 86
   and woman taken in adultery 122
Christian/s (*see also* church)
   faith of 186
   language and theology 123–4, 126–7, 213–27
   Life of a 293 extract 11–13
   rule for 129–30, 231, 236
   true 167, 247
   varieties of 160, 163
church (*see also* apostasy; *Concerning... Church State; Of the Church;* "Some Misrepresentations..."; *Some Queries... Church of Christ;* "Somewhat Relating to...")
   Christ and 98, 164
   conflict in 42–3, 44, 160, 165
   early 221

government 168, 190
life/Spirit in 134, 168, 211
true 98, 168
unity and diversity 160–7
Church of Scotland 4
City of London *see Some Considerations*
Civil War 4, 7, 129, 244
Coale, Josiah 45
Common Prayer, Book of *see Consideration...*
"Compulsion in Religion, Some Queries Concerning" 285
    extract 176
Concerning... Church State 248, 280
Concerning God's Seeking out His Israel 150, 280
    extracts 155–6, 190
Concerning Persecution 150, 170, 197, 215, 219, 280
    extracts 176, 200–01
"Concerning the Rule of the New Covenant" *see under* "Reply to Queries..."
Concerning the Sum or Substance of Our Religion 280
    extracts 191–2, 223, 258
Concerning the Worship of the Living God 150, 205, 218, 219, 232, 280
    extract 152–3
conflict/disputes
    in church 160, 165
    disputes among Quakers: Chalfont 57, 73–4; Horton 82–6; Perrot and hat 39–45, 57, 94; Wilkinson-Story 100–5
conformity (*see also* freedom; liberty; unity)
    in actions 166
    to the letter 221
Congregationalists *see* Independents
conscience
    and final judgment 248, 266
    God in 55–6, 74, 128, 276; in God's sight 22, 28, 82, 97; power of God in 152–5, 157, 259
    liberty of 160, 164–5, 173
    life/light/spirit in 149, 152, 160, 164, 214, 225
    open to Christ 162
    perfection of 263
consciousness (*see also* awareness, being, experience, feeling, unconscious)
    levels of 136–7, 213–4
Consideration... the Book of Common Prayer 246, 275, 281
    extracts 200, 222
contentment 146, 149, 153, 189
Conventicle Acts
    First 47
    Second 89
conversion 149, 152
    convincement (becoming Quaker) 229, 273
    transformation by Spirit 246
    turning to the life 154
Conway, Anne, Viscountess: "To the Lady Conway" 290
    extract 157
Council, IP letter to 26–8
covenant (*see also* New Covenant of the Gospel; "Reply to Queries...")
    of blood 262–3
    of light and life (Christ) 82–3, 153, 194, 223, 259–60
    new 92, 194, 201, 224–5, 236
    outward and inward 251–2
creation/creature 10
    creator Spirit (ruach) 148, 234
    God's creating/preserving power 248, 265, 276
    new (*see also* birth) 24, 106, 129–132, 224, 261, 264–6; in Christ 236; and life, measure of 229, 231; metaphor 218; true religion is 214, 222; and salvation 247–8
    story 231–2
    unfinished 130, 131
creativity 149
creed (*see also* belief; doctrine) Quakers without 242
Cromwell, Henry, letter from Mary to his wife 28–9
Cromwell, Oliver 7, 11, 26, 27, 29, 31, 286
Cromwell, Richard 29
Crook, John, 16, 17, 72

General Index

cross, taking up (*see also* daily spiritual exercise) 137, 141, 161, 200
Crossan, John Dominic 64, 228
Culler, Jonathan 219
Curtis, Thomas 15, 29, 44–5, 54, 102–5
    IP letter to 40

daily spiritual exercise 128, 141, 144–5, 147–9, 152, 154, 188, 201
    "getting low" (*see also* everydayness) 124, 137, 200
    perfection in 247, 262
    waiting on God 175
    wisdom, fresh 198–9
    work of salvation 255
darkness 138, 189, 267
    Voyce out of Thick Darkness 7, 8–10
Datchet 13
"day of small things" 52, 130, 131, 149, 152, 155, 229, 233
death and resurrection 272
deception *see* appearances; self-deception
Declaration of Breda 31
Declaration of Indulgence 93
depths
    deep knowledge 140
    of being, sacred 207
    of life 122–3, 147, 225, 247
    of spirit 144, 150
Descartes, René 179, 184, 220
desire (*see also* affections; passions) 148, 233
    and Fall 212, 254
    for life/God 152, 253
Devil *see* Satan
discernment (*see also* leadings; judgment; waiting) 41, 58, 81, 108, 155–6, 166–7
    from/in the life 183–4, 198–9, 214, 244–5
    in meetings 160–1
    about scripture 237
disobedience (*see also* obedience)
    and sin 245, 257
disputes *see* conflict
Dissenters 93
distressing thoughts 83

divine *see* God; life; mystery; nature
doctrine 128, 193, 229, 240, 242–52
    assent to 188
    contradictions in 268
    Quaker attitude to 124, 242
domination (*see also* authority; oppression)
    in church government 158–61, 243
    kingdom not triumphal 233
    "system of" 122–3, 150
    by veiled self 137, 170
doubt 144, 166, 181, 190
duty *see Some Questions . . . Showing Man His Duty*

Eden, Garden of 245
Elgar, Sarah 85, 116
Eliade, Mercea 180
Ellwood, Thomas 15, 18–20, 29–30
    arrested and imprisoned 33
    IP's letter to him in prison 34
    Testimony to Isaac 38
    tutor to Isaac's children 39, 117
Ellwood, Walter 18
Elgar, Sarah, letter to 116
end of the world *see* eschatology
"end of words" 92, 127, 217
enemy *see* Satan
An Epistle to All Serious Professors 247, 281n
equality
    and difference 59
    in justice 31
    Quakers and 14, 16, 126
equity in government 170, 172, 175, 176
eschatology 248–9, 265–6
estate
    father's, loss of 33, 34
    forfeiture of (praemunire) 89
eucharist 134
everyday/small things (*see also* daily spiritual exercise; lowness)
    deeper life/reality underlying, 122–3, 147
    divine presence in 130, 131, 148–9, 152, 155–6, 184
Eve (*see also* Adam) 231
Evesham 113

evil 63, 65; good and 8, 10, 233; goodness 196
Examination...Boston 158–60, 231, 281, 293
    extracts 161–5, 188–9, 221–2, 238–9, 261–3
existence *see* being
experience (*see also* senses; "Some Experiences") vii, 148
    experiential/experimental knowing 139, 167, 178–9, 219, 249, 274–5; and thought 125, 242–4
    of deliverance from error 105
    of God 115, 139, 141, 143, 222, 225, 273–5; of God/life, in church/meeting 134, 168; IP's 24, 99, 156, 250; in nation 171; as salvation 247; in true light 271; in worship 210
    inward, in religion 115, 124, 129, 135, 192–3, 218
    of the life 167–8, 183
    and language/words: Christian 127; metaphors 121–2, 218; theological 123–4
    and scripture 238–9
Expositions with Observations Sometimes on Several Scriptures
    extract 7–8
eye (*see also* sight)
    of child 24
    pure 220
    of God 84, 95
    inward/outward 106, 208, 235, 251
    of life 101
    pure salve 100
    right/wrong, true 10, 103, 174

faith
    and belief 139, 149, 185–7, 201
    and conscience 164
    definition of 149, 201
    feeling of 153
    obedience 50, 153–4, 201–2
    and salvation 255–6
Fall of Adam and Eve 131, 232, 254
    Protestant/Quaker interpretation of 245
family *see under* Penington
fanatics 75, 76

Farnworth, Richard 45
Father, Son and Spirit (Trinity) 250, 266–72
fatherhood *see* parents
fear 173, 197–8, 201, 203, 207, 212
feeling (*see also* experience; senses; touch) 178–95; synonymous with sense 179
    with conscience 128
    and consciousness 181, 213–14, 216
    in discernment 160–1, 166
    divine mystery 274
    of faith 153
    God within 143, 182, 213–14; of spiritual/divine presence/glory 126, 127, 130, 147, 182, 188, 207 242; refusal of, as sin 245; salvation 246
    inward 90, 211, 260; "sensible plant" sown by God 190
    not knowledge/letter/notion 180, 192, 234
    leadings and drawings 130, 139–40, 150, 155, 218
    life 136, 140, 144, 151, 190, 218, 220, 226, 229, 238, 246; and senses 181
    miracles, felt not interpreted 251
    openness to 148
    and reason/thought 137, 189, 215, 219; as child 83
    and wisdom 198
    and words 140, 216–17, 218, 269; in Bible reading 228, 232, 234, 240
Fell, Margaret 6, 14, 16, 45, 54, 128
fellowship 159
Fiennes family 289n
Fiennes, Celia 107
Fifth Monarchists 4, 33
Fines, Frances: "To the Friend of" 247, 249, 289, 292
    extracts 226, 271–2
Fiorenza, Elisabeth Schussler 228
First Conventicle Act 47
Fisher, Samuel 66, 231, 286
Fleetwood, Ann, to friend of 72–3
Fleetwood, Sir George, regicide 72
flesh (*see also* body; incarnation) 134, 162, 165, 197, 238, 247

General Index

of Christ 187, 250, 256, 270–2
desires, fleshly 20, 21, 27, 28
silence and 206, 209, 225
spirit and life 268
will of the 108
wisdom, fleshly 198
Flesh and Blood 94n, 150, 178, 183, 184, 281
extracts 167, 182, 192–3
flexibility (pliable soul) 149–50, 153, 161, 197–8, 200, 219, 274
"For Friends of our Meeting" 160
forms (*see also* appearances) 133–8, 198, 215–7, 243–5, 252–3
in religion 12, 115
fountain/spring/wellspring 250
everlasting 211, 264
God is 125, 144, 207, 248, 264, 275–6
of life vii, 130, 140, 166, 276
of light 266
"no straitness in" 125, 137, 144
Fox, George 14, 17, 43, 128, 230
administrative reforms 72, 100–01
authority of 103, 104, 159
Bible, being interpreted by 230
disagreement with Perrot 39, 40
epistles of 26, 45
letter from IP to 65–6, 77–8
support by IP 57, 102, 103
freedom (*see also* liberty) 196–204
and grace 258
of the will 196, 253
freshness *see* life
Freud, Sigmund 216
fullness
of Christ 263
of God 125, 142–4, 278
of life 68, 129–30, 137, 276
redemption 140
sense of 148
of words 241
Funk, Robert W. 64, 228
"Further Testimony to Truth" 246, 281
extract 208–11

Garden of Eden 245
gentiles 231
gifts
different 59, 67
of ministry 98
"give over thy own willing" 141
God (*see also* being; Christ; experience; fountain; life; love; pleasure; presence; seed; Spirit; sweetness; wisdom; words) 273–8
alienation from 106, 192, 225, 230, 234
authority/power 56, 58, 59, 61–5, 240
and Bible 239–40
breath 142, 145, 146, 148, 151, 207, 265, 276; as light 267
and church 168
creating/preserving powers 248, 265
dependence on 254
eye of 84, 95
Father, Son and Spirit/Trinity 249–50, 266–8
fullness of 125, 142–4, 278
gifts of (*see also* grace) 59, 67
in government/political world 169–77
image of 165, 177, 214, 222, 225, 246, 255, 266
inward (in heart/in self/within) 141, 176–7, 240, 247–8, 249, 252, 263; that of God in you 59, 74, 133, 149, 173, 226; working 192
judgment/justice of 12, 56, 64, 81, 85, 149, 263, 275; mercy 223, 250, 259
live like 132, 222
meeting with 24, 130
is mystery 128, 180, 274, 277
pleasure of 239–40, 246, 253, 275
Quakers and 128, 277
separation from 52, 245
and sin 10
in small things (*see also* day of) 130
teaching 149, 194, 224–5, 240
union with 184, 195, 225–6, 258, 261
use by 143
voice of 51, 61, 189
will of 163
good and evil 8, 10, 233; evil 63, 65; goodness 196
Goodnestone, Kent (Mary's estate) 94, 115, 116
Goodwin, John 6

309

gospel (*see also* Bible; index of Bible refs) 88, 158
  fellowship 267
  message 240, 278; of apostles 153, 200, 229, 232
  ministry 113, 165, 167
  state 175–6, 246, 248
government 93
  equity in 170, 172, 175, 176
  of church 168, 190
grace 30, 142, 150, 167, 195, 196–8, 246–7, 253, 258–9
Grange, The (Chalfont St Peter) 18, 33, 47, 48
Great Question Concerning... Swearing 247, 281n
growth, spiritual 124–6, 139, 145, 147–57, 185–7, 220–2, 244, 263
guidance *see* leadings

Habeas Corpus application 71
Hall, Robert 81, 82, 83
haste *see* waiting
hats
  customary removal of 20
  wearing of, during prayer 39–41, 45, 69–70, 94
hearing (*see also* senses) 181
  Christ 268
  invisible one 225
  hearing others 219
heaven (*see also* kingdom) 99, 190
  Christ in 98, 270
  inward 177
Hebraic Wisdom 198
hell (*see also* predestination)
  IP's experience of within 18
  IP's 17th-century attitude 60, 249
Hemmings, Widow 289, 290
  letter 26 Oct 1670: extract 194
  letter 28 Nov 1670: 89, 150; extracts 90–91, 208
Hersent, Anne, Guli's maid 35, 45
Hick, John 130
Hill, Christopher 129
Holy Truth 246, 247, 275, 281n
hope 202, 256
Horton, 50–52, 81, 82, 207–8

"To My Friends at Horton and Thereabouts" 206, 289; extract 207–8
Howgill, Francis 43–45
Hubberthorne, Richard 14
human nature *see* nature, human
humility *see* lowness
Hunt, Richard 45
hurry *see* waiting

immediacy 136, 183, 188, 235
  in God's creating power 248, 265
  in silence 206, 211
immortality *see* "Life and..."
imprisonment *see* prisons
incarnation (*see also* body; Christ; flesh) 187, 250, 256, 270–72
Independents (Congregationalists) 4, 6, 43, 164
Inner Temple 6
intellect (*see also* knowing) 91, 126, 129, 137, 178, 184, 215
invisible / visible 139, 198–9
inward / outward (*see also* Christ; conscience; God; life) vii, 135–6
  authority of 159, 231
  beauty 138, 230
  covenant (inward Jew) 91–2, 114, 251–2
  creation 106, 265, 276
  experience 115, 124, 129, 135, 192–3, 218
  eye 106, 208, 235, 251
  food 145
  freedom 203
  growth begins 147, 246
  heaven 177
  kingdom 97, 253
  knowledge 140, 178, 182
  light 135, 214, 225, 226, 231, 235, 278
  in nation 169–77
  nature 225
  prayer / worship 205, 208, 211, 212
  salvation 247–8, 258
  Satan (enemy) 189, 249
  substance 12, 276
  teaching / wisdom 86, 149, 225, 261
  unity of church 103, 160, 165–6

General Index

Ireland 28
Israel *see* Jews (*see also Concerning God's
    ...Israel*; *Some Deep...Israel*)

Jerusalem (Heaven) 99, 190
Jesus (*see also* Christ) 234
    as mentor 158–9
    parables of 269
    sacrifice/suffering 246, 248
    Spirit fully revealed to 247
    and woman taken in adultery 122
Jew Outward 184, 233, 249, 251–2, 282
    extracts 220, 235, 268–9
Jews (*see also To the Jews Natural*; *Some
    Questions...Jews Natural*)
    Christ and 21, 268
    "inward" 91–2, 114, 251–2
    Paul and 231, 239, 261
    return to England (1655) 286
    and scriptures 234
    worship 135
Jordans Farm 74
joy 162, 203, 218
    despite suffering 157
    finding lost sheep 108
    made full 263
    in worship 207
judging/judgment (*see also*
    discernment; justice; legal
    system)
    final 56, 90, 248, 265–6
    of God 12, 56, 64, 81, 85, 149, 263, 275;
        mercy 223, 250, 259
    of Jesus 251, 268
    one another 163
    oppression in the seat of 173
Jung, Carl 216
justice (equity) 31–2, 169–70, 172, 175, 176
Justices (*see also* legal system)
    Berkshire, letter to 93
justification 91, 187, 246

Keenan, John P. 228
Kendal 45
Kent, Mary's connections with 13, 94,
    115, 116
Kerr, Charles, 2nd Earl of Ancram 53, 54
King *see* Charles I, and II

King and Parliament *see Weighty
    Question*
kingdom (*see also* God; heaven; seed;
    "Seed of God", *Some of the
    Mysteries*)
    expected/hoped for 7, 10–11, 154–5, 257
    here and now 276
    inheritor of 25
    inward/within 97, 253
    leaven of 141
    life is the 233
    mystery of, in meeting 160
    openings concerning 91
    receive as a child 82, 87
    righteousness of 67
knowledge/knowing (*see also* intellect;
    letter and spirit) 178–95, 215
    of Christ 271
    deep 140
    through experience 139, 167, 178–9,
        219, 249, 274–5
    God 220, 224, 275
    inward 140, 178, 182
    living 151
    through metaphor 218
    Tree of 188, 230, 232, 233, 245
    true/of truth 24, 80, 224
Lancaster Gaol 45n
language (*see also* metaphor; words)
    religion/theology and use of 123–4,
        126–7, 213–27
    sacrificial 247
last things 248–9, 265–6
Laud, Archbishop William 3, 4
law
    of Christ 194–5, 240
    Paul on 231
laws, equitable/just 170, 173, 175–6
leadings and drawings/guidance (*see
    also* discernment; judgment;
    waiting)
    darkness, out of 189
    and desires 152
    Fall, since the 260
    feeling 130, 139–40, 150, 155, 218
    of the Spirit 58, 122, 134, 209, 222, 232;
        particular 162–3; reading scripture
        232

311

humble attentiveness 137
IP's experience 14, 20; expression of 27
in lawmaking 176
of life 144, 150, 155
in meetings 108; lack of (hat controversy) 40–2
obedience 149, 153
and reason 189
salvation through 246
spiritual growth 147
leaven of the kingdom 141
legal system
assizes 47, 76, 89
Boston, *see Examination...*
justices/magistrates 34–37, 38, 93, 174–5; need for 170
Leloup, Jean-Yves 64, 228
letter and spirit/literal knowledge 133
basis of religion 221, 225
knowledge of Christ 271
in politics 169
in reading scripture 92, 186–7, 230, 234–5, 238–40, 259
patriarchs had inward spirit 260–1
letters of IP: *see under names or places of recipients*; unknown, *see "To _____"*
editions of x–xi, 296
manuscripts 294–5
letting go (*see also* lowness) 130
levels *see* depths
liberty (*see also* freedom) 172, 203
of conscience 160, 164–5, 173
life (*see also* breath; Christ; covenant; everyday; feeling; fountain; God; measure; mystery; quickening; seed; Spirit) 121, 133–46, 207, 213, 275
authority of life 49
in the church 158–68; meetings in God's power/life 107–8, 161
and death, power of 130–32, 209; and resurrection 272
depths of life 225, 247
desire for life/God 152, 253
discerning/judging of (*see also* Bible) 166–7, 183–4, 244–5

divine: partaking of 121, 198–9, 214, 247, 272; as seed 275
dwelling in the 184
experience of the 167–8, 183
eye of 101
flesh of spirit and 268
and forms 134–5, 138, 244–5; "before all forms" 217
freshness of 68, 136, 138, 144, 148, 182, 210, 230; apparent 253
fullness of 68, 129–30, 137, 276
inward 102, 178, 183, 186–8, 192–3, 233, 251, 260, 270; conscience, seated in 214; in politics 169; divine seed 246, 275
kingdom, life is the 233
leadings and drawings 144, 150, 155
light from 140, 155, 256–7
and love: "our life is love..." vii, 59; from root of 167; visitation of 255
oppression of 128
power of 80, 154–5, 184, 201, 226, 244; and death 209
redemption 256–7
rule of 236
savour/sweetness/taste of 111, 131, 141–3, 155–6, 190, 202, 219, 223, 233
seeing 240
self-led 137, 249; transformed 128
stirrings of 147, 152, 154, 169, 181, 233, 274; in IP's early life 214; words from 127
stream of 153
Tree of 115, 188, 199, 230, 232, 233, 245
"Life and Immortality" 149, 231, 247, 249, 282
extracts 212, 278
Life of a Christian 293
extract 11–13
light vii, 38, 14, 164
Christ as 266–8
covenant of light and life 82–3, 153, 194, 223, 259–60
in/on conscience 149, 152, 164, 214
of God 64, 88, 118, 157, 163, 227, 232–3; God becoming 250, 266; God's breath 267; God is 278

and hope 256
inward 135, 214, 225, 226, 231, 235, 278
from life 140, 155, 256–7
of Messiah 240
as metaphor 121–2
and power 51, 167–8138
and reason 155, 191
reprovings of 155
seeing 92, 167
understanding
vessel of 253
walk in the 141
literal knowledge *see* letter and spirit
littleness (*see also* day of small things; lowness) 147, 154–5, 169, 172, 199; "savour this little" 150, 208
liturgies 134, 217
London (*see also* Some Considerations)
Peningtons and 3, 4, 6, 13, 33, 75–6, 95, 117; IP's father in Tower 32
love (*see also*: Salutation of Love; Warning of Love)
brotherly 74, 99–100
Christ's 12, 223, 259; for Christ 255; Christ in heart teaches 223; Christ as fountain of 250
definition 202
fatherly (IP to children) 64
within fear 201
of friends 79
God's: 32, 78, 82, 250, 259, 263, 277–8; our being in/partaking of 79, 197, 247, 264, 278; clouded by doubt 38; as Father 146; fullness of 144; as mother's 275 God's nature is 246, 259, 277–8; in the Spirit 194; visitation of 255
humility of (to GF) 78
law is 170
natural expression of (IP to Mary) 76
of neighbour 135
"our life is love..." vii, 59; from root of life 167
seed of (vs seed of enmity) 223
transformative 198
and unity in church 70, 164–5, 261
words, beyond 203

lowness/humility (*see also* day of small things; littleness)
and IP's style 125
getting low (letting go) 130, 131, 137, 141, 161, 189
God's work 153
lowest seeds 194
poverty of self 209

magistracy 170, 174
Many Deep Considerations
  see Some Deep... Israel
marriage of Quakers 101, 110, 196
measure
of gospel 88
of grace 258–9
of life: greatest in Jesus 160; hidden 84; in our hearts/selves 82, 129, 130, 142, 144; judgment 166–7; not by words 138; relieving 83; as seed 157
of Spirit 161, 164
of truth 114
meeting for worship *see* worship
men's meetings (*see also* women's meetings) 104
mercy, God's 153, 223, 231, 250, 259, 266
Merleau-Ponty, Maurice 217
Messiah 240
metaphor (*see also* language; words) vii, 121–3, 133, 180, 181–2, 248, 274
in Bible 249
for Christ 250
levels of awareness in 216, 218–9
military defence 170
ministry (*see also* Christ)
of the church/gospel 113, 164–5, 167; true 226
gift of 98
in meeting for worship 111
miracles 251
Moore, Rosemary 229
Muggleton, Lodowick 277 (*see also* Observations...*)
Myers, Ched 228
mysteries (*see also Some of the Mysteries*)
of Christ 250
of God, stewards of the 227, 263–4

mystery vii, 136, 234, 275
   being/reality and 136, 147, 180, 184, 197, 220
   Bible 234
   Christianity is 167
   in church (truth/kingdom) 160, 168
   of darkness/death/deceit/sin 226, 237, 240, 267
   experience of 87, 183–4, 274
   of God/divine 128, 180, 274, 277; dwelling in 150, 215, 276; and of humanity 133
   of life 127, 178, 180, 226, 227, 273; in earthly Jesus 259; hidden 87, 192–3, 224; in inwardness 233; power of 154; words and 252
   of light 226, 227
   metaphor/symbol 182, 250, 275
   of religion 193–4, 214–5, 224; faith a pure mystery 220; Quakers seemed far from 14
   of silent worship 208
   stewards of 216, 227
   within 276
   words awaken to 218; manifest 252

Naked Truth 206, 247, 248, 250, 275, 282
   extract 167
nakedness 15
nation (*see also* government; legal system; Parliament)
   life in the 169–177
   spiritual work in 12
natural (*see also* To the Jews Natural; Some Questions . . . Jews Natural)
   desire and understanding 148, 150, 159, 184, 197
   exercise 187
   goodness (mercy) 176
   lives becoming 150
   love 76, 197, 247, 278
   self 134, 137
   virtue 197
nature (*see also* human nature)
   of Christ, hidden 187
   of God/divine 184, 250, 259; is love 246, 259, 277–8; soul changed to 264
   inward 225
   light in 257
   human: corrupt/fallen/old 157, 161, 185; natural man cannot receive Spirit 141; improvement of 186; lamb-like 156; new 261; will 200
   of things 139, 140
   wisdom of 248
Nayler, James 29, 30
new covenant 92, 194, 201, 224–5, 236
"New Covenant, Concerning the Rule of" *see* "Reply to Queries"
New Covenant of the Gospel 231, 282
   extract 152
new creation *see* creation; *see also* birth
Niebuhr, H. Richard 73, 245
Noye, Nicholas, letter to 69–70
Nuttall, Geoffrey 14

Oath of Allegiance and Supremacy 34, 35, 36, 89
oaths, refusal of Quakers to take 33, 46
obedience (*see also* disobedience)
   definition 149, 202–03
   and faith 50, 153–4, 201–2
   to God 20, 22, 143
Observations on Some Passages of Lodowick Muggleton 170, 274, 282
   extract 277
Of the Church in its First and Pure State 218, 283
   extract 258–9
oppression
   no advantage to government 93
   in Bible 122, 228
   of creation 249, 266
   of God in conscience 248, 266
   God works against 169–70, 172, 275–6; vengeance for 56
   of IP's "captivity" 18
   of life 128
   righteousness, passing for 173
outward *see* inward

Pagels, Elaine 228
Palmer, Ruth 89–90
parables of Jesus 269
parents 20–1, 61–5

General Index

Parker, Alexander 17, 26, 45
Parliament 27, 30, 93, 156
passions (*see* affections; desire)
Paul 206, 231, 239, 261, 274 (*see also* Index of Bible Refs)
peace 171, 174, 175
   doctrine of 251
Penington, Abigail (mother) 3
Penington, Arthur (brother)
   becomes a Catholic 96
   letter to 97–9
Penington, Edward ("Ned", youngest son) 54, 75, 117
Penington, Sir Isaac (father) 2 (ill), 3, 4
   Isaac's letter to 20–3
   imprisonment and death of 32
Penington, Isaac
   biography: birth and youth 3; religious crisis, state of 7–10; marriage 13; convincement as Quaker 14, 17; breach with his father, in letter 19, 20–23; brothers and sister 23; father's imprisonment and death 32; IP's imprisonment and loss of father's estate 33, 34; legal security for good behaviour 36; imprisoned in Aylesbury Gaol (1664) 46–71; family forced to leave The Grange 48–9; release from prison then re-arrest 53–4; supports George Fox 57, 66; writes to dissident Quakers 81–5; arrested in Reading, imprisoned 89; death of second son, Isaac 89; moves to Woodside, Amersham 94–5; pamphlet war with Baptists 94; controversy with John Pennyman 95–6; relations with John Story 101–3; death 116; testimony of Elizabeth Walmsley on IP 117–18
   IP's brothers, letters to 23–4, 66–9, 97–9
   IP's children at school, letters to 61–5
   IP's father, letter to 20–3
   IP's impracticality 33
   IP's style of thought and writing ix, 125–6, 218, 248

Penington, Isaac (son) death of 89
Penington, John (son) 13, 17, 20, 116, 117
Penington, Judith (sister) 5
   letter to 105–7
Penington, Mary (wife, previously Proude, and Springett) 13, 16
   becoming a Quaker 17
   estate business 89
   IP letters to 35–8, 47–8, 75
   letter to Henry Cromwell's wife 28–9
   letter to King Charles II 31–2
   letter to Women Friends 109–13
   London visit and illness 75
Penington, Mary (daughter) 13, 117
Penington, Robert (grandfather) 3
Penington, William (brother) 23, 40, 95, 117
Penn, William 5, 77
Pennyman, John 40
   letter to 95–6
Pepys, Samuel 4, 105
perfection 10, 143, 153, 247, 254, 261–4
   in Christ 98
   day, perfect 88
   love, 203, 250
   redemption, in fullness 140, 257, 264
Perrot, John
   relations with viii, 39–42, 57, 65–6, 68, 104, 105, 159
persecution (*see also* oppression; sufferings) 46–7, 72, 89, 176, 200–201
Peter 239 (*see also* Index of Bible refs)
"Phanatiques" (fanatics) 75, 76
Pharisees, Scribes and 200, 235, 268
philosophy, Penington's contribution 178–9, 180
pleasure of God 189, 212, 220, 258
pliability 150, 153, 274
Polanyi, Michael 215
politeness, customary forms 19
political upheaval 11, 26–45, 169–171; and religion 7
power (*see also* authority; kingdom)
   and forms/appearances 133–4, 138, 216–7
   and freedom (new life) 203

315

God's 86, 223; creating/preserving 248, 265; and early Quakers 15; through fear 201; in meetings 14, 17, 104, 107–8, 113; church unity in 43, 95, 166; in conscience/heart 152–5, 157, 259
of life 80, 154–5, 184, 201, 226, 244; and death 209
and light 51, 167–8
regenerating 97–9
true or profane 215
praemunire (forfeit of estate) 89
prayer 205–8 (*see also* worship)
continual 128, 129–31, 208
hat-wearing and 39–40
and hope 202
in meetings 59, 111
for oppressors 156, 223
in the Spirit/living substance 222, 270; true spirit of 25
against temptation 114, 263
predestination 4, 30, 196–7, 259
Presbyterians 4
presence of God/Kingdom/mystery/ truth 56, 59, 141–3, 188, 212, 242, 247–8
appearances/appearings of 17, 114, 154, 183, 191–3; Frances Howgill quotes IP on 44; misunderstanding 138, 257
awareness of 17
"in the midst" 252
revealed measure 209, 274
salvation 246
in everyday/small things 130, 131, 148–9, 152, 155–6, 184
wait/prepare for 99, 114, 190
present time 183, 218, 246
prisons
IP Snr in Tower of London 32
IP in Aylesbury Gaol 46–71, 81; writings from 15, 34, 36, 283n, 286n, 287n, 295n
IP in Reading Gaol 72–93; writings from 38, 89n, 90–1, 282n, 290n, 295
Margaret Fell in Lancaster 45n
prisoners 248

Protestantism 227, 229, 231
interpretations of sin 245
language 123
Proude, Mary, *see* Penington, Mary
psychology 216
punishment
God's 54, 63; everlasting 248
of offenders 170, 176
purification 262
Puritanism 249
purity vii, 215

Quaker faith and practice, list of extracts 292–3
Quakers
and Christ 258
God of 277
gravity of 18–19
in Ireland 28
Quaker Act 46, 47
"Question Answered Concerning Reading the Scriptures Aright" 283
extract 241
Question Propounded . . . England 30, 276, 283n
Question to the Professors 218, 249, 283n
extracts 224–5, 239, 270–71
quickening (*see also* life)
God's 209, 222; of the dead 17
of grace 259
of life 80, 140, 255; Christ's 224, 260
in ministry 111
of the spirit 144, 205, 207, 225, 250
truth, nature of 191

Radway 113
Ranters 8, 10
Reading 13
arrest and imprisonment of IP 38, 89–93
Friends in 15, 102
writings from prison 38, 89n, 90–1, 282n, 290n, 295
reality *see* being; everyday; God; mystery; sacred
reason/reasoning (*see also* feeling) 125, 178–9, 189, 214, 218, 287

carnal/fleshly/human 42, 153, 165, 175
 and laws 170, 175
 and light 155, 191
 spirit 83
redemption (*see also* salvation) 91, 131, 140, 149, 153, 264
 from God, not Christ's manhood 272
 in this life 262
 work of 256–7, 277
religion (*see also Concerning the Sum or Substance; Some Queries... Compulsion*) 7, 91, 99, 125, 128, 213–27
 mystery of 193–4, 214–5, 224
 outward forms 12, 115
 true 213–4, 221–4, 226
repentance 60
 and conversion 255
"Reply to an Answer... concerning the Gospel-Baptism" 150, 283
 extract 226–7
"Reply to Queries and Animadversions [Concerning the Rule of the New Covenant]" 127, 150, 183, 219, 231, 232, 247, 273, 283
 extracts [ii/frontispiece], 193–4, 226, 239–40, 260
revelation (*see also* presence; for Book of Revelation *see* Index of Bible Refs)
 arising within 215
 Christ: power of 250, 258; revealed in soul 223, 224, 249
 continuing 232, 274; denial of 221, 237
 in gathered meeting 160
 of mystery 183
Ricoeur, Paul 182
righteousness (*see also* virtue) 12, 131, 196–7, 215, 256, 261
 Christ's 225–6
 everlasting 262, 265–6
 hunger and thirst after 67
 and lawmaking 56, 170–7
 original 245, 247
rituals and practices 134, 217
Roberts, Gerrard 14

Robinson, Bishop J. A. T. 6, 127
Roman Catholicism *see* Catholicism
root, sink down into 23
Royal Society, Some Things... 150, 248, 287
 extract 225
ruach (creator Spirit, breath) 148, 234
rule for a Christian 129–30, 231, 236
Russell, William 74–5

sacred, the 180, 207
 body as sacred space 133
 in daily life 147
sacrifice 196–7, 246–7, 250, 264, 272
Salutation of Love 248, 283
 extract 266
saints, *see* Anselm; apostles; Paul; Peter
salvation (*see also* redemption) 51, 98, 106, 116, 153, 167, 263
 definition 246–7, 255–7
 history 230, 247, 250
 inward 247–8, 258
 with/without Christ 234, 260, 271
sanctification 98, 130, 149, 186, 246
Satan (Devil/enemy/wicked one) 99, 138, 145, 249, 254, 262
 distinguishing appearances from God's 188, 189
 and temptation 58, 64–5
savour (*see also* taste)
 "be a good savour" 60
 of life/savoury life 111, 141–2, 143, 155–6, 190, 219, 223, 233
 "savour this little" 150, 208
Scattered Sheep Sought After 219, 229–30, 232, 245, 248, 249, 250, 276, 284
 extracts 138–9, 220, 229, 252–3, 261, 266–8
"Short Catechism" extracts 151, 199, 233–5, 255–6
Scotland
 Church of 4
 "To My Dear Suffering Friends in Scotland" 149, 289n
Scribes and Pharisees 200, 235, 268
scriptures *see* Bible
Second Conventicle Act 89
seed vii, 24, 70, 246

Christ as, 236; metaphor for 250, 275
of God (*see also* "Seed of God..."
below) 11, 28–9, 58, 209, 275;
experienced in Quaker meeting
17, 24; in nation 171; sink down to
141
growth of 132, 224, 246, 255, 257, 275
of the kingdom 224, 261
of life 109, 157, 276–7
little 152, 154, 246
two seeds: true/profane 215; love/
enmity 223
"Seed of God and of His Kingdom" 150,
197, 217, 284
extract 278
seeing *see* sight
Seeker groups 4, 43, 97
self 213–27
-deception 126, 137, 149, 150, 196, 275–6
poverty of 209
"veiled" 134, 148, 150, 159, 183, 214,
219, 229, 249; letting go of 246;
and lusts 170; judgment by 160;
self-led life 137, 249; wisdom of
198
sense/sensing *see* feeling
sense (modern philosophical usage) 179
senses (*see also* hearing; feeling; sight;
smell; taste; touch): combined or
general 80, 139, 144, 181, 274, 275
benumbed 246, 253, 276
literal and spiritual 182
strengthened 144, 150, 181
sermons 134
prepared 217–18
service/work
Christ as servant 161, 251
peculiar 163, 184, 192
use by God 143
shadow *see* appearances
"Short Catechism" *see* Scattered Sheep
Sought After
sight (*see also* eye; invisible/visible; light;
senses)
comparison of senses 181
God onscience in) sight of 22, 28, 82,
97; image of God 225; seeing God
or Christ 270

and know in the thing 225
life, to see 240
mystery 87
Spirit seen/not seen 131, 183
taste and see 180
silence
and the flesh 206, 209, 225
immediacy 206, 211
of Jesus 251, 269
and the unconscious 128, 182
waiting/abiding in 48, 73, 84, 107,
189
and words 244
worship in 30, 126, 136–7, 147, 184,
205–12, 242
simplicity 169, 171
Simpson, William, 15
sin 245–6, 252, 257, 262, 266
and death 23
original, and original righteousness
245, 247
sinking (*see also* lowness)
down 145, 161, 184; into root 157; seed,
141
inward 157
in spirit 218, 250, 269
Skippon, Katharine 115
letter on death of child 85–6
small things *see* day of; everyday;
littleness
Smallwood, Allan ix
smell *see* senses
Smith, William 45
social
hierarchies 134
relationships 18
*Some Considerations Proposed to the City
of London* 26n, 170, 284
extracts 172
Some Deep...Israel 43, 284
extracts 14, 165–6
Some Directions to the Panting Soul 246,
284, 293
extracts 141–2, 222
"Some Experiences" 285
extracts 195, 227
*Some Experiences in the Life of Mary
Penington* ix, 293

Some Few Queries... Cavaliers 170, 198, 285
    extract 172–3
"Some Misrepresentations of Me Concerning Church Government" 247, 252, 285
    extract 260–1
Some Observations upon that Portion of Scripture, Romans 14:20 170, 181, 214, 285
    extract 222–3
Some of the Mysteries of God's Kingdom Glanced At 150, 205–6, 218, 249–50, 274, 285, 292
    extracts 201–3, 207, 254–5, 263–4, 269, 277
"Some Queries Concerning Compulsion in Religion" 285
    extract 176
Some Queries Concerning the Order and Government of the Church of Christ 286
    extracts 166–7, 190–91
Some Queries Concerning the Work of God in the World 170, 286
    extract 173
Some Questions... for the... Jews Natural 245, 248, 249, 250, 252, 275, 286–7
    extracts 142–3, 256–7, 276
Some Questions... Showing Man His Duty 160, 184, 247, 276, 287
    extracts 153–4, 276
Some Things of Great Weight 150, 287
    extract 224
Some Things... Royal Society 150, 248, 287
    extract 225
"Somewhat Relating to Church Government" 160, 287
    extracts 168, 278
Somewhat Spoken to a Weighty Question 170, 171, 246, 287, 292
    extract 174–6
Son of God (*see also* Christ; God; Jesus) 256, 266–7, 271
soul (*see also* flexibility; redemption; salvation; satisfaction; *Some Directions to...*; spirituality)
    begotten of divine breath 151, 234
    centred in/united with Christ 131, 152, 224, 235–6, 263–4
    in darkness 138, 267
    God's work in the converted 153, 255
    growth of 144–5
    looking/turning to God 25, 52, 58, 203, 209–10, 267
    prepared for fullness 143–5, 276
    and religion 224
    and senses 181, 188
spa resorts 107
speaking 206
    of the Spirit 210, 211
Spears, Joanne and Larry 228
Spirit/spirit (*see also* God; leadings; life) vii, 130, 134, 160–1, 174–5, 222, 239
    and Bible 236–7, 239
    and body/flesh 27, 133, 162
    breath of (*ruach*) 148, 234
    depths of 144, 150
    of God 92, 220, 226
    letter and 133, 187, 221
    and life 150, 164, 215, 259
    in meeting 211; and unity 166–7
    reasoning 83
    stirrings of 152, 228, 242, 24
    Trinity 249–52, 266–8
    wisdom of 198
    and words 218, 275, 277
spiritual life (*see also* birth; growth; soul) 147–5
    God, live like 132, 222
    task 137
"Spiritual Travels" 24, 250, 288
    extracts 15–16, 18–19
spirituality (*see also* daily exercise; lowness; waiting) 125, 128, 137, 182
    or religion 124, 213–4
Springett, Gulielma (Guli) 13, 16, 18, 35, 45, 49, 65, 75
    and William Penn 77, 94
Springett, Mary, Lady, *see* Penington, Mary
spring *see* fountain
stillness 142, 145–6
stirrings (*see also* life; Spirit)
    in nation 171
Stonar, Elizabeth, 90

Stonar, Nathaniel 90
"To Nathaniel Stonar" 289; extract 226
Story, John, 101, 103, 104
   letter to 101–2
substance (*see also* being; *Concerning the Sum or Substance...*)
   of God/Christ 145, 234, 236, 239, 266–7, 270; a mystery 276
   inward 12, 276
   living 270
   truth 11
suffering/s (*see also* imprisonment; oppression) 33, 56, 79, 156, 243
   Bridget Atley 50
   to Thomas Ellwood on 34
   and God 273
   Jesus and 248
   John Perrot's 41
Swarthmoor Hall 16, 45
swearing *see* oaths
sweetness (*see also* taste) vii, 240
   of brotherhood/fellowship 60, 163, 165, 208
   of Christ 12, 250
   of God 132, 171, 180, 264, 277
   of life 202; of living vine 154, 201
   salvation/communion with God 107
   of Satan's appearances 188
   of scripture 241
symbol 182–3, 230, 245, 249, 274

"tacit dimension" *see* unconscious
taste (*see also* savour; senses; sweetness) 144, 179–82, 184, 230
   and discerning of the kingdom 142
   of God/life/power, 138, 188, 222, 269; under Commonwealth 171
Taylor, Christopher, Quaker school 60
teachings of God (*see also* "Treatise Concerning God's Teachings") 61, 79, 87, 99, 149, 161, 164, 193, 205
   in experience 218, 224
   from fear 173, 212
   love to enemies 223
   parables 251
   peace in nation 174
Temple, Inner 6
temptation 58, 64–5, 114

tempter *see* Satan/Devil/wicked one
theology, Penington and (*see also* doctrine) 123, 124, 127, 242–72, 274
Thomason, George 8, 10
"thou" and "you" 20
Three Queries 216, 217, 288
   extract 156
Tillich, Paul 127
tithes 134
"To..." Letters to known individuals and meetings, see under names
"To _____" (27 Nov 1670) 150, 247, 288
   extract 264
To All such as Complain that They Want Power 147, 246, 288
   extracts 154–5, 201, 257–8, 276–7
To Friends in England, etc 159, 275, 288
To the Jews Natural and to the Jews Spiritual 171, 289
   extracts 142–3, 176–7, 203–4, 204(ill)
To the Parliament 170, 290
touch 181, 188
Touchstone and Tryall of Faith 6
Tower of London, Isaac Sr dies in 32
transformation 128, 135, 219, 234, 246, 261
   intention of IP's writing 125
travel (travail) vi, xii, 15–16
"Treatise Concerning God's Teachings" 181, 290n, 293
   extracts 194, 240
Tree of Life 115, 199
   and Tree of Knowledge 188, 230, 232, 233, 245
Trinity (*see also* Christ; God; Jesus; Spirit) 249–52, 266–72
"True and Faithful Relation" *see* "Spiritual Travels"
truth (*see also* Ancient Principle; "Further Testimony"; Holy Truth; Naked Truth") vii, 11, 176–7, 188–9, 222, 241, 274, 277
   covenant of light and life 259, 260
   discerning 191
   quickening, nature of 191

unconscious/tacit knowing 128, 136, 182, 215–7, 219, 228 (*see also* consciousness)

understanding *see under* Bible; light;
        natural; *see also* knowledge;
        reason
union/unity
    and diversity 160–7
    with God 184, 195, 225–6, 258, 261
    inward (church) 70, 103, 160, 164–6,
        261
    in knowing 238
    with whole of being 207
universalism (*see also* liberty; salvation)
        160, 231, 251
    God not limited by church 168, 226

veil 143, 193, 276
    covering the self 206
    of flesh 152
violence (*see also* peace)
    causes of 171, 174
virtue (*see also* power; righteousness)
        197–8, 219
    17th-century usage xiv
Voyce out of Thick Darkness 7, 8–10

waiting
    daily exercise 144–5, 149, 152
    for discernment / guidance /
        leading / sense 14, 23, 51, 59, 90–1,
        163–5, 222; in controversy 40–42,
        166; women's meetings 104
    for gift, 24; use of 67
    on God/Life/Spirit 6, 86–88, 143–4,
        190, 208–9, 211, 220; for divine
        awakening 137, 142; faith and
        obedience 153, 202; for great
        appearance (mistakenly) 131, 152;
        in heart/within 84, 139, 151, 219;
        nation/authority 174–6; voice of
        God/Christ 189, 268; for wisdom
        24, 86
    for meaning (Bible/words) 87, 124,
        140, 230, 238
    nature of things, to know/*see* 139,
        220
    in religion 215
    Seekers 4
    in silence/worship 48, 111, 189, 207,
        209–11

in writing ix
Walmsley, Elizabeth, 52
    letters to 53, 114–15
    testimony on IP 117–18
Walmsley, Thomas, letter to 78–81
Waltham Cross, school at 60, 94
war 174, 175, 266
Warning of Love from the Bowels of Life
        150, 246, 248, 276, 290
    extracts 140, 253, 264–5
Watkins, Morgan 45, 54–5, 71
Way of Life 26, 120(ill), 229, 231, 233, 236,
        290
    extracts 129–32, 214
*Weighty Question Propounded to the King
        and Parliament* 219, 291, 291 (ill)
    extracts 189, 223
wellspring *see* fountain
Where is the Wise? 150, 181, 197, 291
    extracts 140–41, 151–2, 199–200
Whitehead, John, imprisoned with
        Penington 35
whole (*see also* being; God; unity) 207,
        210, 274
Wilkinson-Story separation 100–5
will
    freedom of 196, 253
    "give over thy own willing" 14
    of God 163
    natural human 200
Wink, Walter 123, 228
wisdom 50, 51, 103, 131, 140, 215, 275
    of the Bible 123
    earthly 214
    "fear" 207
    of God 23, 49, 143; and power 27, 28,
        86, 87, 143, 168
    and knowledge 233
    of man 24, 155, 174, 175, 259
    of nature 248
    of Penington 126, 199–200
    of the Spirit 275
    of the veiled self 198
    womb of *see* birth
Wise, *see Where is the Wise*
Wittgenstein, Ludwig 217
women Friends, letter to 107–9
women's meetings 101, 104, 109–13

321

word/words (*see also* language; metaphor)
    beyond words: God's teaching 224; love 203; Spirit 127, 140, 145, 239
    of Bible 86, 229; IP's use of 150
    "end of words" 92, 127, 217
    fullness/weight of 239–40
    for God 160, 273–5; of God 117, 172, 234, 240, 247, 269; of God's Spirit 91–2, 218, 275
    IP's use of ix. xiii–xiv
    knowledge/learning from experience not words 218–9, 224–5, 275
    "let your words be few and weighty" 49
    and life: not measure of 138; mystery of 218, 252
    in prayer 205–6, 208
    taken for a rule 236
    in worship 111, 206, 210
    of wisdom 86
work/service, peculiar 163, 184, 192

Works of the Long-Mournful and Sorely-Distressed IP x, xi (ill)
"world turned upside down" 129, 243
worship (*see also* prayer) 152, 205–12
    forms of 134, 138
    hat controversy 39–45
    meeting for worship, Quaker 126, 159; mystery of kingdom in 160
    IP and Mary's first experiences 14–17
    openness to Spirit in 136, 147–8
    "mind our peculiar work" in 184
    nature of 206, 208–12
    set liturgy eliminated 217–8
    waiting in 48, 111, 189, 207, 209–11
Wright, Joseph, letter to 99–100

yoke *see* daily spiritual exercise
"you" and "thou" 55
youth 61–2

Zachary, Thomas, letter to Quaker meetings at TZ's 86–8